FEDERATIONS

FEDERATIONS

*The Political Dynamics
of Cooperation*

CHAD RECTOR

Cornell University Press
Ithaca and London

First published 2009 by Cornell University Press
First printing, Cornell Paperbacks, 2009

Printed in the United States of America

Library of Congress Cataloging-in-Publication Data

Rector, Chad.
    Federations : the political dynamics of cooperation / Chad Rector.
        p. cm.
    Includes bibliographical references and index.
    ISBN 978-0-8014-4736-5 (cloth : alk. paper) —
    ISBN 978-0-8014-7524-5 (pbk.)
  1. Confederation of states.   2. Federal government.
3. International cooperation.   4. International relations.   I. title.

    JC357.R43 2009
    320.4'049—dc22

2008043694

Cornell University Press strives to use environmentally responsible suppliers and materials to the fullest extent possible in the publishing of its books. Such materials include vegetable-based, low-VOC inks and acid-free papers that are recycled, totally chlorine-free, or partly composed of nonwood fibers. For further information, visit our website at www.cornellpress.cornell.edu.

Cloth printing   10 9 8 7 6 5 4 3 2 1
Paperback printing   10 9 8 7 6 5 4 3 2 1

CONTENTS

ACKNOWLEDGMENTS

I treat the formation of federal unions as a puzzle for theories of international relations, so this research project spans traditional subfields in political science. I therefore count myself very lucky to have been in two political science departments—UC San Diego and George Washington—full of scholars who take a unified approach to our discipline and who take ideas about institutions and strategies seriously, whether their particular expertise is in international relations, comparative politics, American institutions, or area studies. I will always be grateful to my advisers, peers, and colleagues who continually helped, and sometimes pushed, me to see a larger world. Chief among these is David Lake. Without his guidance, encouragement, insight, and patience this book would not have been possible.

Many, many other friends along the way generously gave their time to read and comment on the project. I deeply appreciate help from Deborah Avant, Bruce Buchan, Chris den Hartog, Erik Engstrom, Henry Farrell, Tanisha Fazal, Martha Finnemore, Jim Goldgeier, Peter Gourevitch, Henry Hale, Michael Hiscox, Ethan Hollander, Miles Kahler, Scott Kastner, Steven Kelts, Gina Lambright, Erik Lawrence, Andrew MacIntyre, Ian Marsh, Stephanie McWhorter, Kimberly Morgan, Pablo Pinto, Stephanie Rickard, Philip Roeder, Marc Rosenblum, Marian Sawer, Melissa Schwartzberg, Susan Sell, John Uhr, Erik Voeten, Barbara Walter, Joel Watson, and Daniel Ziblatt. I also thank seminar participants at the Australian National University, Columbia University, and the University of Maryland, and the many panelists and attendees at the Midwest Political Science Association conferences for their feedback at various stages. Regular participants at GW's Generation X political science faculty workshops gave me some much-needed reality checks. At Cornell University Press, Roger Haydon and two reviewers provided extremely valuable advice, and I am especially thankful to Patricia Sterling for her thorough copyediting and Teresa Jesionowski for production editing. I also thank several excellent research assistants: Erin Barrar, Matthew Broadhead, Colby Clabaugh, Joseph Clark, Daniel Dye, Mark Moll, Courtney Robbins, and Robert Sickel.

I acknowledge, with thanks, institutional support from the political science departments at UCSD and GWU, as well as financial support from the University of California Institute on Global Conflict and Cooperation, the American Consortium for European Studies, and the UCSD Friends of the International Center, and administrative help from the Research School of Social Sciences at the Australian National University, the British Library of Political and Economic Science, and the State Library of Victoria.

This book is dedicated to Sarah and Milo. I love you both.

C.R.

FEDERATIONS

INTRODUCTION

Half the world's people live in federations made up of states that at one time had a choice between remaining independent countries and merging into federal unions, and some scholars speculate that the European Union (Gillingham 2006) or even the world as a whole (Rodrik 2000; Wendt 2003; Deudney 2006) may eventually become constitutional federations.[1] Yet political scientists have only rarely asked why states form federations— and studies that do consider federation nearly always conclude that states choose it because they can be wealthier or more secure if they govern larger territories. States can get the benefits of size in many other ways, however, including cooperation through international organizations such as customs unions or alliances. A complete theory of federation must explain why states choose to federate when there are several other possible options.

In some instances, states are unable to cooperate without binding political institutions. Cooperation always requires states to bargain with one another, to divide among them the gains they reap by cooperating. Cooperation itself, however, sometimes changes the states' bargaining power because cooperation can require states to make investments in assets that are relationship-specific, meaning the assets are valuable only while cooperation persists. Examples of such assets include militaries designed to fight with the help of a particular ally, and economies geared toward

---

[1] The estimate of half the world is from Riker (1975); Lemco (1991) counts forty-four federations since 1787. Furthermore, most Latin American and African states were once part of proposed federations that went unimplemented.

production for a particular market. States that are more heavily invested in relationship-specific assets than their partners find themselves held hostage by the partnership: the more they cooperate, the more they have to lose if cooperation ends. As a consequence, these states' bargaining positions erode over time, exposing them to extortion by their less heavily invested partners. Fearing extortion, states sometimes reject cooperation altogether when cooperation would breed unequal vulnerability.

Federations can form when states benefit from cooperation, but cooperation requires unequal levels of relationship-specific investments. Creative leaders propose federal constitutions as tools to *contrive symmetry* by eliciting large, relationship-specific investments in political institutions from those states that would otherwise be less tied to a relationship. Only a federation, which creates high political costs to exit as a substitute for other exit costs, can rebalance bargaining and make cooperation mutually appealing. My theory explains, for the first time, not just why states form federations instead of pursuing self-sufficiency but also why they form federations instead of pursuing international cooperation.

I also explain how states in pursuit of their individual interests can reach a federal agreement in the first place. States that would be at risk of extortion in a relationship avoid it by turning the extortion around, demanding up front, as the price of cooperation, political integration that is as deep as they can get from their partners. Their partners give in when the benefits of cooperation are great enough that they are willing to subordinate themselves to political integration, thereby getting otherwise unattainable economic or security gains.

I test my theory by studying groups of states in which federation was actively discussed as a real possibility. The groups vary, both across states in the group and over time, in the leaders' perceptions of their prospective gains from cooperation, and also in their potential vulnerabilities. In what are now Australia and New Zealand, governing coalitions on the Australian mainland at first dismissed the idea of federation but by 1901 had embraced it, whereas New Zealand's leaders expressed interest but then stayed out. A group of South American states met at several constitutional conventions throughout the 1850s, but ultimately only some of them joined the Argentine federation, and even then only after sustained fighting. The two waves of German federal integration in 1866 and 1871 also involved force, although many of the states joining in 1871 did so by negotiation. Finally, in the early 1960s, newly independent states in East Africa and the Caribbean produced federal constitutions, but eventually they chose to remain apart.

In this introduction, I define federation and show that existing studies of federal origins are incomplete, discuss the gains that states can enjoy by cooperating, foreshadow the theoretical argument, explain my research design, and preview the rest of the book.

Federations

Federalism is a political system in which regional governments coexist with a national government, and the regional and national governments each have some independent authority, mutually recognized. Regional governments exist in a rough balance with the central government, dividing responsibilities among themselves and providing some checks on each other's behavior (Weingast 1997; Filippov, Ordeshook, and Shvetsova 2003; Bednar 2008). Scholars generally agree that it is impossible to define federal systems in terms of any one necessary, specific institution—such as a bicameral legislative body or constitutional court (Franck 1968, 169; Sawer 1969, 2; Duchacek 1970, 189)—but that federalism generally refers to any set of political institutions in which a balance is maintained between center and regions.

Balance is necessary, according to leading contemporary federal theorists such as Jenna Bednar (2008), because although the central government must be strong enough to compel regions to contribute to common national goals rather than free-ride, a center that is too strong will erode regional autonomy and exploit individual regions for private gain. Either danger, shirking by the regions or predation by the center, creates the risk of stagnation or even dissolution.

Although the specific features of federal constitutions vary, there is a consensus among scholars of federalism on several points. First, federal systems are artificial creations. In one of the first attempts at a scientific study of them, Edward Freeman (1863) traced federal processes in Italy and Greece and emphasized their artificiality. Scholars since have noted that institutions such as courts and legislatures are "mechanical contrivances" (Bryce 1888, 357) or "political contrivances" (Dicey 1885, 143). These institutions are the means by which federal bargains are implemented; they are not ends in themselves, and there were no prior conditions that make federalism inevitable (Livingston 1952).

Second, although the formal constitutional features of federal systems differ, one necessary feature of a stable federal union is a party system that joins local and national politicians (Truman 1962; Wildavsky 1967), since parties influence the incentives of politicians and other elites to organize political coalitions that favor or oppose the continuation of a federal union (Riker 1964). If local leaders know that the surest way to advance their careers is to work cooperatively with allies in other regions and at the federal level, the preservation of an effective union will be a byproduct of their personal ambitions (Sawer 1969; Filippov, Ordeshook, and Shvetsova 2003, 235).

Third, federal states are at one end of a continuum ranging from independence to loose alliances to formal treaty organizations to confederations to federal republics to unitary states. Federalism is an intermediate form between independence and unity, but scholars early on (Freeman 1863; Sidgwick and Sidgwick 1903, 433; Maddox 1941) recognized that it is only one of many possible intermediate forms, differing from them only by degree, and contemporary scholars concur (Riker 1975; Elazar 1998b; Lake 2007).

Finally, federalism and federation are distinct ideas. Federalism is a political system. Federation is a description of the merger of states, and can refer both to the process of merging and to the political system resulting from the merger (King 1982). Federation—my interest in this book—is fundamentally different from administrative decisions about centralization or decentralization. It is, rather, a prior choice that states make about whether to have a common government at all (Riker 1987, 10; Stepan 1999, 21–22).

Several contemporary examples illustrate these ideas. The European Union is one of the most far-reaching and widely studied examples of an intermediate political system in the world today. Somewhere between a treaty organization and a federal union, and sometimes called a confederation (Lister 1996), the EU is the product of a conscious decision by national leaders after the Second World War to bring their states into closer cooperation. As David McKay (1999, 34) argues, the leaders of the European movement used the language of federalism to explain what they were doing and as a means to achieve cooperation; they were not pursuing federalism for ideological reasons, as an end in itself. European institutions have thus been designed, intentionally, to create incentives for politicians to coordinate their activities across national borders in a way that reproduces the union as a byproduct of their ambitions (Moravcsik 1998), even if the specific institutions they chose did not always have the consequences they intended (Goldstein 2001).

An early federal theorist, Albert Venn Dicey, concluded that the conditions in which states choose federation are that "they must desire union and must not desire unity" (1885, 141). The foundation of the contemporary

EU, the Treaty of Rome, was itself a response to the failure of Western European states to agree to a more nearly complete political and military union, the European Defense Community (Ruane 2000); the less centralized institutions that followed were an alternative to deeper federal integration. In Chapter 3 I discuss the Australian political system where, two decades prior to the federation in 1901, the states enacted a formal international organization quite similar to the contemporary EU precisely because, like the Europeans, they had been unwilling to commit to unity. The Australian Federal Council, a loose institution formed in 1881, was a panel of legislators from the member states empowered to propose laws on certain subjects, similar in form to today's EU Council of Ministers (although, in practice, the Federal Council was less successful than the EU at eliciting economic cooperation from its members). In both Europe today and Australia initially, leaders contemplated designing a federal union but instead chose an international organization.

The People's Republic of China and Taiwan, two independent states de facto although not de jure, have been tacitly negotiating reunification under a federal system since 1982, when the PRC first publicly stated its proposal for a "one country, two systems" arrangement. The two sides have also developed deeper trade and investment ties, leading to a high degree of economic cooperation, despite the lack of a political settlement (Kastner 2003). Taiwan is unlikely to agree to a formal union with the PRC, however, unless the agreement can make credible the PRC's commitment to respect Taiwanese autonomy and interests. Taiwan's dilemma today is quite similar to that of some of the smaller German or Argentine states in the nineteenth century when confronted with federal proposals from their stronger neighbor, Prussia or Buenos Aires: they had to decide between, on the one hand, having a tenuous international relationship with their neighbor, mediated by international organizations and treaties, and, on the other hand, a risky domestic relationship mediated by an untested federal constitution (see Kastner and Rector 2008 for a detailed comparison).

Finally, following the removal of Saddam Hussein's regime in 2003, Iraq has been moving in the direction of disunity and civil war. Even though (as of 2008) there is a recognized central government, with the United States as a powerful outside patron, there are widespread fears that the country may fracture into three functionally independent states (Byman and Pollack 2007; Fearon 2007). Like the Argentine states after Spanish colonial rule ended, the Iraqi Kurdish, Sunni, and Shiite regions, following a reduction of U.S. security commitment, may find themselves in a situation in which they each have the potential to be fully independent, and must decide what kind of relationship, if any, they wish to negotiate with one another: complete self-sufficiency, a loose alliance with an economic union under the auspices of a regional grouping (such as the Gulf Cooperation Council or the Arab League), a complete federal republic, or something in between. Lacking strong institutions or a national party system that could make commitments to respect minority rights credible in a unitary state (Bouillon, Malone, and Rowswell 2007), some speculate that Iraq's leaders may eventually face a choice between a loose federal union and no union at all (Biden and Gelb 2006).

These three examples illustrate the strengths of existing scholarly theories about the origins of federations but also reveal a key problem: states do not have a binary choice between federal union and complete independence. The European states and China and Taiwan can get the benefits of economic integration without forming a federal union, and Iraqi regions could in principle cooperate on security without a reconstituted Iraqi state. Nevertheless, most scholars explain federation simply by noting that there are gains from cooperation: William Riker (1975) and Murray Forsyth (1981, 160) maintain that states federate when they can be made more secure by pooling their resources. Critics of their views argue, correctly, that these theories cannot distinguish between federation and alliance, since there are many other ways apart from federation to unify in the face of a common threat (Davis 1978, 132; King 1982, 36).

The foregoing examples also illustrate the thesis of this book, that problems of credibility and mistrust can account for states' sometimes choosing federal union over international cooperation. I address the first issue, how the presence of potential gains from cooperation cannot account for any one particular form of cooperation, in the next section; I consider the issue of credibility and outline my theoretical argument in the subsequent section, where I preview the theory I develop in Chapter 2.

Gains from Cooperation

William Riker (1975) asserts that states federate because a federation will be more secure or wealthier than states that remain self-sufficient. Alberto Alesina and Enrico Spolaore (1997, 2003) generalize this argument by hypothesizing that states merge for the sake of efficiency gains. They begin with the premise that states provide important services with increasing returns to scale, benefiting from size, since if they are larger they can spread the costs across more taxpayers. This logic can drive federal unions when leaders seek to capture further cost savings from scale (Alesina, Angeloni, and Etro 2001).

One public good that larger states can provide more cheaply is security. National defense is nearly a pure public good (Olson 1965), and security threats may provide an incentive for states to merge (Alesina and Spolaore 2003, 111; Parent 2006). William Riker's causal theory of federations rests on security interests, either common defense or common offense (1964, 1975, 1987). He assumes, implicitly, that states can at times make themselves more secure by working together than by working separately. A large common market is another possible public good: the greater the number of people enclosed within a market, the more opportunities they will have for exchange (Smith 1776), so that each additional citizen added to the market increases the average value of the market to every other citizen (Alesina and Spolaore 2003, 4).[2]

Size can have drawbacks as well, however. There may be declining returns to scale as a state's administrative apparatus grows past a certain size (Lake 1992). Alesina and Spolaore assume that because citizens have diverse tastes for public goods, in a large state many citizens will end up with public goods that are not well suited to their tastes; they conclude that states past a certain size will be inefficiently large (Alesina and Spolaore 1997). There is some empirical evidence that people form political jurisdictions in response to considerations of scale economies as well as homogeneity, at least with respect to school districts, where race is a proxy for diversity of preferences over varieties of public spending (Alesina, Baqir, and Easterly 1999; Gordon and Knight 2006), and by some measures scale economies (such as railroad networks) are related to the average size of new countries over time, although there is still considerable variation in state size (Lake and O'Mahony 2004).

Other empirical studies, however, have failed to find clear evidence that size matters; for example, by a variety of measures, small countries seem no worse off on average than large countries (Rose 2006). This may be so because states can achieve any of the gains from scale, at least in principle,

---

[2] Other economic theories exist. Larger size may also provide states with insurance against shocks to particular regions when a central authority can redistribute surpluses (Oates 1972). Friedman (1977) argues that multiple states along a single trade route will overtax the route, whereas states along parallel trade routes will undertax them, relative to the revenue-maximizing rate; see Chapter 5. Bolton and Roland (1997) assume that states merge for (unspecified) efficiency gains and analyze the consequences of regional redistribution.

simply by cooperating with other states either through informal cooperation or through international organizations. Customs unions, military alliances, and other functional institutions abound; states do not face a simple choice between, on the one hand, federal integration, and, on the other hand, isolation and self-sufficiency. A complete theory of federation, therefore, cannot logically rest only on the observation, however true, that the size of a region for which a public good is produced matters.

The disconnect between existing theories about the origins of federation and existing theories about international cooperation is strange. For example, Riker's argument that military threats drive federation assumes that groups of states will not be able to achieve those same military gains through alliances. Although alliances are sometimes problematic (Snyder 1997), they have clear advantages over complete self-sufficiency, and standard theory suggests that states can form alliances with one another to defend against common threats (Walt 1987). States can also, in principle, achieve all the economic gains from a common market by cooperating, whether tacitly or through a formal international organization. In practice, states often take advantage of the potential gains from regional cooperation while still maintaining their independence (Mansfield and Milner 1997), and there is a large theoretical literature that examines the nature of international organizations generally (Keohane and Martin 1995; Martin and Simmons 1998; Koremenos, Lipson, and Snidal 2001b).

States can opt for self-sufficiency, providing for all their military needs autonomously and keeping their internal market separate from their neighbors. Or they can cooperate with other states on core goals. Cooperation can be tacit, as when states informally coordinate their security policies and maintain low trade barriers. Cooperation may take the form of ongoing negotiations over adjustments, with details and changes subject to negotiation as the need arises (throughout the book I refer to this as cooperation through ad hoc arrangements). Or cooperation can also take the form of explicitly negotiated cooperation, implemented through formal international organizations (IOs) with regular administrative apparatuses and decision-making procedures. Other options states have for gaining the benefits of scale include free-riding on their neighbors' efforts at providing security or markets, threatening their neighbors to win concessions, or conquering them outright.

Federation is an inefficient way for states to cooperate. Negotiating and implementing a federal constitution is itself costly—for example, I show in Chapter 4 that the government of New South Wales, the largest Australian state, gave up its ambitious agenda for social reforms, involving goals that its leaders valued highly, in order to build a domestic coalition in favor of federation. Federation also imposes long-term costs on states, as it impedes their future freedom of action. If federations are tools for achieving economic or military cooperation, why would states use such inelegant tools?[3]

Credible Contracts

States can get just as much of a gain in security or prosperity by cooperating through an international organization as by federating—the only difference is how the states arrange the institutions. A growing literature addresses the different outcomes produced by different kinds of institutions and the reasons people choose the ones they do. This scholarship includes theories of firms (Klein, Crawford, and Alchian 1978; Williamson 1985; Hart and Moore 2005), states (Tilly 1990; Spruyt 1994), and the relationships among states (Lake 1999; Cooley 2005).

In the literature on federation only one study explicitly asks why states form federations instead of alliances. Peter Ordeshook and Emerson Niou (1998) suggest that an inability to commit to a potential alliance partner may drive states to form federations instead of alliances for security when the military stakes are high. Their argument does not, however, explain why commitment is a problem in the first place and why federation solves it. With a different dependent variable, Daniel Ziblatt (2006) asks why states sometimes merge into federations and at other times merge into unitary states. He concludes that they form federations when the smaller states have the administrative capacity to carry out commitments, but he does not specifically question why they do not instead form international organizations.

I describe cooperation in abstract terms, making as few assumptions as necessary in order to support a logical argument as to why states would ever choose a federation over cooperation via ad hoc arrangements or through an international organization. The theoretical argument is therefore like a possibility theorem, showing that a logically consistent set of assumptions can account for an outcome where states reject international

---

[3] Faced with the inability of any existing theory to provide a complete explanation for the origins of federations, a leading textbook on federalism argues that a generalized and parsimonious theory may be impossible and that the best explanation we have for federation is "circumstantial causation": that is, states that federated did so under unique conditions that cannot be generalized (Burgess 2006, 97).

organization in favor of federation—something that has not yet been
done in the study of federal unions. As an empirical matter, the theory has
several observable implications, which can then be tested against available
evidence.

Sometimes, cooperation necessarily leads states to invest in relationship-
specific assets, whether economic (roads, pipelines, factories) or military
(specialized equipment, strategies). These assets are more valuable if cooperation persists than if cooperation ends; as a result, they make it more
costly for states to pursue an outside option should they or their partners
end the relationship. If the investments in relationship-specific assets are
unequal, states that have a higher stake in the relationship become more
dependent than their partners. In tacit cooperation or in an international
organization, this unequal level of relationship-specificity can lead vulnerable states to lose bargaining power gradually over time, allowing their
partners to renegotiate the terms of the agreement. Such asymmetry in
relationship-specific investments makes cooperation risky and can lead
states to reject cooperation in the first place. They can, however, use political institutions to create what I call contrived symmetry, artificially ensuring that all sides have something to lose if cooperation ends. Because
federal agreements make exit costly for all members, vulnerable states are
put at less of a bargaining disadvantage. These states have an incentive to
refuse to cooperate in international organizations, and when cooperation
is valuable, their potential partners have an incentive to accept a federal
constitution as the price of cooperation.

Economic studies of contracts between firms provide a powerful analogy. Two corporations contemplating a joint venture will think carefully
before making an agreement, since although they will have some common
interests (both want their venture to succeed), they will have some competing interests as well (each wants more of the benefits of success). Since
contracts are not always perfectly enforceable by third parties such as
courts, a firm with more at stake than its partner—such as a manufacturer
that relies for critical parts exclusively on one supplier, who in turn has
many possible manufacturers it could sell to—is at risk of opportunistic
behavior. In one famous example, Fisher Body, the sole supplier of a critical component for General Motors, found itself able to use GM's position
of dependence to effectively renegotiate the terms of an agreement in order
to capture more of the profits from GM automobiles, enriching Fisher
while putting GM in a difficult position (Klein, Crawford, and Alchian
1978). In general, those parties more at risk tend to demand contracts that
create more constraints on behavior (Schwartz and Watson 2004).

Similarly, states form federations when they would benefit from cooperation but some fear that they will be exploited if they enter into an agreement that leaves them more dependent than their partners; these potentially vulnerable states hold out for a federal commitment, up front, as the price of cooperation. Whereas existing explanations for federation emphasize common interests as a factor leading to union, my argument suggests the opposite. Just as James Madison observed that if men were angels there would be no need for government, and Thomas Hobbes explained that people create governments not from mutual love but from mutual fear (1968, 183), I show that federations are born of mistrust—not affection.

Research Design

Some studies of federal origins focus on just one case (Allin 1913; Maddox 1941; Birch 1965; Watts 1966; Kurtz 1970; Lister 2001), while others are primarily theoretical (Grodzins 1966; Elazar 1998a). In setting out his own theory, Riker defines two necessary conditions—that states find federating with neighbors easier than conquering them, and that the states face a common military threat—and describes his methodological problem this way:

> The hypothesis…is that these two predispositions are *always* in the federal bargain and that each one is a necessary condition for the creation of a federalism. I am tempted, on the basis of my immersion in this subject, to assert that these two conditions are together sufficient. But, since I cannot possibly collect enough information to prove sufficiency, I am constrained to assert only the more modest hypothesis of necessity. (Riker 1987, 14)

He then briefly surveys the history of every federal system and in each case describes a common external military threat that the member states, as a group, faced.

This research design is limited for two reasons. The first is the reason Riker suggests. Without data on control cases—states that did not form a federation—it is impossible to test his argument fully. The second reason Riker's design is limited is that the selection of cases (only those in which states actually formed federations) makes it difficult to measure the key independent variables convincingly, since he cannot show that the threats faced by states that federated were more severe than threats faced by similar states that did not. Thus, Riker (1975, 120) finds that the Australian federation in 1897–1900 was due to the accumulation of aggressive imperialism in the Pacific by France in the New Hebrides, by Germany generally, and by Japan in Korea; but he does not show why similar threats did not lead New Zealand to join Australia. He finds that a threat from Ghana drove Nigerian federation but does not explain why Ghana's closer neighbors, Togo and Benin, did not also join Nigeria. He finds that threats from the South American interior drove Argentine federation but does not explain why the same threats did not drive Paraguay and Bolivia together (1975, 122–25). In the absence of rigorous comparison, any empirical conclusions are tentative.

One solution to this problem is to conduct paired case studies. Daniel Ziblatt (2006) contrasts Prussia, which formed a federation with its neighbors, and Piedmont, which conquered them. Another solution is to trace variation over time in one case. Daniel Deudney (1995) follows the development of the American system from the Articles of Confederation through the outbreak of the Civil War. These kinds of case studies have the advantages of variation on the independent and dependent variables, as well as assurance that the cases are in many ways comparable.

They have, of course, some drawbacks as well. For one, the cases are not randomly selected but chosen on the basis of variation on the dependent and independent variables, at least within a certain range. Ziblatt, for example, uses a group of states for which federation was a "real" possibility (I do this as well). That is, leaders at the time discussed federation, and contemporaneous observers seemed to take the possibility seriously, allowing a process-tracing exercise: what went "wrong" to prevent a federal bargain in the case of Italy or East Africa? The drawback is that if these near-miss cases truly were *near* misses, they might have characteristics that make them more like the successful cases than like most other groups of states that did not attempt to federate at all.

I use comparisons across and within groups of states in a region and also trace the evolution of particular regions over time. So, for example, the chapters on Australia and New Zealand contain variation among the states—some Australian states joined the federation quite willingly; others were ambivalent; and New Zealand stayed out—as well as variation over time: some of the state governments adopted one position on regional integration at one time but changed it later following exogenous economic or political changes. Where possible, I gain additional leverage by examining the actions and preferences of social groups within particular states, in order to draw out counterfactuals—for example, I argue in Chapter 3 that had New Zealand been governed in the 1890s by an agricultural, rather than a pastoral, coalition, it might have joined Australia.

More important, my theory has several observable implications about the political process that leads to federation, beyond just the prediction that states will federate under particular conditions. Six specific predictions about the process of federation, where it happens, are independently falsifiable, even for cases in which a federation actually formed. The six predictions (which I derive in Chapters 1 and 2 and state more precisely at the end of Chapter 2) are these: (1) the motives for states to form federations involve excludable goods; (2) federations are never the first choice of all member states; (3) leaders of nonvulnerable states, those that would have few relationship-specific investments in cooperation, prefer international organizations or ad hoc arrangements; (4) leaders of vulnerable states, with large relationship-specific investments in cooperation, prefer to cooperate via a federation; (5) vulnerable states resist cooperating until after federal institutions are in place; and (6) nonvulnerable states joining a federation will invest more heavily in federal institutions by, among other things, making more substantial changes to their party systems.

Plan of the Book

From here, I proceed in six chapters and a Conclusion. Chapter 1 frames the problem by examining how states divide the gains from cooperation. Divisions depend on each state's bargaining power, which in turn depends on what each can get by walking away from a deal. When cooperation requires investment in relationship-specific assets, cooperation necessarily makes outside options worse. A commitment problem arises when a cooperating state makes larger relationship-specific investments than its partners do, since its partners can renegotiate terms once cooperation begins. Highly vulnerable states can be worse off by joining in cooperation than by remaining self-sufficient. Lack of symmetry in relationship-specific investments, therefore, can lead states to pass up opportunities for mutual advancement.

Chapter 2 considers political institutions. When lack of symmetry is a problem, states can contrive symmetry by using institutions as mechanisms that impose costs on states if cooperation ends. These institutional exit costs are low or even negligible in an international organization but are higher in a federation. In federations, they arise from the institution-specific investments that political parties and individual politicians make in securing power at the federal level, investments in joint military forces and other bureaucratic organizations, and, possibly, changes in national identity. Federations make exit costly for all partners, so states that would otherwise be vulnerable suffer less bargaining disadvantage. These states reject IOs, preferring to pursue self-sufficiency; they accept cooperation only if it takes the form of a federation. When the gains from cooperation are high enough, their less vulnerable partners agree to federation as an acceptable compromise. I conclude with six independently falsifiable predictions.

Chapters 3 and 4 consider the formation of the Australian federation and New Zealand's decision to stay outside it. Chapter 3 tests the observable implications of my theory by focusing on Australia. Functionally independent from Britain from the 1850s, the six Australian states and New Zealand at first cooperated via ad hoc commercial treaties, but after the 1870s they failed to form a customs union, despite a strong desire in each state's governing coalition for market integration. Victoria, with firms poised to make large relationship-specific investments in a common market, led the smaller states in holding up economic integration until less vulnerable New South Wales agreed to federate in 1901.

In Chapter 4 I test an alternative explanation for federation that involves the presence, or deliberate construction, of a common political identity in a group of states. In the Australian states and New Zealand, a liberal transnational progressive movement pushed for political reforms such as female suffrage, and some Australian historians have argued that this transnational change in political ideology led to a normative shift that resulted in federation. Evidence from parliamentary divisions, party strategies, and newspaper editorials, however, indicates that market motives, rather than a prior identity change, drove the initial federal movement—although identity politics may have played a role in helping the states commit to a union.

Chapter 5 examines instances of coercion. Even states able to use force to rule their neighbors may instead choose to negotiate federal agreements with them, but their choice of federation is puzzling when they could instead coerce their neighbors into joining alliances. Nineteenth-century Buenos Aires and Prussia both perceived large gains from expanding and faced potential partners that could, in principle, have gained from economic and security integration. A common trade route in the Argentine case, however, and a diplomatic union in the German case would have caused the smaller states to be more dependent on cooperation than the larger states, resulting in difficulty for Buenos Aires and Prussia to commit, in advance, to a division of gains that would make cooperation beneficial for all. Although Buenos Aires and Prussia could each have tried to coerce an international organization, they concluded that a federal union would face less resistance from their potentially vulnerable partners.

I look at two near misses in Chapter 6. Two groups of former British colonies in East Africa and the Caribbean negotiated postcolonial federal constitutions in the 1960s, but neither was implemented. The largest state in each group—Kenya and Jamaica, respectively—was initially interested in federation when nationalist leaders valued regional integration. Economic integration would have led to large asymmetries in relationship-specific assets, driving the smaller states' demands for federal institutions to levels that, from the perspective of the larger states, were unacceptably high. In both cases, the way the union unraveled demonstrates the logic of the theory, since some states—Tanganyika in East Africa, Trinidad and Tobago in the Caribbean—changed their positions on federation following changes in their exposures to relationship-specific investments.

The Conclusion presents some broader implications of my argument and speculations about the future of the European Union, China and Taiwan, the two Koreas, Iraq, and the prospects for world government. I also detail how both theory and evidence pose challenges to some broader ideas in international relations theory. First, structural realist interpretations argue that states uncomfortable with the influence of a neighbor will form balancing coalitions to ensure their security, but I show that they can use institutions as an alternative way to create credible assurances. Second, most existing work in the liberal institutional tradition argues that states use institutions when they are already inclined to cooperate but seek to enhance the value of cooperation by reducing transactions costs, but I show that states can agree to use institutions to give one side a bargaining advantage and thus reduce the risk of opportunism. The logic of contrived symmetry can therefore help sharpen our understanding of international politics.

1

COOPERATION AND COMMITMENT

States have more than one way to work together, so how can we explain any one particular form of cooperation? I present my theory in two steps. This chapter shows conditions in which states cannot agree on cooperation that could be mutually beneficial because they face a commitment problem in dividing the gains from cooperation. Chapter 2 shows how federal institutions can resolve this particular problem. Taken together, these chapters argue that there are instances in which states agree to form a federation not just *despite* their inability to agree to cooperate through an international organization or ad hoc arrangement but rather *because* they are unable to reach such an agreement.

A fundamental dilemma states face when they contemplate cooperation is that cooperation requires them to divide the gains they reap by cooperating but sometimes changes the states' respective bargaining power. Cooperation sometimes requires states to make investments in assets that are relationship-specific (more valuable while cooperation persists). States that are more heavily invested in relationship-specific assets than their partners are held hostage by the partnership. The more they cooperate, the more they have to lose if cooperation ends. As a consequence, these states are exposed to opportunism by their less heavily invested partners, who can renegotiate cooperation later for a larger share of the gains. This contracting problem can prevent states from cooperating even when cooperation is in their common interest.

The assumption I begin with is that states are governed by leaders or coalitions that act in pursuit of a consistent set of economic and security goals. In order to make meaningful generalizations about international organizations, I analyze cooperation in the abstract by assuming that all cooperation is accomplished through ad hoc agreements, without any international institutions. (In Chapter 2 I expand the analysis by describing the effects of institutions and concluding with an argument about why states choose the institutions they do.)

This chapter proceeds in three steps. First, I describe gains from cooperation. I discuss the problem of division and show how, according to standard theories of bargaining, a state in a cooperative arrangement gets a share of the benefits from cooperation in proportion to its ability to walk away from the deal—its outside option. Second, I consider outside options in more detail by discussing self-sufficiency, free-riding, and conquest as alternatives to cooperation. Third, I describe relationship-specific investments and argue that states that build up relationship-specific assets in cooperation are vulnerable to extortion by their partners, sometimes making them worse off than they ever would have been had they never joined in cooperation in the first place.

Division of Gains

States can produce more security or wealth, or both, working together than they can separately, but gains from such joint efforts can be divided in any of a number of ways. Even if the natural technology of joint production creates some particular allocation of gains—such as when market forces distribute wealth among members of a common market—states can find other ways to redistribute. Most goods are themselves divisible, so that, for example, states can allocate among themselves the costs of military preparations for common defense, but even when they are not they can be linked to other issues through side-payments.[1]

In dividing gains, states have a range of possible decisions that are consistent with preserving their relationship. The boundaries of this range are determined by how well each member would fare if cooperation were to come to an end, so that states will continue to cooperate as long as they are each, individually, at least as well off by staying as by walking away. For example, two member states would face a simple trade-off: they can make a division so unfavorable to one that it is indifferent between staying and

---

[1] On the importance and limits of side-payments see Mayer (1998), Gruber (2000), and Rector (2001).

leaving but extremely favorable to the other; they can make a division at the opposite extreme, favorable to the other but unfavorable to the one; or they can choose any point in between.

As a result, the actual division of gains—the policy decisions that the states make—depends on the outside option that each state has. This is a common way of thinking about bargaining; for example, work by Howard Raiffa (1982) describes how bargains are shaped by each side's best alternative to a negotiated settlement. States that would be relatively well off without cooperation—those that would be militarily secure and have access to large markets even without cooperating with partners—have a better outside option than states that would fare poorly without cooperation. States with better outside options need a more favorable division of the benefits in order to entice them to cooperate; they are in a better bargaining position (Hirschman 1970; Gehlbach 2006). States, furthermore, have the ability to adjust the distribution of benefits among themselves in order to rebalance the division of gains as their outside options change. If a state's outside option improves over time, that state will be in a position to extract a better bargain from its partners. If, on the other hand, its outside options worsen, it will find itself getting a poorer and poorer division of benefits over time.

Figure 1.1 illustrates how states bargain over the gains from cooperation. The horizontal and vertical axes represent the payoffs to two different states. If they choose not to work together, they get the "payoff to no cooperation." If they do choose to work together, together they move to

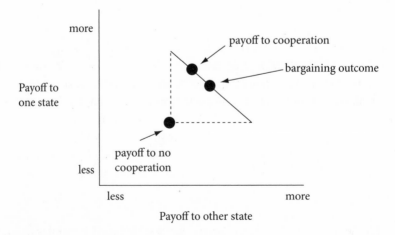

Figure 1.1 Distributing joint gains

the point labeled "payoff to cooperation." Cooperation makes both better off: the one state can get more by cooperating than it could by not co-operating (it moves to a payoff that is higher along the vertical axis) and the other state also gets more by cooperating (it moves to a payoff that is further to the right along the horizontal axis). Because the two states can redistribute the gains from cooperation between themselves, they can achieve any payoff along the 45-degree line going through the "payoff to cooperation" point. If the transfer is negotiated at the same time that the states decide whether or not to work together, the two states must simul-taneously decide whether to cooperate or not and, if they do cooperate, how they will divide the gains.

The outcome they choose will be somewhere along the diagonal line segment. Neither state will accept a bargain that leaves it worse off than the payoff to no cooperation, so the line segment does not extend beyond the two dashed lines. Each state, of course, would ideally prefer a solution in which, as they work together, it gets all the benefits to itself—so that the one state prefers a solution near the upper left of the 45-degree line, whereas the other state prefers a solution to the lower right. Assuming that the states always agree to split the difference between the two minimally acceptable outcomes, they end up at the point labeled "bargaining outcome."[2]

Outside Options

The value of a state's outside option is simply the value that it would de-rive from managing its affairs without securing cooperation from a part-ner. Suppose a state and its potential partner begin with a relationship of complete self-sufficiency. How well a state will fare—how much wealth and security it will have—without ever cooperating depends on three fac-tors: the state's ability to provide for itself, its ability to free-ride on the contributions of others, and its ability to take value from others by force. These factors, in turn, depend on the state's size, the excludability of the particular goods in which it is interested, and how well its military capa-bilities are matched to the kind of good it wants.

---

[2] Splitting the difference is (in this case) the Nash Bargaining Solution, the divi-sion the states would reach in the most commonly modeled forms for noncooperative bargaining (Watson 2002), such as an Osborne-Rubinstein bargaining game in which discount rates approach zero (Osborne and Rubinstein 1990). This assumption is used commonly in studies of international cooperation generally (Milner 1997) as well as in models of contract negotiation similar to mine (Hart 2007).

Self-Sufficiency

The simplest outside option is pure self-sufficiency. In principle, a state can always produce more by acting in concert with other states, but the extent of the gain depends on how much it could make alone. A state that merges its market with that of a partner will become wealthier from having a larger market, but the gains will be only marginal if its market was large to begin with. A state that integrates its military and defense policy with that of a trusted partner will be safer from attack, but again the gains will be marginal if the state was already relatively secure.

In their work on state size, Alesina and Spolaore (2003, 23) and David Lake (1992) assume that the public goods that states produce (such as markets, defense, and others I catalogued in the Introduction) have diminishing returns to scale.[3] As states get larger, or as more states join an international organization, the marginal benefits of each new member decline.[4]

The economic finding that states with larger internal markets have smaller international sectors (that is, trade as a proportion of economy) than states with smaller internal markets, all else equal, is commonplace. Diminishing returns in security can be present for at least two reasons. First, the expansion of a commonly defended territory, either through conquest or through a network of alliances, can lead to declining returns past a certain point if expansion threatens neighboring states and leads them to coalesce into an opposing alliance (Snyder 1991). Second, defending or deterring a particular threat requires a fixed investment in military capabilities, so adding more capabilities adds little beyond the level at which deterrence is achieved. Thus, larger states both are able to provide more for themselves than smaller states and have less to gain than smaller states by expanding or by securing cooperation from partners.

Self-sufficiency, the ability of a state to provide for its own prosperity and security autonomously, is sometimes thought of as a basic feature

---

[3] Specifically, Alesina and Spolaore (1997) assume that the public good a state produces has a fixed cost that is paid by levying taxes on all citizens who enjoy it. Adding an additional citizen to a small jurisdiction lowers the per capita payment more than by adding an additional citizen to a large jurisdiction. They also assume that tastes for public goods are heterogeneous, which limits the value of one public good extended to ever larger numbers of citizens. Other models assume administrative costs that create negative returns with more territory (Bean 1973; Lake 1992).

[4] An exception is global "weakest link" public goods, like controlling infectious diseases or denying sanctuary to terrorists, where there are large gains to enlisting the cooperation of *all* the states in the world rather than *all-but-one* (Sandler 2004, 62).

of states, but it is also a matter of choice. Kenneth Waltz, for example, defines self-help in a way that includes balancing behavior, as when states seek support from allies (1979, 111), suggesting that self-sufficiency is a means to an end rather than an end in itself. When states face demands from rivals that they do not wish to accommodate, they have a choice: they can counter threats by joining with allies, or they can invest from their domestic resources in the ability to counter threats. Both responses have drawbacks, and neither is by definition always superior to the other.

Self-sufficiency, then, the first outside option a state has, depends on the state's size and on the state's willingness to bear costs to develop its internal capabilities.

Free-Riding

The states that have the worst outside options, however, are not necessarily those that are least self-sufficient. In many situations, small states may actually have a quite favorable outside option if, in the absence of formal cooperation, they can simply free-ride on the investments of larger states. For example, when the United States and its European allies cooperated to provide joint defense during the Cold War, the outside option available to the smaller states was to free-ride, since they knew that the United States would be likely to defend them against a Soviet attack regardless of whether or not they had contributed to the joint defensive efforts. The ability to get defense free gave smaller allies a bargaining advantage by allowing them to get what they wanted outside of cooperation (Olson and Zeckhauser 1966). Here, the states with the poorest bargaining positions are those, such as the United States in the European defense example, that enjoy enough benefit from a public good and have enough of the means to produce it that they can be better off, individually, providing the public good themselves, even if no other states contribute (Olson 1965, 49).

Free-riding follows from the characteristics of public, or collective, goods. Although public goods are typically defined as being nonrival (the enjoyment of the good by one consumer does not reduce the availability of the good to other consumers) and nonexcludable (one consumer cannot easily prevent another consumer from enjoying the good), the key is nonexcludability. Since the United States directly benefited from defending Western Europe from the Soviet Union (thereby preventing a growth in Soviet power), there was no way it could achieve this goal while excluding free-riding European states from its protection.

A security regime is also nonexcludable. Great Britain in the nineteenth century, for example, went to great effort to suppress piracy on the high seas. Piracy was both a commercial and a security threat to the major trading powers, but it was a diffuse one: British military commanders could not know in advance which country's vessels would next fall prey to any one particular pirate ship (or Barbary state), so they took military measures against all pirates (Lowenheim 2003). In this case, excluding a trade-dependent state from the security Britain provided would have been impossible even in principle.

If a large state produces a nonexcludable good that free-riders then consume, instituting cooperation to share the costs only redistributes costs without yielding any net gain for the group. Free-riders would therefore never agree to any such system. Cooperation in this instance is sustainable only if the large state and the free-riders can devise some trade-off that makes both better off, as in the case of NATO when small states traded contributions for voice in the decision-making process (Keohane 1971). In this case, though, the issue is no longer a collective action problem but simply an example of gains from cooperation in which states collectively benefit by exchanging tasks.

Small groups of states can overcome collective action problems in a variety of situations (Shivakoti and Ostrom 2002), and international cooperation to provide public goods is more common than the first-cut logic of collective action suggests (Snidal 1985). Under many common conditions, a single actor can start contributing to a public good and stimulate a critical mass of cooperators as long as the benefits are nonexcludable (Oliver and Marwell 1988, 2001). For example, the American states under the Articles of Confederation were still able to supply necessary collective goods such as defense, even though they lacked both a hegemonic leader and a centralized enforcement mechanism (Dougherty 2001).

Situations in which collective action problems completely inhibit cooperation present a paradox from the standpoint of scholars investigating the origins of institutions: if a collective action problem prevents a group of states from producing a public good, there will also be a collective action problem that prevents the group of states from creating an institution that produces the good (Heckathorn 1989). Robert Keohane (1984) got around this problem by positing that institutions created by one dominant state could persist even after that state had lost its dominant position. His answer, though, cannot explain how states might overcome a free-rider problem to create an institution when the reason they need an institution in the first place is that, without one, they are unable to overcome free-rider problems.[5]

Conquest

A third outside option, after pure self-sufficiency and free-riding, is conquest. One state may destroy another state and directly seize its territory, population, and resources. Obviously, a state that has the ability to conquer its neighbor will have more bargaining leverage with that neighbor than a state that does not, since it makes the potential conqueror's outside option better and the potential conqueree's outside option worse.

The benefits from conquering a neighbor are not entirely straightforward, however. Conquest is costly for the state that does the conquering, because it requires a large military force to subdue, occupy, and police a territory. In addition, a state that can fight back and inflict damage on its conqueror, even if it cannot prevent the conquest, can thereby reduce the *ex ante* (pre-conquest) bargaining advantage that a potential conqueror enjoys.

Furthermore, the manner in which territory is acquired can influence its value. If the gains that come from controlling territory arise because the territory itself has strategic value or contains resources that are easily extracted, then land taken by force is just as useful as land voluntarily ceded. For other goals, however, the gains will be less: it is more difficult to raise an army from a conquered state than from a voluntary ally, and conquering a state violently may render it less economically productive.[6]

So, the extent to which a state has the outside option of conquest depends on its military capabilities (how easily it can conquer and administer its target while containing any costs its target can impose on it) and

[5] Krasner (1983) discusses problems of regimes more generally. Small groups of states can always, in principle, overcome collective action problems in ways that large groups cannot, meaning that a single leader may not always be strictly necessary (Russett and Sullivan 1971; Snidal 1985). There is a similar problem for theories of federation specifically, since federal unions are both forums for bargaining and the products of bargains (Filippov, Ordeshook, and Shvetsova 2003, 76); federations therefore suffer from the general paradox of institutional origins (Riker 1980).

[6] Although conquerors may be able to exploit occupied territories well enough that the net gains from conquest outweigh the costs (Liberman 1996), the relevant comparison for this section is whether there might be even more gains from negotiated cooperation.

on the kind of good it seeks from the target state (whether it is something that can be seized or looted by force or something that requires the acquiescence of the conquered population).

In his theory of federations, elaborated in the 1960s and '70s, Riker (1975) argues that states federate with neighbors when they do not wish to go through the effort of conquering them. His insight is that even if one state could conquer another and would be willing to do so in principle, conquest is not the inevitable result. Rather, states might be able to reach federal bargains that are better for both of them than war. Riker's argument is ultimately incomplete because it cannot explain why a federation is necessarily the alternative to conquest. Rather than coercing a smaller partner to join a federation, a strong state could coerce its partner to join an unequal alliance (such as, for example, the Warsaw Pact). The puzzle of why a federation instead of an international organization is still unexplained.

Relationship-Specificity

After the value of outside options generally, a second important and predictable influence on the value to a state of pursuing its outside option is the extent to which it is invested in relationship-specific assets. When a state cooperates with partners, it sometimes builds up assets that lose value if cooperation ends. If the act of ending cooperation is itself costly because it erodes the value of relationship-specific assets, then the state's outside option is worse than simply the static value of self-sufficiency, free-riding, or conquest. A state with investments in relationship-specific assets will have a worse outside option than a state without such investments.

Cooperation sometimes requires states to invest in relationship-specific assets. Allies build militaries that are more effective when used in conjunction with their partners and less effective when used independently, and firms invest in economic sectors that are profitable when they have access to particular markets but less valuable without such access. If the relationship ends, states have to start over in order to become self-sufficient again; they suffer losses greater than that of simply forgoing the benefits of cooperation and must pay the costs to make up the functions the ally had previously served (Lake 1999).

Established procedures, joint training, and informal contacts between militaries are all relationship-specific assets that raise the costs of losing a partner (Weber 1997; Wallander 2000). Security investments that depend on territory controlled by an ally are relationship-specific as well. During the early Cold War, American land-based, intermediate-range ballistic missiles could not reach targets in the Soviet Union from the continental United States and so were valuable as a deterrent only as long as they could be stationed on the territory of allies who were closer to the Soviets. Similarly, Soviet short- and medium-range missiles were most useful as a deterrent if they could be stationed on Cuba. The loss to either side of the ability to use allied territory would make the missiles far less useful.

Economic forces can also create relationship-specific investments. Trade patterns in a common market can make a state so dependent on its trading partners that it would be forced to make a costly readjustment if those partners were to sever ties. Such a readjustment might be more costly than the gains from trade in the first place, both for firms (Alt et al. 1999) and for the economy as a whole, as the state might have to restructure its economy entirely around trading with other partners or around producing for the home market in autarky (McLaren 1997).

Some economic assets related to trade (in addition to the production that trade itself creates) are also relationship-specific. Jeffrey Frieden (1994) notes that mines are site-specific, and so an ownership stake in a mine in a foreign country generates revenue only if the mine is not expropriated by the host state. Gas and oil pipelines are likewise potentially lucrative but only if they are in friendly territory (Yarbrough and Yarbrough 1992; Hancock 2001). Thus, the nature of the relationship between two or more countries determines the value of the assets.

Economic integration can also lead to demands for economic policy changes in order to bring a state more into line with its economic partners. These additional policy changes, which make sense in a unified market even though they are not what a state would choose if left to its own political process, are costly to undo. In the lead-up to European Monetary Integration, for example, European economies changed their wage-setting institutions in order to take account of currency unification, sometimes in ways that ran counter to the interests of otherwise powerful groups (Enderlein 2006).

Much of the literature on security and interdependence recognizes, at least implicitly, the way in which political relationships between states influence the value of particular economic assets (Cerny 1995, for example, discusses some of the broader consequences). Where trade requires specialization, firms have an interest in avoiding investments likely to be disrupted by future international conflict. Joanne Gowa and Edward Mansfield (2004) trace one implication by exploring inter- and intraindustry trade, finding that intraindustry trade, which results from economies of scale in specialized niches (and is therefore attributable to firms' conscious investments in building up specific assets) is higher between states that have close security relationships than between states that do not. They reason that private actors will invest in relationship-specific assets only when they believe that the relationship will persist.

If two states entering into a cooperative relationship *both* must make costly, relationship-specific investments, they know that ending it would create extra losses for both of them. Oliver Williamson shows that when external contract enforcement is uncertain or costly, mutual specificity of this sort can make contracts more stable (Williamson 1983), even in an uncertain environment (Riordan and Williamson 1985; Williamson 1994).

Policy coordination, though, may require one state to make a highly relationship-specific investment while a partner's is much less specific, as when market integration leads one state (often the one with the smaller market) to make a larger adjustment than another. In choosing whether or not to enter into cooperation, the state with the higher potential level of specificity faces a dilemma: the vulnerable state (state V) has a valuable hostage at stake in the relationship, but its partner the nonvulnerable state (state N) does not.

Once states are already cooperating and one is vulnerable to high adjustment costs if cooperation ends but another is not, the state with less at stake (state N) can use the threat of ending the relationship in order to take a larger share from V. Similarly, V (with more at stake) has a greater incentive to give up concessions in order to preserve cooperation. If V's outside option is poor enough—that is, if its potential losses from ending cooperation as a result of relationship-specific investments are great enough—it may be made worse off by a division of benefits than it would have been had it never started cooperating with N in the first place.

A number of studies in economics have clarified the risks to vulnerable partners in contractual relationships (Williamson 1985; Grossman and Hart 1986; Hart and Moore 1990), including a seminal work by Benjamin Klein, Robert Crawford, and Armen Alchian (1978) on the "appropriable quasi-rents of specialized assets." When two firms engage in joint production, they may create a situation where one makes a greater initial investment in specialized assets than the other. For example, from 1910 until 1926, Fisher Body and General Motors had an agreement whereby Fisher produced closed bodies, a critical component for the new GM cars coming on the market. Once production was under way, Fisher, as the sole supplier for GM, discovered that it was in a powerful position to renegotiate the terms of its agreement in order to capture for itself more of the profits from GM's sales. Fisher's production delays were attempts, in effect, to extort rents from GM. Fisher's advantage came from the fact that whereas GM's investments in its production process depended on cooperation from Fisher in order to be profitable (since without Fisher's bodies GM could not maintain its position in the new market for fully enclosed cars, and the resources it had invested in creating and marketing a production line would be lost), Fisher's investments in body production did not depend on cooperation from GM (since it could easily shift to supplying other manufacturers, as it had contracts with most of GM's competitors as well). Having a smaller specialized investment at stake gave Fisher the ability to enter into an agreement with a partner at terms favorable to the partner but then to change the terms to be more favorable to Fisher later. As a result of such a difficulty in making initial contracts credible, firms will often avoid investments or relationships that would put them at risk.

Extensions to this insight have shown that the firm seeking to renegotiate does not need to threaten to break the contract to get a better deal (though such a threat will help); all it must do to compel its partner to make concessions is find ways to hold up its contributions, thus undermining cooperation while the contract is being tacitly renegotiated (Hart 2007; Hart and Moore 2007). Klein (1978) concludes that appropriable quasirents of specialized assets—unequal levels of relationship-specific investments that leave one partner at risk—lead firms to integrate vertically.[7]

Like firms, states that can be made worse off by entering into a cooperative arrangement in which they are likely to be exploited have a clear interest in refusing to cooperate at the outset.[8] Instances of states actually entering into cooperation and subsequently being exploited should therefore be rare. Occasionally, though, either because leaders make mistakes or because institutions sometimes produce poor decisions, states do enter into these unwise agreements, providing examples that show how

---

[7] Klein (1978) argues that GM's purchase of Fisher Body (partial in 1919, full in 1926) shows that contractual cooperation was unsustainable, but Coase (2000) argues that vertical integration does not follow, and that firms could rely on long-term contracts since vertical integration involves substantial upfront costs that firms would rather avoid paying. Klein (Klein and Murphy 1988) disagrees. Coase's argument assumes that courts provide third-party enforcement of a contract, a condition not present in international politics.

[8] By "exploited," I mean that N is better off, but V is worse off than it would have been had it never entered into cooperation in the first place. I do not imply a moral judgment.

nonvulnerable states can explicitly renegotiate the terms of cooperation
or link the continuation of cooperation to some other concession.

Prior to 1939, Germany used the implicit threat of ending economic
ties with weaker East European states to extract military commitments to
which these states otherwise would have been unlikely to agree (Hirschman
1945). Relations between the United States and the Hawaiian kingdom are
another example. Although an early trade reciprocity treaty provided Hawaii with a generous division of economic benefits, those benefits came at
the cost of orienting the Hawaiian economy toward the U.S. mainland. As
a result, Hawaii later agreed to cede Pearl Harbor in return for an extension of the agreement, a territorial concession the kingdom's leaders had
previously resisted (Abdelal and Kirshner 1999). Some Canadians argued
against ratifying the U.S.-Canada free trade agreement on the grounds that
the gains from specialization would be dependent on continued access to
U.S. markets providing the United States with the potential future leverage
to renegotiate the agreement in terms less favorable to Canadian interests.
Given this potential for future exploitation, a country might sensibly reject
a trade agreement, even when short-run gains are large (McLaren 1997).

In more abstract terms, relationship-specific assets change the alternatives to cooperation of each state, thereby changing the outcome of bargaining over the division of benefits, as illustrated in figure 1.2. Two states,

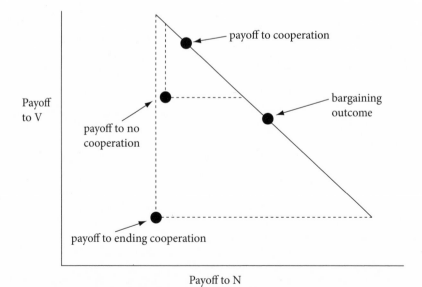

Figure 1.2 Distributing joint gains with unequal relationship-specific investments

V and N, are contemplating cooperation. If they choose not to cooperate at all, they receive the payoff labeled "payoff to no cooperation." If they do cooperate, they produce a joint gain labeled "payoff to cooperation." Cooperation, however, requires both states to invest in relationship-specific assets, though V must invest more in such assets than N. So, if the states choose to begin cooperating but then end their cooperation, not only do they give up the benefits of cooperation but each also has to pay the costs of adjusting. When cooperation ends, both states are worse off than they would have been had they never started cooperating in the first place—the point labeled "payoff to ending cooperation."

Since V has more to lose than N (by assumption), when V and N bargain over the division of gains from cooperation, V is willing to accept a deal that benefits N greatly while making V worse off than it would have been had it never agreed to cooperate in the first place—the lower right end of the diagonal line—because even this unpleasant bargain is better than ending cooperation entirely. If the states split the difference as before, they end up with a bargaining outcome that N would be happy with but would cause V to regret ever having cooperated.[9]

Anticipating just this sort of exploitation, many states in V's position have declined to enter into cooperative arrangements that had the appearance, at least at first, of being generally beneficial. The American decision to leave the British Empire was motivated in part by the desire to pursue a more self-sufficient path to economic development, since Americans expected that development within the empire would lead to more dependence upon it (de Figueiredo, Weingast, and Rakove 2000). This rationale was repeated by postcolonial Indian leaders, who sought economic independence as a means to ensure political independence (Grieco 1982); by Latin American rulers who pursued import substitution policies; Taiwanese leaders today who seek to diversify their economy's ties away from the PRC; and France's decision in the Cold War to preserve military

---

[9] One possible objection is that any threat N makes to end cooperation is not credible, since ending cooperation would make N worse off. States, however, can threaten to "lose control" in a crisis, risking an unpleasant outcome that neither side in a bargaining situation wants. Brinksmanship can get leaders what they want even in nuclear crises, when the costs of an uncooperative outcome (war) can be very high (Schelling 1966). Disputes over redistribution always have the potential, if they are mishandled, to lead to the dissolution of any system of cooperation, whether it is an alliance, an economic union, or even a state composed of regions bargaining over economic redistribution (Bunce 1999, 14).

capabilities outside of NATO in order to reduce its dependence on the United States.

In other words, N has a credibility problem; it cannot commit, in advance, to a cooperative agreement with a division of gains that would benefit both sides. This credibility problem is as much a problem for N as it is for V, since it means that both states wind up with self-sufficiency and thus are worse off than they might have been, in principle, from cooperation. The two states have a common interest in finding ways to solve N's credibility problem, thereby making cooperation possible.

In principle, the problem would be solved if N could commit, in advance, to self-restraint. The conditions under which such a commitment could be made credible, however, are quite limited; the credibility advantages sometimes attributed to democracies (Martin 2000; Lipson 2003), for example, do not apply in this instance. Democracies, the argument goes, are selective about which agreements they enter into. Because of broad domestic accountability and procedural hurdles in the legislative process, they enter only into those agreements that they expect they will prefer to uphold in the future. N's credibility problem, however, does not stem from a possible future preference to leave an agreement, but rather from a likely future bargaining advantage stemming from V's vulnerability. Democracies are just as able as nondemocracies to behave opportunistically by taking advantage of their partners' negotiating disadvantages (Gruber 2000), especially given their inability to commit even to core procedures (Schwartzberg 2004); this is especially true once the selection effects of the initial decision to make an alliance commitment are controlled for (Gartzke and Gleditsch 2004).

The nature of the outside option—self-sufficiency, free-riding, or conquest—has a substantial impact on the strategic importance of relationship-specific assets. Suppose states N and V cooperate, and both know that the alternative to cooperation is self-sufficiency. Since ending cooperation would cause V's investments in relationship-specific assets to be irretrievably lost, N could exploit V while cooperation persists. If, on the other hand, the alternative to cooperation were that V free-rides on N, then both sides know that if cooperation were to end, V would not lose its relationship-specific investments. As a consequence, V's investments in cooperation would not give N a bargaining advantage, and there would not be the potential for exploitation. Finally, V's relationship-specific assets likewise do not uniquely erode V's bargaining position if the alternative to cooperation is that N conquers V. V's alternative to cooperation—being conquered—is surely unpleasant but is so because of the nature of conquest rather than the loss of relationship-specific assets. V, once conquered, would presumably continue to be part of N's provision of markets and security. So the potential for one state to change the terms of the agreement over time is most severe when the alternative to cooperation is self-sufficiency.

Because of the potential for exploitation, the leaders of states sometimes have an interest in passing up opportunities for cooperation: they fear that the deals they agree to may get worse over time, since in the future they will be more vulnerable to the end of cooperation, allowing their partners to extort more in exchange for maintaining the relationship.

Conclusion

Cooperation is risky, because it can lead states to invest in assets that are valuable only as long as cooperation lasts. When a state is more vulnerable than its partners in cooperation, it can be exploited when its partners use their leverage to renegotiate the terms of cooperation, leaving the state worse off than it would have been had it never entered into cooperation in the first place. When cooperation would lead states to invest in assets that are highly and unequally relationship-specific, potentially vulnerable states have an incentive to refuse to cooperate; if they do refuse, both vulnerable and nonvulnerable states are made worse off by missing out on the potential benefits of military or economic cooperation. The problem is one of asymmetry: one side is vulnerable and one side is not. The next chapter considers institutional mechanisms that can artificially create symmetry between states—contrived symmetry that makes cooperation possible.

2

CONTRIVED SYMMETRY THROUGH INTERNATIONAL AND FEDERAL INSTITUTIONS

States sometimes forgo opportunities for mutual gain when cooperation would cause them to be unequally vulnerable in their relationship-
specific investments. With a partner able to exploit a state's vulnerability
by renegotiating the terms of cooperation once it has begun, that vulnerable state can lose more through extortion than it can gain by cooperation.
This lack of symmetry leaves both vulnerable and nonvulnerable states
worse off, since they miss getting the gains possible from military or economic integration. Both can therefore be better off if there is some way
for them to make their outside options, and therefore their bargaining
leverage, more symmetrical.

One method of doing so involves *contrived symmetry*. States contrive
symmetry when they artificially manufacture a situation in which all
states are vulnerable, rather than just one or a few of them, giving confidence to states that would otherwise be vulnerable.[1] Contriving symmetry
is costly and difficult; it can require creative leadership on the part of political strategists who devise ways to tie the political fortunes of the leaders
of nonvulnerable states to the interests of constituents in their otherwise

---

[1] The symmetry is "contrived" because it is something leaders "create in an artistic
or ingenious manner" and "bring about by stratagem" (*Merriam-Webster Collegiate
Dictionary,* 11th ed., 2003). Both Bryce (1888, 357) and Dicey (1885, 143) describe
federal systems as "contrivances" to emphasize that they are complex, artificial creations designed to meet particular needs. By "contrived," I do not mean to imply that
the strategies of constitutional framers are nefarious or improper.

vulnerable partners. To contrive symmetry, leaders make valuable invest-ments in institutions. These investments, which can take the form of po-litical parties, bureaucratic organizations, or possibly political identity, can create new possibilities for mutual gains that would otherwise have been unworkable.

This chapter presents the central argument of this book, that states choose federations rather than international organizations when they would benefit jointly from cooperation but cooperation requires high and unequal levels of relationship-specific investments. The first section discusses bond-posting as a metaphor for the way states create artificial relationship-specific investments, and describes how federations can hold bonds. The second section considers the variety of federal institutions and incorporates insights from existing studies of how federal systems operate in practice. The third section summarizes the expected consequences of federations and international organizations and combines these expecta-tions for how states cooperate with the discussion of the commitment problem that formed the basis of Chapter 1, to derive the preferences of state leaders for particular institutional arrangements. The fourth section describes how states bargain over different institutions, highlighting the importance of creative and flexible leaders who build federal agendas to bring new institutions into place. I conclude with observable implications of the theory, which I then test in subsequent chapters.

Bond-Posting Mechanisms

States contrive symmetry by manufacturing an institution that they can all invest in together. Investing in an institution is like posting a bond. In-stitutions are relationship-specific: they can be linked to continued coop-eration among states, and they can be costly for states to leave. Although institutions influence politics in other ways as well, part of the power of institutions comes from adding to the costs that members must pay if and when they leave.[2] Not only is political integration costly to undergo, but it creates costs of secession that are distinct from those costs that arise from either the benefits of cooperation forgone or from lost investments in other relationship-specific assets.

---

[2] Institutions can also alter outcomes by promoting transparency, creating com-mon expectations, and helping states to link issues and facilitate side-payments. These generally fall under the category of reducing transactions costs (Keohane and Martin 1995).

Suppose, for example, that Mexico were to exit the North American Free Trade Agreement (NAFTA). The costs of such a decision for Mexico's political leaders would arise from several distinct sources. First, leaving the agreement would mean that Mexico would pass up the future benefits of economic integration with the United States and Canada, including both the direct economic benefits from cooperation and any spillovers from trade, such as closer political relations with a neighbor. These are the gains from cooperation. Second, there would be a costly economic adjustment, as firms that had specialized in producing for export to the United States (or in using or distributing imports from the United States) either closed or adapted. These are exit costs that stem from relationship-specific investments. Both of these first two kinds of costs stem from the logic of cooperation generally, and so Mexico would have to pay these costs regardless of how NAFTA as an institution had been structured—whether as a federal union, an international organization, or ad hoc cooperation.

A third type of cost is political and follows from the nature of international or federal institutions themselves. In the case of Mexico, political costs might include a loss of credibility for political parties that had supported the treaty, the loss of a relevant issue to campaign on for those parties that had organized their political strategies around issues related to NAFTA, or a loss in relevance for lawyers, policy entrepreneurs, and bureaucrats who had developed expertise in the workings of laws and procedures related to NAFTA (such as dispute resolution procedures). For this third kind of cost it would matter a great deal whether NAFTA was a formal international organization, a federal union, or a series of ad hoc agreements, because the deeper the political integration, the more specific adjustments people will make to it. The economic costs (the first two) do not vary with the form of cooperation, but the political costs do.

As another example, if Quebec were to secede from Canada, it too would pay three kinds of costs. The first two, the loss of the benefits of cooperating with the other provinces (both economic and security) and the adjustment costs of developing alternative market niches and a new security strategy, would not depend on whether Canada was a federation, a customs union and alliance, or an ad hoc cooperative arrangement. The third kind of cost would stem from the nature of Canadian political institutions. The obsolescence of Quebecois political organizations at the federal level, the administrative expense of dividing specialized bureaucracies, and the losses to private actors who had adapted to specific political institutions (such as Canadian law) would all make separation highly costly, even more so than for a Mexican withdrawal from NAFTA.

The European Union is an intermediate case. A state exiting the EU might lose the benefits that come from being part of a common market.[3] Likewise, if an existing member of the European Monetary Union decided to withdraw from use of the euro and reissue its own national currency, it would both lose the benefits of lower transaction costs to trade and investment (the gains of cooperation) and pay the costs of making a transition (the exit costs due to relationship-specific investments). It would also have to pay some costs derived from the institutional arrangements that governed the euro, such as lost credibility in regional diplomacy and lost investments in gaining representation in monetary institutions such as the European Central Bank; Barry Eichengreen (2007) argues that these political costs are distinguishable from the economic ones. Exit costs that stem from institutions would likely be greater in the EU than in NAFTA, although not as great as they would be in Canada.

The costs of leaving that stem from political institutions have a key characteristic: they are automatic in that they do not depend on an affirmative decision of any one actor (a federal government or IO secretariat) to levy some punishment. Such a threat to punish would not be inherently credible beforehand, since the very act of leaving an organization undermines that organization's capacity and leverage in the first place. Bond-posting is an analogy commonly used to describe a mechanism that enacts punishment automatically. A bond—a payment that is forfeited if the payer reneges on a commitment—makes leaving costly; it is valuable to political leaders in one state only as long as they preserve their relationship with another state.

Jenna Bednar (2007) describes federalism as a system in which policy cooperation is enforced by the states themselves. In her model of federal unions, when one state violates the terms of the agreement, or attempts to free-ride on the efforts of others, other states act together to punish it. She notes that since carrying out a punishment is costly, states may have an incentive to secede rather than carry out their commitments to punish. As a result, she argues that when exit costs are low, the commitment to federal action is weak. The logic here is similar to the problem of second-order free-riding, where enforcement of contributions to a public good is itself a public good (Heckathorn 1989). Bednar's argument, however,

---

[3] This loss assumes that a state leaving the EU would also no longer be a member of the common market. Several nonmembers, however, are economically integrated either because they are "associate members" (such as Turkey and Iceland) or because they have negotiated separate agreements (such as the Mexico-EU Free Trade Agreement).

assumes that states must make affirmative decisions in order to punish one another. If federal institutions are thought of as fixed investments—like bonds that are automatically forfeit for a state that exits—then this restrictive assumption is unwarranted.[4]

Bonds have been studied extensively in other political contexts such as legislative bodies,[5] as well as economic organizations such as firms (Williamson 1985) or Better Business Bureau–style associations (Kreps 1990). A bond is a useful metaphor for the process of joining a federation as well, since federal institutions have many of the key features of bond-holding mechanisms. Joining an institution of any sort—whether a political party or union for a person, or an international organization or federation for a state—is costly. Adapting to success in a new environment takes time and energy that could otherwise be spent elsewhere. States therefore have little interest in putting down a larger bond than is absolutely necessary.

Federations and international organizations are different in degree rather than in kind, and identifying degrees of integration is difficult, even in principle. Riker (1975) sketches a range from anarchy through international law, treaties, international organizations, federations, and finally to unitary states, but scholars at the time disagreed about which label to apply to, for example, the North German Confederation (Hudson 1891) and the Caribbean Federation (Springer 1962). International organizations such as NAFTA or NATO are similar to federations in that groups of states join them in order to achieve some gains even at the expense of giving up some of their autonomy. In terms of holding bonds, the difference between federations and international organizations has to do with the differences in the costs of exit. In international organizations the costs to exit are lower (or nonexistent) than in federations.[6]

---

[4] Bednar does not assume enforcement by a central federal agent, but federal executives do have an encompassing interest in maintaining cooperation (de Figueiredo and Weingast 2005).

[5] For example, members of the U.S. Congress are better off if they cooperate with each other, but they need assurances that all will honor agreements. Joining a legislative party requires an upfront investment (in time, money, or position-taking) that eventually pays off (in producing a record of legislative accomplishment, or electoral support). Because legislators' reputations and policy positions are tied up with those of their parties, they are dependent on the party organization they have built their careers around. This makes them vulnerable to censure from other members or party leaders, which in turn makes their promises to the party credible (Cox and McCubbins 1994).

[6] I treat federation as a contract among states and avoid raising the issue of the origins of political authority within states. Following Riker (1975), I assume that it is harder for member states to defy a federal government than an international organization;

Another key characteristic of the mechanisms that can hold bonds in a federation or international organization is that the cost of each state's bond can differ. To contrive symmetry, the states devise a system that elicits a higher bond for the state (N) that would otherwise be less vulnerable and a lower bond for the state (V) that would otherwise be more vulnerable. This has the effect of offsetting the bargaining disadvantage that the vulnerable state would otherwise have.

Investing in an institution is a political project, rather than a legal decision. The formal documents that set up a federal constitution do not have magical properties that instantly create investments that will constrain states and their leaders in the future. Rather, investing in a federal institution, and thereby making a federal commitment credible, is a process that involves changes in the organization of political parties and bureaucracies as well as changes in popular ideas about national identity. In the case of the West Indian Federation (see Chapter 6), for example, the states signed a federal constitution, but then, contrary to expectations, the leading politicians from Jamaica chose not to seek office at the federal level and resisted the creation of a real federal civil service. Formal agreements notwithstanding, a federal system was never actually created.

I therefore focus on the actual investments that states make when they implement a federation, rather than the legal codes they adopt. Three specific institutional mechanisms can hold bonds among states and meet the necessary criteria for contriving symmetry among states: political and legal organizations that adapt to specific rules and institutions, military and bureaucratic organizations, and political identity. I conclude the section by discussing the ways states adjust these bonds so that they create more new constraints on some states than others.

Parties and Leaders

When a state joins a federation, it goes through a period of transition as people and organizations adjust to a new set of laws and institutions. The

---

I propose below some reasons why this might be. Other scholars (Elazar 1988, 1998b) work from a legal tradition and simply take enforcement as a given (through, in Elazar's formulation, a "covenant"), although it is a tautology to say that at higher levels of authority the center can enforce its rules and decisions more effectively. My argument is consistent with any conception of political authority that attributes to it two characteristics: political leaders can create new authority structures, and defying authority is costly.

closer the union—that is, the more like a federal union and the less like an ad hoc agreement—the more the political system adjusts to the change. These changes, costly to undertake and then costly to undo, give politicians an incentive to maintain the new status quo.

Party systems in particular can create incentives for elites to invest in maintaining a union. Politicians and parties in a federation have an incentive to invest their scarce political resources in acquiring representation at the federal level. They also modify their political strategies at the state level to take account of politics at the interstate level. For example, American political parties at the state or district level pay some cost for being associated with a particular national (federal-level) party or faction when that affiliation leads them to defend positions taken by the party's national platform which are unpopular in their own districts. This cost, however, is balanced against the benefits of being associated with broader party name recognition and record of governance, along with other private goods that party membership can provide (Ansolabehere, Snyder, and Stewart 2001; Snyder and Ting 2002). If the federation ends, these local parties will be left with the worst of both worlds: policy positions inappropriate to winning locally and lacking broader support from federal allies. Adopting a position suited to winning at the federal level is like an up-front investment: it costs, in terms of local support, but pays dividends in the long run, since it allows a politician to steer benefits to supporters. This dividend, however, exists only as long as the federal institution survives.

The political adjustment costs that come with the end of an institution give parties incentives to support the status quo, even when underlying preferences within a state point to secession. Many regional political parties in places where secessionist movements are pertinent use their leverage with their constituents to try to suppress the desire for autonomy or secession, because the leaders of those parties have a specific investment in the national political system as it exists (van Houten 2003).[7] By giving political parties much to lose if institutions fail, federal political systems create incentives for nearly any successful party or faction to support the continuation of the federal system.[8] In a federation, a party system that is national, rather than regional, is more effective at giving politicians

---

[7] An example is the enormous resources national parties in Canada invested to defeat secessionist measures in Quebec (Dion 1996; Martin 2003).

[8] Big decisions can be influenced by small political costs as long as those costs are focused on political leaders. See, for example, the literature on how audience costs (Fearon 1994) or organizations (Howard 2004) influence decisions about war and peace.

incentives to maintain the federal system as a means of preserving their own careers (Chhibber and Kollman 2004).[9]

Bonds posted via political parties make leaving an institution—whether an international organization or a federation—more costly. States do not design systems that make leaving so prohibitively costly as to be impossible, for at least two reasons. First, political institutions are costly to create, and the cost of joining an institution rises with the level of political integration: federations are costlier to join than international organizations, which are in turn costlier to join than ad hoc arrangements. Second, an institution from which it would be impossible to secede would not be in the states' interests anyway. Once the outside options for everyone become so bad that no one side has a large enough bargaining advantage to subject another to extortion, there is no reason to make those exit options even worse.

The leaders of one state in a federation might be challenged by a rival group of potential leaders who wish to take the state out of the federation. This possibility reinforces the importance of institutional investments. Domestic competition within a state that is in a cooperative relationship (whether a federation, an IO, or some other form) contributes to the costs to leaving, since deeply institutionalized cooperation between a state and its partners means that incumbent politicians within the state are tightly linked to that cooperation. The status quo creates winners, and those winners are willing to expend resources defending that status quo. Daron Acemoglu and James Robinson (2006), for example, show how incumbents are often able to prevent the adoption of new, social welfare–enhancing measures such as trade, technology, or political reforms. Think of "the ability to credibly threaten secession" as a kind of new technology that a state could in principle use to win benefits for itself by renegotiating the terms of a federal union with its partners. Any credible threat to secede, however, runs the risk of leading to an actual secession (Bunce 1999, 14; Laitin 2007, 29) and thereby threatens entrenched elites. Federal elites impose costs on any of their domestic competitors who seek to bargain

---

Existing literature on federalism highlights the importance of federal institutions' influence on elite incentives (Filippov, Ordeshook, and Shvetsova 2003, 163).

[9] Pradeep Chhibber and Ken Kollman (2004) note that not all federal party systems are equally effective at inducing parties to make investments in issues and organizations at the national rather than local level. Still, all else being equal, federal unions provide more of an incentive for political parties to invest in the center than international organizations do.

harder with other states in a way that would put the continued survival of the federal union at risk.

The reverse is also true. The survival of incumbent politicians who stand to be hurt disproportionately if the federal union ends and who, as a consequence, fight to defend it against domestic challengers will be increasingly tied to the survival of the federation itself. The fact that few if any federal constitutions specify secession procedures does not make secession impossible, but it does make it costly (Filippov, Ordeshook, and Shvetsova 2003, 104; Bednar 2007). Were there to be an actual secession from the Australian or Canadian federation, the outcome would be ambiguous and potentially risky for political leaders (Clarke, Kornberg, and Wearing 2000). Prior to the American Civil War, the legitimacy of and procedure for secession from the Philadelphia constitution was unclear, although most party leaders seemed to understand that secession would be extremely disruptive to the existing political parties (Deudney 1995).

The American Civil War superficially appears to be an example of federal institutions failing to prevent secession, but in fact, American antebellum institutions worked surprisingly well, preventing a breakup of the union for some seventy years. Historians have typically argued that the second party system in the United States maintained confidence in the union by incorporating local politicians and governments into a national party structure that was invested in the national government (Holt 1978; Kornblith 2003). The national parties, recognizing their interest in preserving the union, simultaneously fought off regional rivals and formed coalitions between northern and southern interests. Both parties (Democrats and Whigs), for example, ran balanced tickets composed of pro- and antislavery candidates for president and vice president, and the Democrats, the dominant party, kept rules that gave southerners an effective veto over national candidates and policies (Aldrich 1995, 133). The nationalization of political parties prior to the war not only held the union together but also protected southern states from opportunistic behavior on the part of northern states that might have preferred to renegotiate the original constitutional bargain in order to end slavery.

The extent to which leaders suffer if their state leaves the organization depends on the nature of the institution. Federations are costlier to leave than international organizations. In a federation, where parties are tightly integrated at the federal level, the political losses to breaking the organization can be quite high. In an international organization they are much lower but may be consequential in some cases. The European Court of Justice and the European Court of Human Rights produce decisions that are difficult for states to undo or evade precisely because they work through commitments made by leaders within their states to uphold judicial procedures; hence, national leaders in Europe cannot ignore international legal rulings without undermining the legal basis of their authority at home (Alter 1998; Mattli and Slaughter 1998). At still lower levels of political integration, such as alliances or customs unions, the costs to leaders of exiting a bargain may be slight, but even here, some scholars have argued, the institutions themselves can shape leaders' calculations either because their domestic publics value commitments for their own sake (Fearon 1994), or judge leaders' competence by the extent to which they live up to commitments (Smith 1998), or value the process that leads to commitments (Lipson 2003).

Militaries and Other Agencies

A second way states can post bonds is through the creation of specialized bureaucracies—in particular, joint military forces. Joining militaries has strategic implications that go beyond the merging and creation of other governmental organizations, but many of the initial consequences are the same. Once agencies are merged, leaving that cooperative arrangement is costly for each state because it has to manage disentangling its administrative apparatus from those of its former partners. In one sense, this is little different from the bonds posted through political parties or other kinds of institutions that adapt to cooperation, but agencies in general—and military forces in particular—have important strategic effects of their own.

Before considering these effects, however, first note that even though military integration may be a means to make it costlier for states to exit an organization, and can therefore be a part of a federal agreement, military integration is not synonymous with federation. The American states, for example, kept their own militias after 1787; the constitution, federal in other respects, did not specify that the militias had to be merged into a single army for administrative purposes, and there was no uniform trend toward a national military even after the Civil War (Riker 1957). Similarly, the Australian states maintained separate standing armies for the first fourteen years of federation (Coulthald-Clark 1988, 121–23). Just as federation does not necessarily imply military integration, military integration does not necessarily imply federation. Most NATO members participate in a unified military chain of command, and there are proposals for a common European defense force, even though the states have not formed a federal union.

The same is true for bureaucracies and agencies generally. The existence of specialized organizations is not itself a defining characteristic of federations; for example, the European Union has many such organizations, whereas the United States did not—even relative to the state governments at the time—until the growth of the federal bureaucracy in the 1840s (Basinger 2003).

Integrating militaries or other administrative agencies raises the costs of exit for several reasons. First, the ability to regulate society is a basic characteristic of states. A state that merges its administrative apparatus with that of another state and then later unmerges it will be at least temporarily without the means to exert control. In the transition to reasserting control, it bears all the administrative costs of taking control over state functions generally plus the additional costs and risks that follow momentary weakness or uncertainty.

A second reason has to do with the way governments control agencies. All organizations are controlled either through formal or informal mechanisms, whether the organizations are state agencies controlled by political bodies generally (Calvert, McCubbins, and Weingast 1989), or through military officers appointed by civilian governments and socialized to respect particular kinds of decisions (Huntington 1957). Consider an extreme case in which one of two states merging takes on complete control of the joint bureaucracy, and the other state gives up all control. If the relationship were to end, the state that had control of the bureaucracy would have an easy time adjusting, since its mechanisms of control would remain essentially intact. Russia, which inherited most of the Soviet Union's military and executive institutions, emerged from the dissolution of the USSR making far less adjustment than many of the other republics. The state that had no control of the bureaucracy (including the military), however, would be left not only without a means of defending itself but also without a means in place of controlling any military forces it did raise or new agencies it did create.

Other ways in which agencies can act as bonds are particular to militaries. When states merge their militaries, there are additional costs to secession beyond simply the administrative costs of dividing a bureaucracy. States can use their control of military organizations to raise the costs to other states of dissolving the union, either by using their military dominance to threaten with punishment a state that defects (for example, Russia's use of its military against Chechen separatists) or by using their control of a military to resist punishment (for example, most American officers before the Civil War were southerners, making it easy for the

Confederacy to field an army without much warning and difficult for the Union, at first, to punish the secession attempt).

Finally, an integrated military may increase the costs to states of ending cooperation if the process of military integration has led to social integration. The Roman army, for example, was an instrument not just of coercion but of social engineering, since it brought together men from across the empire who then established a common Roman identity; some historians argue that the army was as important a tool of Romanization as any other (Goldsworthy 2003). Integrated militaries that actually see combat may have an additional effect on both soldiers and citizens, solidifying bonds across a region: examples include the Australian military in World War I and the reunified American army in the Spanish-American War. To the extent that integrated militaries condition individual soldiers, who later become citizens, to identify with the wider community instead of just their home state, they make it more difficult for leaders to leave that community.

Identity

A third possible way that states can post bonds is through a general change in the political identity of leaders or citizens. My argument so far has been explicitly rationalist in assuming that the leaders of coalitions that govern states pursue specific goals, such as wealth or security. Suppose that, in addition, either leaders themselves or the citizens to whom they are accountable make choices based on their understanding of their identities as members of political communities. Although not a necessary part of the theory, national identity can play an intervening role in establishing federal bonds.

Political communities are groups defined by the way members feel about one another. People identify with others in their community, believing themselves to be alike in fundamental and exclusive ways. A community, or *demos,* is therefore characterized by a common "we-feeling" (Finnemore 2003) or a cognitive community in which individuals are prepared to internalize the welfare of others, knowing that they recognize one another as legitimate members of the group (Adler 1997).[10]

---

[10] Alexander Wendt (1999, 2003) describes moves toward mutual recognition within an ever expanding community in teleological terms, as part of an inevitable process that will eventually lead to a global or near-global federation. Political leaders in such a world would have a much harder time seceding from organizations. His argument

In practice, how people define themselves and their community can vary. Any one individual has a variety of potential identities (such as Catalonian, Spaniard, Catholic, or European), each of which suggests that the individual is part of a larger community of similar individuals (Catalonia, Spain, Christendom, or Europe). Which of these identities is activated at any one particular time is at least partly a product of politics. In general, the historical and sociological evidence suggests that elites have the ability to influence, at least at the margins, which particular identity is most relevant to the people. As a consequence, elites can influence the size and shape of a political community (Laitin 1986). Once constructed or activated, shared political identities can create constraints or imperatives for leaders, regardless of how those identities arose in the first place (Fearon and Laitin 2000). Most scholars, in any case, reject the idea that political identities are primordial (inherited from a distant past and not subject to change); they agree that shared political identity is often socially constructed in a process that involves not only symbolic actions by elites to shape a national community but also adoption of national identities by individual citizens seeking security, acceptance, or status within an environment made up of both elites and their fellow citizens (Anderson 1983; Laitin 2007).

Whether shared identity in a community is a deliberate construction by political elites, as it may have been in postwar Europe (Parsons 2003), the result of a dialogue between elites and masses over cultural symbols (Jones and Fowler 2007), or a consequence of other institutional choices (such as military integration), it can constrain future leaders by making leaving a community more costly than staying. Communities, then, whether in a federation or international organization—that is, whether we call them nationalisms or international communities—can be tools for posting bonds. At the very least, the effect of political identity is that, all else being equal, higher levels of political integration will lead to greater community or we-feeling, making exit more difficult.

Establishing a national political identity for a new federation is, at best, a difficult and risky project for political leaders seeking to bind themselves to a new set of institutions, especially when there are preexisting political

---

leaves room for agency. Individual political choices, such as democratization in his terms, can lead to a greater or lesser feeling of community among states and their people. Similarly, decisions about how to institutionalize cooperation may lead to a stronger or weaker affective community, resulting in more or less constraint on future choices. The development of a political community in Europe may be an example (Wendt 1999, 297).

or cultural differences among the member states (Laitin 2007, 81). The experiences of those federal unions that have successfully remained unified despite initial ethnic or cultural diversity (such as the United States, Canada, India, and Malaysia) suggests that national identity has the potential to be just pliable enough to accommodate federal institutions, although there is nothing to indicate that success is inevitable. (On the role of identity as an intervening factor, see Chapter 4.)

Binding Non-Vulnerable States

If federations are tools to contrive symmetry, political institutions need to impose higher exit costs on nonvulnerable states (N) than on vulnerable ones (V). Nonvulnerable states have an incentive to allow such imposition to happen. Because N is unable to commit credibly to being restrained once its potentially vulnerable partners are themselves locked in to cooperation, N is better off making itself more vulnerable, up to the point where its partners have confidence in their ability to bargain effectively.

Three examples of how institutions can be structured to create a higher bond for N than V are, first, ensuring that leaders from N are brought into political coalitions that separate them from the parochial interests of their constituents; second, tying N's interests to specifically federal bureaucracies; and, third, causing N to invest in physical assets that are specific to the federal institution, such as a capital city in a federal district.

First, states can make federal institutions that are costlier for N's leaders to leave than V's leaders by the way they structure political competition at the federal level. Suppose that in order to win federal power, politicians have to strike a balance between the interests of their local constituents and those of other federal politicians (from different states) with whom they need to form a governing coalition. Investing in achieving influence at the federal level is costly because it forces politicians to adopt positions other than those that would be most popular in their local constituencies. To achieve balance, the federal system needs to be set up in a way that gives leaders from state N more incentive than leaders from V to advocate policies contrary to those favored by their local constituencies. This can be done by establishing two conditions: first, leaders from N are likely to be in any governing coalition, and, second, leaders from N cannot govern the federation without drawing substantial support from other states with different interests.

In all the successful examples of federations surveyed in the empirical chapters of this book, vulnerable states in the federation outnumbered nonvulnerable ones. In Australia, for example, the leading vulnerable states (Victoria, South Australia, and Queensland) formed a bloc that acted more or less in unison in order to bargain effectively with the major nonvulnerable state, New South Wales. Prior to federation, all parties understood that the leaders of that nonvulnerable state would be key players in a governing coalition, but that the governing coalition would advocate much higher tariffs than its leaders would have chosen had they remained in power solely in New South Wales. In Germany, potentially vulnerable states such as Bavaria were more likely to join the federation voluntarily when there were already other vulnerable members such as Saxony in the federal group; these likely coalition partners gave the states confidence that they would be able to work in concert to protect their own interests.

In effect, political elites from state N are offered a bargain: they can rule the new federation, but in order to do so they must rely on political support from representatives of the more vulnerable states, and as a consequence they must advocate policies that are different from the ones their home constituents would ideally prefer. N's leaders thereby invest in a federal union by making themselves less popular at home; their most winning political assets become their connections to federal governance. They know that if the union ends, they will lose that key asset and be left powerless.

Second, the institution can lead N, the nonvulnerable state, to invest heavily in particular kinds of relationship-specific federal bureaucracies, creating a more vested interest among elites who specialize in handling legal issues (lawyers, accountants, lobbyists, and so on) in state N than in state V. On the surface, this result seems paradoxical, since stacking the federal bureaucracy with civil servants from state N should increase N's influence in the federation as a whole, rather than making N vulnerable. Having N penetrate the bureaucracy would increase N's bargaining ability if the bureaucratic organizations in which it had disproportionate influence were to control divisive issues, such as allocating tax payments or distributing scare resources. But if the bureaucracy N penetrates is one that provides public goods for the group of states as a whole with fewer distributive consequences, and is subject to oversight by representative institutions—such as a military organization providing a pure public good like area defense—then this disproportionate investment can reduce the value of N's outside option relative to V's outside option. If the federation ends, N's investment in agencies that produce regional public goods either is lost (in which case N has to pay high adjustment costs to revert to self-sufficiency) or persists (in which case N continues to provide the public good and V can free-ride on it); either way, the institution worsens N's exit options relative to V's.

To have this effect, the institutions N invests in must be most useful as means to produce regional public goods, and less useful as tools to pursue self-sufficiency. For example, in the West Indian Federation, the smaller, more vulnerable states tried to entice Jamaican elites in the civil service to join the federal agricultural services agency and specialize in developing farming techniques appropriate to the geography of the Leeward Islands. Once specialized, these educated elites in Jamaica would have been a voice for keeping Jamaica in a system where it provided public goods for the region as a whole—but once the federation ended, this Jamaican-led bureaucracy was left without a function. A related example is the investments that New South Wales, the leading nonvulnerable state in the Australian federation, made in regional defense. Specific units of the New South Wales military invested in fixed coastal defenses for parts of the Australian continent in Queensland and Western Australia in order to defend mail routes and telegraph installations that benefited the region as a whole. These investments gave the (albeit small) military establishment in Sydney a fixed investment in regional cooperation.

Third, the states can use the development of particular territory as a bond. Consider capital cities in special districts in certain federations, such as Canberra, Ottawa, and Washington. Placed either near or within the territory of a nonvulnerable state—New South Wales, Ontario, and Virginia—these cities were created for the sole purpose of being the federal capital and have little commerce or industry that does not specifically service the federal government. Upon joining a federation, the state that gets the capital city in or near its territory receives the economic benefits of a new city, but these benefits are tied to the preservation of the union and require costly adjustment if the union ends.[11]

Although these three mechanisms are not each, independently, necessary for a federal agreement, they are examples of ways states can devise federal institutions to ensure that N's federal bond is higher than V's.

Making the federal institutions costly for states to leave and costlier for N to leave than V are necessary parts of federal designs for contriving symmetry. When states decide to cooperate, they may choose to implement that cooperation through an institution. Institutions require an

[11] National capitals built in already-existing cities, such as Buenos Aires and Berlin, are evidence against my argument; I discuss them in Chapter 5.

initial investment to start up, and they raise the potential costs to their members of ending cooperation. In this sense, they are like bonds that states post. States can choose large bonds that will make substantial changes to their outside options (institutions more like federations), or they can choose small bonds that will make smaller changes to their outside options (institutions more like international organizations). For two states, N and V, with a credibility problem that prevents them from agreeing to mutually beneficial cooperation, a large bond can solve their credibility problem if potentially vulnerable states are able to ensure that their otherwise nonvulnerable partners would bear most of the costs of ending the institution.

Federations in Practice

The previous section explained why federal unions have characteristics that make them useful tools for contriving symmetry among states contemplating cooperation. In this section I describe the differences between federations and international organizations, explain why states would choose a federal institution rather that a unilateral institution to restrain a state, and discuss problems of voice and centralized encroachment within federations.

Federations and International Organizations

Both federations and international organizations are groups of states that have made commitments to cooperate under a given set of decision-making procedures. Politicians in a federation can advance their careers most easily by rising through parties that are tied to this center, so that those leaders with the ability to take their states out of the federation have a strong incentive not to do so. Potential challengers for political power might try to capitalize on secessionist sentiment, but they will do so without support from, and in the face of resistance of, all established political parties. Secessionist states will face the costs of rebuilding specialized bureaucracies, including a military, and of convincing their publics to change the way they think about their political identity. These costs of leaving are consequences of political institutions themselves, as opposed to consequences of the end of cooperation.

These same kinds of costs may apply to leaders of states that contemplate exiting from an IO, although they will be much smaller because in less extreme forms of political integration, the political system is less oriented toward the center. Most of the advantages commonly ascribed to international organizations have to do with reducing transactions costs, thus effectively increasing the value of cooperation. Since the specific commitment to an IO is low for most state-level political parties or bureaucracies, the exit costs to leaving an international organization are unlikely to be higher than the losses from cooperation forgone or from investments in relationship-specific investments. These costs, to be sure, may in some cases be quite high, and they may be enough to give states an incentive to maintain cooperation (Gourevitch 1999); however, the relevant question is not the magnitude of the exit costs but the symmetry. Exit costs in an international organization are unlikely to be much more symmetrical across the member states than exit costs from an ad hoc agreement.

The key distinction is between those exit costs that stem from the nature of cooperation itself and those exit costs that stem from lost investments in institutions. Leaving a weakly institutionalized organization that provides a desperately needed service may be costly, but such costs do not necessarily arise from the institution itself. In some cases it is possible, for example, to imagine politicians even gaining, at least in the short run, from leaving an unpopular institution. In 2006 the Iranian president contemplated ending his state's cooperation with the International Atomic Energy Agency. Doing so would have been costly, since it would have ended security cooperation with the West and heightened suspicions about Iran's nuclear program. These prospective costs, stemming from the end of cooperation itself, would probably have been quite large. The specific institutional costs to leaving, on the other hand, would be negligible; if anything, Iran's leaders might have benefited in domestic political competition by demonstrating their independence from international agreements.

Several existing studies of the workings of federal systems describe federalism in terms that do not completely distinguish federations from international organizations. In their thorough project on federal systems, for example, Mikhail Filippov, Peter Ordeshook, and Olga Shvetsova (2003) at times describe federal institutions as investments that are costly for state leaders to make, and therefore costly for them to leave, in a way that is consistent with my theory (34, 104, 191–94, 235). At other times, however, when they discuss the effect that federal institutions have on how states bargain with each other, they describe the institutions in terms suggesting that their main effect is reducing transactions costs by serving as a venue (118) or a point of coordination (147). The benefits to federations of transactions costs, however, can be gained through international organizations, and without a commitment problem there is little motive for states to invest in a federation in the first place.[12]

Multilateralism

If the whole point of contriving symmetry is to increase the exit costs to N more than to V, then why include V in the institution at all? In principle, the states could simply devise a system that elicits a bond from N, committing N to particular policies that N knows will be reassuring to V, but that does not elicit a similar bond from V. Leaving aside any practical considerations (such as that it is not clear how a unilateral commitment device would work), problems of incomplete contracting would prevent any unilateral bond from being credible.

States that cooperate to form a common market or to provide for their common security face many additional decisions once cooperation has begun. In a common market, they must constantly make regulatory decisions about the rules of competition, how private contracts are negotiated and enforced, and how their common external trade policy reacts to a changing environment. With a common security strategy, they must adapt to new technology and new threats and opportunities. All these unanticipated choices may have different implications for the partners, and they will be unable to fully foresee what their future preferences will be at the time they begin cooperating.

The usual solution to problems of incomplete contracting, like this one, is the allocation of residual rights (Williamson 1985; Hart and Moore 2005). In a firm, the contracting parties will designate either a single manager or a committee to arrive at decisions when new situations arise, whereas states in a union may write rules to specify in advance how to respond jointly to new issues (Koremenos, Lipson, and Snidal 2001).

Consider a situation where N and V agree to an international organization and N promises, in advance, that residual rights of control will be jointly shared between N and V. V knows that N's promise is not credible, since once V is invested in the relationship more heavily than N is, N

---

[12] Rui de Figueiredo and Barry Weingast (2005) posit that federal governments create more transparency among states than international organizations do, making it harder for states to free-ride, but other scholars have shown a variety of less costly mechanisms for IOs to promote transparency (Martin and Simmons 1998).

will have an incentive and an ability to renege on its commitment and reserve rights to itself. Scholars studying unequal international relationships have often found that one state reserves to itself the right to interpret the contract and decide how to deal with unanticipated situations (Lake 1999), especially if it is strong enough relative to its partners that it has the ability to establish separate contractual relationships with each of them (Nexon and Wright 2007).

Unequal relationships between a strong state with disproportionate residual rights and a weaker state are often called empires, although scholars differ on precise definitions (Doyle 1986a; Nexon and Wright 2007; Lake 2008). Traditionally, federations are thought of as distinct from empires, since federations formally lack a core state, and all members are treated as juridical equals. Alexander Cooley (2005), for example, says that his argument about the configuration of hierarchical organizations does not apply to federations because of this formal equality. As a practical matter, however, federations do arise from conditions of inequality, as tools to bind states, suggesting that ideas about unequal or hierarchic relationships are still relevant (Lake 1999).[13]

Voice and Governance

In federations, where exit costs are high, the stakes for states in acquiring a voice at the federal level are also high. A state that lacks an effective voice in federal governance, for any reason, will be at risk from its partners or from a rogue center. Because exit costs are higher in federations than in international organizations, states entering federations will place a higher value on protections from opportunism.

A federal government designed along simple majoritarian lines would therefore be unappealing to many potential members, because they would have no guarantee that their preferences would be taken into account in future decisions. Governance through minimum winning coalitions creates the potential for some states to be permanent losers. Proposed federal institutions therefore disperse power widely enough to give parties incentives to govern through supermajority coalitions. The separation of executive and legislative functions, bicameralism, and supermajority rules

---

[13] Cooley argues that territorially decentralized empires, as M-form organizations, are more flexible and adaptive than unitary, U-form organizations. Similar arguments about adaptability have also been made in defense of federal systems (Bednar 2008).

are all designed to give minorities a say; institutions that tie national parties to local parties—such as local control of elections, voter rolls, and legislative districts—give national parties incentives to maintain ties with local organizations across the union (Lijphart 1999; Filippov, Ordeshook, and Shvetsova 2003, 189, 235).

A related fear for potential member states is the risk of exploitation by a predatory central government. This is the flip side to the problem of disunity that may stem from central institutions that are too weak (Bednar 2008). Although tyranny by an uncontrolled center is not an inevitable feature of centralized political systems, there is no single solution. Independent judiciaries, for example, cannot by themselves restrain a central government, because courts do not have an independent power base. Dispersing power at the federal level can at least partly solve the problem by making it harder for a central government to gain control of all institutions. Dispersion also makes it easier for courts to use law and other normative constraints that allow disempowered actors to coordinate resistance to federal encroachment (Bednar, Eskridge and Ferejohn 2001; de Figueiredo and Weingast 2005).

Parallel to studies of how states protect themselves from a central government, a growing literature in international politics examines the mechanisms that states and leaders use to control international organizations. At least two kinds of factors have been shown to be important. One is the extent to which international organizations, as agents of governments, are able to act independently to determine a policy in line with their own interests (Barnett and Finnemore 2004; Haftel and Thompson 2006); another is the means states use to control and direct those agents (Nielson and Tierney 2003). Both of these, in turn, are functions of the kinds of investments that states have in the institutions, and the costs to states of exiting an organization and starting up from scratch a new system of cooperation. Where the costs of exit for states are low, executive agents in international organizations will be constrained from acting opportunistically, regardless of how the institution is organized internally, since the center knows that the states will simply dissolve the institution if it behaves in ways contrary to the interests of the members (Voeten 2004). The problem of diffusing power in order to restrain either narrow coalitions of member states or predatory centers is a more pressing problem in federal unions than in international organizations—and it is an independent reason why, all else being equal, states would prefer to cooperate via IOs than via federations—but states have often successfully managed it.

Ex Ante Preferences

Cooperation, whether through a federation, via an international organization, or ad hoc, is something that states must jointly choose. To derive a hypothesis about the conditions in which states will choose one form of cooperation over either another form or no cooperation at all, it is necessary to specify the preferences that states have. This is particularly important here since, as I argue below, federation is the result of a compromise in which at least one state does not get its most preferred outcome.

Consider two states, V and N, contemplating the formation of a common market or provisions for their common defense. This can be a moment before the states begin cooperating or, equivalently, a moment when these two states, already cooperating to some degree, are contemplating deeper cooperation. Assume that for these states the only alternative to cooperation is self-sufficiency (so free-riding and conquest are not feasible alternatives; I relax this assumption later). Should they avoid cooperation and pursue self-sufficiency?

Suppose that if V and N choose to cooperate, they have a choice between an institution with a low bond—call it an international organization—and an institution with a high bond: call it a federal union. (This limited choice is for the sake of simplicity here; in the next section I relax this assumption as well and consider a full range of institutions, from ad hoc cooperation through confederation and union.) Among self-sufficiency, international organization, and federation, V and N have different preferences because each expects that the outcome it gets will depend on which of these three options is chosen.[14] Assume, furthermore, that the states are in the situation I described at the end of Chapter 1: they could both, in principle, benefit from cooperation, but N cannot credibly commit to a distribution of benefits that would make V better off by cooperating.

Vulnerable States (V)

A vulnerable state that cooperates with a nonvulnerable state is at risk that N will use its exit option to renegotiate the terms of cooperation if there are no institutions to prevent it. Given a choice between self-sufficiency and weakly institutionalized cooperation, V prefers self-sufficiency. But

---

[14] By "preferences" I refer to the states' rank ordering of the various possible outcomes. These might be called intermediate preferences, since the outcomes are themselves means to achieving other goals.

V prefers federation to either of those. Since cooperation provides joint benefits, V would be happy cooperating as long as it could be guaranteed enough of those benefits to make it better off by cooperating than not. Only a federation, which makes bargaining between N and V more symmetrical by imposing exit costs on N, achieves this result. Prior to cooperation, then, states that would have high levels of relationship-specific assets in cooperation (state V) will rank possible arrangements by their expected payoffs this way:

> First choice: federation
> Second choice: self-sufficiency
> Third choice: international organization

Scholars have long recognized that actors in the more vulnerable positions prefer strong institutions. Workers and units within firms are better able to cooperate to their joint advantage when they have some guarantee of a positive return from investments in specialization, and the more complete and better enforced intrafirm contracts are, the more likely this guarantee (Stole and Zwiebel 1996; Acemoglu, Antráas, and Helpman 2005). States that have worse outside options, those that are poor (Grieco 1982) or small (Smith 2000), also prefer the stronger institutions. Concluding his study of relationship-specific investments, and the contract between Fisher Body and GM, Klein observed that organizations typically ensure that the parties with greater investments are protected by having more of an ownership stake (Klein, Crawford, and Alchian 1978).[15]

Note that this preference ordering assumes that the gains from cooperation are high enough to offset the initial start-up costs of forming a federation in the first place. V has federation as its first choice as long as the start-up costs are less than the value of what V stands to lose from having the weaker bargaining position that comes from being in an IO instead of the stronger bargaining position that comes from being in a federation. For any state to prefer federation to self-sufficiency, the

---

[15] For example, country clubs in which the members have intangible investments in their social relationships, but hired managers do not, often have a rule that existing members must vote on whether to accept new members. Managers making membership decisions would maximize revenue rather than the intangible value of the community's social network. The analogy to international clubs is weak, since Klein assumes that the courts can enforce the contract, but the point is that the institution is designed to boost the influence of the more vulnerable parties.

joint gains from cooperation must be quite high, as when the issue at stake is major, such as complete market integration or joint defense in a hostile world. Issues that do not implicate a risk of survival or a major swing in prosperity are likely to be dealt with via an international organization or treaty. Many, although not all, IOs deal with just one or a few issues, whereas federations typically involve comprehensive economic and security cooperation.

Non-Vulnerable States (N)

Between cooperation under a federation and cooperation under an international organization, N is always better off cooperating through an international organization: once the relationship is under way, it can get a better deal for itself, since with an IO it has more leverage to renegotiate agreements later. Federations also have higher start-up costs than IOs. N therefore always prefers international organization to federation.

As long as there are any potential joint gains to cooperation (such that the states working in concert can produce more than the sum of what they can produce separately), cooperation through a weak institution is always better than self-sufficiency. International organization offers the best possible outcomes from N's perspective.

When the joint benefits to cooperation are high relative to the start-up costs of federation, states (such as N) that would have low levels of relationship-specific assets in cooperation have this ranking:

First choice:	international organization
Second choice:	federation
Third choice:	self-sufficiency

In reality, states do not face a stark choice between a federation and an international organization as the only two ways to organize cooperation; there is a whole range of options, from ad hoc arrangements through treaties, IOs, confederations, and federal unions. I have been using the labels "federation" and "international organization" to stand in for the two sides of the continuum. In more general terms, the states have preferences for particular points along this range.

Although I have been describing N's preferred arrangement as an international organization, my theory actually predicts that N's first choice will always be the weakest possible form of cooperation: an ad hoc agreement with no institutions at all. In terms of contrived exit costs, however, the difference between an ad hoc agreement and an international organization is probably small; I consider N's preference as being for an international organization because IOs probably have other advantages over ad hoc cooperation in that they reduce transaction costs (this advantage is not captured in my theory, although as I noted in the Introduction, other scholars have explored these advantages at length). Within a continuum of possible agreements, N's preference is simply always for a less institutionalized form.

V's preference is always for a more institutionalized form of cooperation, as long as the gains from cooperation outweigh the start-up costs of forging an agreement. V prefers federation to confederation, confederation to international organization, and international organization to ad hoc arrangement.

Negotiating Federal Unions

If federation were the ideally preferred outcome of all members of a group of states, there would be nothing left to explain. My theory, however, does not predict this harmony of interests. At least some states in a potentially cooperative group—those who would not be vulnerable to relationship-specific assets (state N)—never have federation as their first choice and always prefer cooperation through an ad hoc arrangement or, at most, an IO. No states in groups with similar levels of relationship-specific investments would prefer federation, since there would be no need for institutions to contrive symmetry among states that were already symmetrical. So, where a federation does emerge, it is always the second-best alternative for at least some of the members. Two of the critical elements necessary for states to reach a federal bargain are (1) threats to hold out (V's willingness to reject cooperation via an international organization and demand a federal union instead) and (2) federalists (political entrepreneurs who devise federal agreements and put them on the agenda).

Holding Out

There is a difference between preferences and strategies. As Jeffrey Frieden (1999) explains, actors have preferences as to outcome but are often unable to attain what they see as the best possible outcome. Anticipating that they will fail if they push for their best outcome, they adopt a strategy aimed at securing an outcome that, even if not ideal, is better than the likely alternative.

N and V form a federation when V ideally prefers a federation and, failing that, will choose self-sufficiency over any other form of cooperation. Since cooperation requires the agreement of both parties, V's willingness to veto any form other than federation gives it leverage.

N has a choice: it can propose its first choice, cooperation with a low level of institutionalization such as an international organization, or its second choice, federation. If N proposes its first choice of an IO, V will reject it, preferring that the states not cooperate at all. Both N and V, however, would rather cooperate through a federation than not at all. If N and V are able to negotiate a solution that leaves them each better off, then together they will choose a federation.[16]

In holding out, vulnerable states do not have a credibility problem, since they genuinely prefer self-sufficiency to cooperation under anything less than a federal union, as long as both N and V understand each other's preferences. Suppose, however, that N is uncertain of V's preferences, so that N does not know whether V will accept an IO instead of self-sufficiency (that is, suppose N is uncertain about V's subjective valuation of either the benefits to cooperation or the level of V's relationship-specific investment). When V demands a federal constitution and threatens self-sufficiency if its demand is not met, N does not know whether or not V is bluffing. Even in this situation, all else being equal, as long as actual higher levels of relationship-specific investments for V lead N to an increased estimate of the probability that V's level of such investments is high, then higher levels for V are still related to a greater chance that the states will form a federation.

These kinds of additional informational caveats, however, are probably unnecessary. States contemplating federation are likely to be neighbors, with a history of interactions and a dense network of contacts. Unlike wars involving rogue states or guerrilla armies (common subjects for models using incomplete information), this situation is one in which the players are likely to have a great deal of information about each other. Even if there is uncertainty at first, leaders can take time to figure out the facts. The Australian federal process spanned at least twelve years, and the Argentine and German processes lasted for decades. In each case, political parties, private advocacy groups, and government agencies spent years evaluating the prospects for federation and the bargaining positions of

---

[16] This assumes that there are no other impediments to bargaining, such as incomplete information or sources of mistrust other than the ones I have already taken into account.

partner governments. It is more likely that the preferences of these political systems were relatively transparent to each other, at least with respect to federation, than that the leaders were able to hold multigenerational bluffs.

The logic of holding out is different when the alternatives to cooperation are free-riding or conquest, instead of self-sufficiency. If the gains from cooperation are not excludable, the potential for free-riding complicates the states' strategies. If V can free-ride on N's efforts, then N cannot credibly threaten to cut off V in exchange for concessions, since by definition N would be unable to provide for itself at all without inadvertently helping V. To return to the NATO example from the Introduction, the United States in the Cold War would not have been able to renegotiate the terms of an agreement to suit itself, to the detriment of its European allies, because the United States had no realistic outside option; the only way for it to provide for its own security would have been to prevent the Soviet Union from conquering Europe. Recognizing that their outside option, free-riding, would get them what they needed anyway, Europeans knew they would not be left in a vulnerable position. With little risk of renegotiation, Europeans did not have an interest in contrived mechanisms to worsen the American exit option. The logic of the argument therefore suggests that where the benefits to cooperation are not excludable, states do not choose federation.

Another option is conquest. Supposing that N would be able to conquer V cost-effectively, both N and V understand that N would prefer to conquer V than to be self-sufficient. But since conquering a partner is still costly, there are at least some types of agreements with low start-up costs and few constraints for N that N would prefer to conquest. As always, N prefers a weak institution such as an alliance to a strong institution such as a federation. Supposing that conquest is costly enough, either because of the inherent costs of violence or because conquest would destroy some of V's value as a partner, then N would prefer an international organization to a federation and would prefer a federation to conquest.

V prefers a federal union to a weak institution, although either would be preferable to being conquered by N. But even if V is clearly at a disadvantage, it can be possible, in some conditions, for V to hold out for a federal agreement. By threatening to resist unless it gets a federal agreement, thereby raising N's costs of conquest, V may be able to elicit some concessions. Although N ideally prefers an IO and V ideally prefers a federation, each side would accept the other's preference rather than fight a war, making a negotiated compromise possible. The negotiated entry of Bavaria into Germany and the *litoral* states into Argentina demonstrate this possibility.

Federalists

The reason federal constitutions are so varied is that a federal system must be adapted to particular local conditions in order to be successful. Scholars have generally agreed that the variety of federal systems is so wide that federalism is impossible to define a priori (Filippov, Ordeshook, and Shvetsova 2003, 9). My argument can account for this, since I show that federal institutions need to serve more than one goal, such as guaranteeing representation for all members while eliciting larger investments from some states. Matters of institutional design have important consequences, and federal institutions suited to one situation might not be appropriate tools for contriving symmetry in another situation. Designing a workable federal union is a complex and delicate task, with no practical off-the-shelf blueprint available. As a result, federation requires the presence of creative and motivated leaders, people willing and able to propose a workable system, set an agenda, and coax states into implementing it. I refer to these entrepreneurs as federalists.

The most important problem federalists face is designing a constitution that will *both* lead nonvulnerable states to invest enough to give vulnerable states confidence that integration would not be to their detriment, *and* be politically acceptable to nonvulnerable states. Even where this is possible in principle, there may be a process of false starts and trial and error. In Australia, the final round of negotiations that led to federation lasted over a decade, and at least two initial drafts were rejected before federalists produced a mutually acceptable compromise. Constitutions for Argentina and the West Indies likewise went through multiple revisions. In all these cases, federalists served as intermediaries, negotiating with state leaders on all sides in order to better refine their proposals.

In addition to acting as proposers and intermediaries, federalists can also manipulate the decision-making agenda to further political integration. The process that leads to a decision about whether to federate can be important in situations where there is a range of mutually acceptable options—for example, V prefers a federal union but would be willing to accept a weaker confederation, while N prefers a weaker confederation but would be willing to accept a federal union. If several solutions are possible, the structure of negotiations matters. Similarly, constitutional conventions can be held in ways that allow them to circumvent internal sources of opposition, but only if agenda-setters are clever. In the Australian case, after an unsuccessful attempt at negotiations beginning in 1889, federalists proposed the direct election of state representatives to a constitutional drafting meeting and were careful to ensure that the candidates elected would favor federation (Loveday 1972).

Federalists are also necessary to coax new member states into making political investments in federal institutions. Negotiating interstate party alliances, which then become the foundations of federal parties, are a first step—a step that was never completed in the case of the two failed federations considered in Chapter 6. In order to bind nonvulnerable states tightly to federal institutions, federalists also need to devise ways to ensure that political elites from such states are brought into coalition governments where they must rely on support from representatives from vulnerable states in order to maintain their hold on power. Federalists in Victoria, for example, successfully lobbied that the leading ministers of New South Wales be given turns at serving as prime minister in the new Australian federal government.

Why might creative and talented politicians devote time and energy to federalism? Ideology is one possibility. Although federalism is rarely an ideological end in itself (McKay and McKay 1999, 34), some entrepreneurs may place an ideological value on unification and see federalism as the best available means to that end.[17]

Federalists who are insiders within a region may get private benefits from union, if they are able to take advantage of some slack in the constitutions they write in order to ensure their own futures. Several leading Australian federalists ended up with positions in the federal ministry (including Edmund Barton, who became the first prime minister after leading the Federalist Party in New South Wales) or on the High Court (including Samuel Griffith whose later history of Australian constitutionalism I cite in Chapter 3).

Federalists may also be outsiders who nonetheless stand to gain from political unification because they have a large interest in regional unity or stability. In the West Indies the initial round of federal proposals came from British colonial agents who hoped that a politically unified region would be more prosperous and less in need of British financial assistance. These federalists did not have the power to carry out a federal union unilaterally, since for both practical and ideological reasons they could not force the states together. But they did act as proposers and intermediaries

---

[17] The literature on German unification includes several early studies that privilege ideological factors (Friedjung 1935; Eyck 1950; Pflanze 1963), but ideology cannot account for variation within the German case or explain why similar ideologies in other places, such as Italy, did not produce similar results (Ziblatt 2006).

in an attempt to work out a deal. Contemporary American or UN mediators in post-conflict regions such as Iraq play the same role: they have some ability to set agendas, even if they can only rarely act directly to implement their preferred solutions.

Summary

This chapter and the one before it argued that there are instances where states are unable to cooperate without binding political institutions, circumstances in which cooperation requires one or more of the states, but not all, to invest heavily in relationship-specific assets. Asymmetry in relationship-specific assets can make it impossible for the states to commit to a division of the benefits of cooperation that makes all states better off. Federal constitutions are a way for states to contrive symmetry by making sure that *ending* cooperation would be costly for *all* members. Doing so resolves the problem of commiting to a distribution of joint benefits from working together such that all members can be confident of gaining by cooperation.

States that would be put at risk from extortion once they were in a cooperative relationship demand political integration from their partners as a precondition for cooperation. To avoid being subject to extortion themselves, they turn the extortion around by demanding as the price of cooperation, up front, political integration that is as deep as they can get from their partners. Their partners give in when the benefits of cooperation are great enough that in order to attain otherwise unattainable cooperation, they are willing to subordinate themselves to political integration.

Theory: Federations form when states benefit from cooperation but cooperation requires unequal levels of relationship-specific investments.

This theory has several advantages over the way political scientists have tried to explain federations before. It can account not just for why states form federations instead of pursuing self-sufficiency but also for why they form federations instead of international organizations. By treating the decision of whether or not to federate to pursue common goals as part of the same decision as whether or not to pursue common goals in the first place, the theory explains not just that federations are an efficient solution to particular commitment problems but how states pursuing their selfish interests can ultimately arrive at a federation.

I introduced the theoretical argument as being something like a possibility theorem. In a particular situation—gains to cooperation but asymmetrical relationship-specificity—states might be able to agree to cooperate through a federation but not by any other mechanism. Many groups of states may never find themselves in such a situation, and there is no way, a priori, to predict when, specifically, states will do so. Furthermore, given the importance of political entrepreneurs—federalists—idiosyncratic factors such as the availability of creative leaders can be critical. Still, the theory can be investigated empirically because in places where these conditions seem to hold, it is possible to test several observable implications about the process by which the states formed or did not form a federal union:

1. States form federations in order to achieve joint gains in the production of excludable goods.
2. Federation is not the result of a consensus. One or more members will prefer cooperation by means of less binding institutions.
3. Leaders of states that would have few relationship-specific investments in cooperation prefer to cooperate via weak institutions, such as an international organization or ad hoc arrangements.
4. Leaders of states that would have highly relationship-specific investments in cooperation prefer to cooperate via a federation but reject cooperation via international organizations and other ad hoc arrangements.
5. States that would have highly relationship-specific investments in cooperation will resist making those investments until after their less potentially heavily invested partners have first invested in federal institutions; states that would have few relationship-specific investments in cooperation will seek to elicit relationship-specific investments from their more potentially heavily invested partners before they invest in a federal institution.
6. When joining a federation, states with fewer relationship-specific investments than their partners will invest more heavily in federal institutions, through changes in party systems, investments in bureaucracies, or creation of new federal cities in their territories.

I test these independently falsifiable implications in the following four empirical chapters before returning to some general conclusions.

3

AUSTRALIA'S EXPERIMENTS
WITH INTERNATIONAL ORGANIZATION
AND FEDERATION

Why is Australia one country instead of six? Why are Australia and New Zealand two different countries? Although in retrospect Australia and New Zealand seem to have logical boundaries, there was nothing inevitable about them at the start. The six states that today form the Australian federation were, de facto, separate countries from the 1850s until they federated in 1901. The inability of New South Wales and Victoria, over many rounds of failed negotiations in the 1870s and 1880s, to reach an agreement on a customs union via an international organization but then the success with which they negotiated a federal union are superficially puzzling. A federal constitution to contrive symmetry was necessary, since the root of the problem with Australian proposals for an international organization in the late nineteenth century was the inability of New South Wales to commit to refrain from revisiting the terms of cooperation once it started.

The process that led to Australian federation provides several opportunities to investigate all six of the testable hypotheses listed at the end of Chapter 2. My focus in this chapter is mostly on the politics of federation in the two largest states, New South Wales (a relatively nonvulnerable state, taking the role of state N as I defined it in the theory chapters) and Victoria (state V, more vulnerable to integration), although I also find evidence in the other four states and New Zealand as well.

This chapter proceeds in five parts. First, I provide an overview of the political process that resulted in federation. Second, I discuss possible security motives for federation in order to refute William Riker's argument

about the military origins of Australia and to test the first implication of
my theory, concerning excludable goods. Third, I describe the bargaining between New South Wales and Victoria and show how the differences
in preferences over federation between these major states test the second
through fifth implications of the theory, concerning relationship-specific
assets and varying preferences as to how cooperation is structured. Fourth,
as an additional test, I trace the negotiations over the federal constitution
to show how Victoria and the other, more vulnerable, states held out until
New South Wales accepted federation. Fifth, I explore the federal institution itself, as proposed in the 1890s, to show how it held bonds from the
states and how it was able to extract a higher bond from New South Wales
than from the other states; in the course of doing so, I also account for the
struggle between New South Wales and Victoria over how to approach
New Zealand's candidacy for membership.

Overview

Beginning with New Zealand in 1853, the Australasian states—New South
Wales, New Zealand, Queensland, South Australia, Tasmania, Victoria, and
Western Australia—became self-governing dominions within the British
Empire when the British government began to disentangle from its settler
colonies. By 1860, when Queensland became self-governing, all the states
except nearly empty Western Australia were governed by locally elected
parliaments. The token force of British troops that remained was inconse-
quential, and the last of them withdrew in 1870 (Trollope 1968 [1873], 259).
In general, Australian states had independent foreign policies well before
either federation or official recognition. From the 1870s, nations such as
Germany and the United States pursued their interests with these colonies
"on the basis of *de facto*, if not *de jure* equality of status" (Veit-Brause 1988,
143). Figure 3.1 shows the states with their years of self-government.

The seven states were largely focused on developing their new territories. Diverse by European standards, the states were mixed both religiously
(Protestant and Catholic) and ethnically (English, Irish, Scottish, and some
continental Europeans).[1] Most infrastructure was local, as the states built
railroads connecting the farms, pastures, and mines of the interior to the

---

[1] The colonists did not establish treaty relations with Australia's indigenous inhab-
itants, and Aborigines did not participate in the white political process. The Maoris
in New Zealand eventually won substantial concessions but were still politically mar-
ginalized during the federation period (Buchan 2000).

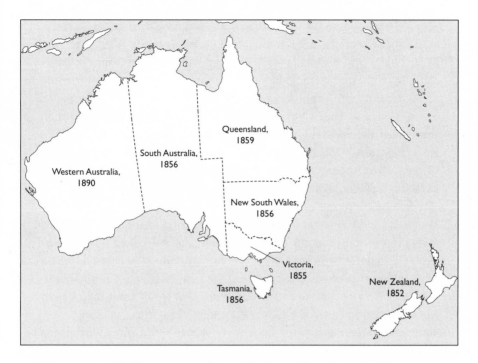

Figure 3.1 Dates of self-government in the Australasian states (distances are to scale)

major port cities; there was little demand for transportation links between the major cities, arrayed along the coast (Clark 1908a,b; Harman 1970).

Still, the states had several common goals, and newspapers and political memoirs emphasizing the importance of regional cooperation led to several regional conferences. At one, in 1863, the states rejected a proposed formal international organization and instead instituted a regularized system of informal meetings. These meetings produced nonbinding resolutions that often went unimplemented, especially on divisive issues such as tariffs, although they did successfully coordinate policies on marriage regulations, agricultural standards, common postal rates and routes, and telegraph lines (Moore 1910; Livingston 1932; Mines 1969; Dalziel 1987). Trade was relatively open throughout the 1860s, but by the end of that decade the states began to erect substantial barriers against one another's products.

In 1881 the premier of New South Wales, Henry Parkes, proposed an IO system incorporating all the self-governing "Australasian" states (a formulation that included New Zealand), whereby a committee of parliamentary delegates would be empowered to make decisions on behalf of the group. The proposal did not, however, contain provisions for an executive authority or administration to carry out decisions (Wise 1909, 164). New South Wales and Tasmania strongly supported the plan, but the other states were not interested and pushed for a more centralized government.

Eventually, both proposals were abandoned, and Victoria, Tasmania, and Queensland began formally cooperating through a new institution they called the Federal Council. The council was a forum for delegates from the individual states with a legislative process similar to today's EU Council of Ministers. Despite the name, it was not really a federal system in that it included neither an executive nor any sort of bureaucracy; nor did it include a proposal for a customs union (Aroney 2000). New South Wales and New Zealand both participated in the negotiations over the formation of the Federal Council, but both states declined to join. New Zealand's delegate observed that there seemed limited benefits, and Sydney's leaders expressed concerns about the legal standing of council decisions and were hesitant to approve anything that would limit their leeway to pursue their own trade policy (Beach 1899). In particular, chambers of commerce and the allied Free Trade Party in New South Wales were always skeptical of the value of a strong central authority (Turner 1904, 332). New South Wales, New Zealand, and the other nonmembers did, however, participate in the council meetings on an informal basis, often holding parallel meetings in the same building.

Throughout the 1880s, market division grew as protectionist parties tightened their grip in Victoria and the other smaller states. New South Wales and New Zealand remained open to trade; although their interests were harmed by lack of regional market access, they benefited from trading on world markets. Still, the lost opportunities for regionalism eventually led the government of New South Wales in 1889 to agree to open federal negotiations. A series of conventions met on and off for the next decade; the states ratified an agreement in 1899; and the federation took effect on January 1, 1901.

Australians studying their origins have long noted that the relevant question to ask is why the Australian states federated when they had an alternative available: coordinated action through decentralized cooperative arrangements (Baker 1897; Reeves 1902; Irving 1999; Hirst 2000). To account for Australian federation, a theory needs to explain not just why the states federated but also why they did not instead choose to cooperate via a system of customs unions and military alliances as they had originally discussed, why each of the six states joined but New Zealand did not, and also why they did not federate sooner.

Writing just after the successful completion of the public referendums that ratified the federal constitution, Premier Alfred Deakin of Victoria cautioned against taking Australia for granted: "All History takes on the appearance of inevitableness after the event. Looking backward the future will be tempted to say that Australian Union was Australia's destiny from the first and that nothing could have prevented its consummation" (Deakin and La Nauze 1963, 172). In fact, there was nothing inevitable about it; studies of the origin of the federal system there are not posing a trivial question. Before 1901 a federation of six of the states and independence of New Zealand was only one of four possibilities.

First, the states could have chosen to remain independent, perhaps cooperating through an IO. In 1901, interested observers certainly did not see a federation as inevitable, and many predicted that it would fail (Parker 1964, 156; Pringle 1975). In his memoirs the attorney general of New South Wales noted "such a sullen and deep-seated hostility between New South Wales and Victoria, that at times it seemed as if the history of the South American republics might repeat itself" (Wise 1909, 162). The drafters specifically considered retaining weak cooperation through an international organization as an alternative to the federation, and in each state there were at least some political leaders advocating this course as an alternative to federation (Beach 1899). They had access to a wide range of historical scholarship, political thought, and prior examples of federations, confederations, customs unions, and military alliances from North America, Central Europe, and the rest of the British Empire, and during the federation period they produced careful and detailed analyses of these various forms (Aroney 2002).[2]

Although it seems implausible in retrospect, at least some leaders expressed concern that relations among the Australian states would be far less harmonious in the twentieth century than they were in the nineteenth. George Grey, then governor of New Zealand, observed the rise of trade barriers and told the New Zealand parliament in 1884 that in the future Australia would still be divided into several states, with militarism and war between them (Sinclair 1986a, 83). The president of the upper house of the South Australian parliament predicted that "the more populous these colonies become the more questions leading to friction and disputes

---

[2] Studies of federal theory by Australians writing prior to the conventions (Baker 1891; Stuart-Cansdell 1891; Willoughby 1891; Griffith 1896a; Baker 1897a; Baker 1897b; Garran 1897) hold up reasonably well in comparison with the theoretical scholarship on federalism that followed in the twentieth century.

between them will arise. Republics are notoriously quarrelsome, and all history and experience have shown that no ties, not even those of a common origin, speech and religion will in the end prevail against self-interest. The most bloody and vindictive wars have been waged between kinsmen" (Baker 1897b, 5). Trade disputes especially were seen as a possible source of friction that could spill over into military conflict (Baker 1891, 5; Galloway 1899).

Second, the states might have formed the federation with a limited membership. The bill to enact the 1901 constitution was controversial in New South Wales and passed only on the second referendum. Some in the popular press predicted that New South Wales would absolutely never join (Vogel 1898). Similarly, as late as 1900, plans for federation excluded Western Australia. In 1899 its parliament rejected the federal constitution, and through 1900 politicians in the other states dismissed any possibility that Western Australia might join (Robertson 1897; Parsons 1899; British Parliament 1900, 29). Finally, in July 1900 Western Australia held a referendum, after a long political battle that raised the possibility of civil war (Battye 1924; Bastin 1964). The federation bill passed, surprising most outside observers, who had assumed that the state would stay out.[3]

Third, the federation might have included New Zealand, which had been settled by the same sort of people, had trade ties with the Australian mainland, and participated in regional meetings and the regular premiers' conferences. Geography alone is an insufficient explanation for its omission. Tasmania, also an island, did join the federation, as did Western Australia, even though Perth (its major city) was farther from Sydney than Auckland (New Zealand's major port) and could be reached only by sea (Grey 1901, 215). Keith Sinclair, New Zealand's foremost national historian, argues that the colonial histories of New Zealand and the rest of Australasia show that separation was not inevitable and that New Zealand and Australia did not have "separate manifest national destinies." Not only did "no one contemplating inter-colonial negotiations in the eighteen-seventies" have "convincing reason to forecast that within thirty years six

---

[3] Rudyard Kipling's poem extolling federation for the *Times of London*, published on October 4, 1900, excludes Western Australia, referring throughout to the "Five Free Nations." Changing the number from "five" to "six" would have required Kipling to alter the couplet "Lit with her land's own opals, levin-hearted, alive / And the five-starred cross above them, for sign of the nations five." He might not have found an adjective for opals to rhyme with "six."

of the colonies would federate, [but] it would have been equally difficult to foresee that New Zealand would stay out" (Sinclair 1970, 153, 175).

New Zealand rejected the proposed Federal Council in 1881, despite active involvement in the negotiations. Its representatives proposed two amendments to the council's charter and withdrew only when Victoria vetoed them. Likewise, New Zealand sent delegates to the federal conventions in 1891 and participated in the constitutional drafting process. As late as 1889 the founder of the Melbourne Chamber of Commerce predicted that New Zealand would inevitably join the union (Westgarth 1889, 371).[4]

Fourth, the states might have adopted the federation sooner than they did. One Australian constitutional scholar writes: "That forty years should have elapsed between the establishment of responsible government in five of the six Australian colonies and their decision to come together in a federation may seem remarkable" (McMinn 1979, 92). Compare the United States, in which the states formed the Articles of Confederation immediately following independence and the 1787 constitution within only a few years. Similarly, the South African, Malaysian, and Canadian (except Newfoundland) states all formed federations almost immediately upon independence.

My theory explains these counterfactuals by accounting both for the New South Wales change from opposing federation before the 1880s to supporting it later and for New Zealand's initial interest in federation but ultimate refusal. Two key changes, in the early 1870s when protectionist industrialist parties took control in Victoria and in the early 1880s when technological changes opened up European and North American markets to New Zealand's exports, account for the outcomes.

Security and Excludable Goods

States federate when there are joint gains to producing an excludable good, but cooperation requires some states, though not others, to invest heavily in relationship-specific assets. The good that the states seek to produce can be anything, although the value of it must be high enough to overcome states' natural reluctance to pay the high start-up costs of federating. (The theory chapters described both military and economic integration.)

My argument differs from that of William Riker (1975), who contends that states federate only when they face a common security threat. The

---

[4] Even after 1901, some observers expected that New Zealand would join (Grey 1901, 220), and proposals for it to do so still occasionally surface (Craig 1993).

particular case of Australia, however, shows some of the weaknesses of this contention. The states federated despite not being faced with a security threat and even though they were perfectly capable of cooperating without a federation to meet any security threat that might have arisen.

Riker argues that the Australians formed a federation in 1897–1900 because of the accumulation of aggressive imperialism by France in the New Hebrides, by Germany generally, and by Japan in Korea (1975, 120). Yet the only time the states perceived any sort of threat was from Russia in the 1870s, when they responded by cooperating on defense preparations but did not seriously consider federating. By the 1890s there were no plausible security threats at all, yet this was when the states finally began negotiating the federal union in earnest. The near-universal consensus among Australian scholars writing on the federation period is that security was not a real motive, given the extreme implausibility at the time of any genuine military threat reaching Australia and the relative ease with which the states could have formed a military alliance had there been a crisis (Serle 1969, 50; Trainor 1970; La Nauze 1972; Johnson 1974, 176; Norris 1975; Martin 1980; Coulthald-Clark 1988, 121–23; Donovan 1990; Grey 1990, 43, 53; Spillman 1996, 155; Grey 2001, 6).

A regular report by the British Colonial Defense Committee in 1890 noted that geography made any attack so improbable as to be unworthy of consideration, given the technological and financial constraints on large-scale amphibious operations, the enormous distances to even the nearest naval bases of other great powers, and the security provided by the British and American navies (Duckworth 1899; Chapman 1961; Johnson 1974, 176; British Parliament, 1890, 30–32). The Australasians did not perceive threats from French (Serle 1969, 16) or German (Veit-Brause 1986) activity in the Pacific, since the Australasians' relations with other great powers were more cooperative than Britain's.

Security motives, furthermore, cannot account for the earlier choices the states made not to federate, or for New Zealand's choice to stay out entirely. And although Western Australia was the most exposed to an attack, it was highly unmotivated to join the federation; likewise, the westerners around Perth, the most exposed to invasion, resisted federation the most (Crowly 2000). By contrast, Tasmania and South Australia, on the south side of the continent, were sheltered from any plausible invasion route and in any event, as small states, could have easily free-ridden on security from the others—but they were strong supporters of federation.

Security, for the Australians at this time, was nonexcludable. The best way for the larger and wealthier states to ensure their own defense was to ensure the defense of the smaller and poorer states. New South Wales, the most populous, had been the first to contribute troops voluntarily to British military campaigns in the Sudan and in South Africa, which were seen as important for preserving Australian access to trade routes and communications lines to Europe (Connolly 1978; Saunders 1985). Conventional alliance theory suggests that with an anarchic arrangement, New South Wales would bear a disproportionate share of the costs of providing security (Olson and Zeckhauser 1966), especially since that state had a greater investment in vulnerable overseas trade routes than the others. If security had been the motivation, then New South Wales should have been the most enthusiastic about federation as a way to commit the other states to contribute to the common defense. In fact, though, New South Wales was extremely reluctant to join the federation and, for a long time, held out.

Before federation the Australian states occasionally paid jointly for defensive installations that would bolster the defenses of the continent as a whole: on several islands near the Torres Straits off the nearly uninhabited northern tip of Queensland; around the new port at Darwin, where the states had jointly installed a telegraph cable linking the continent to Singapore; and at Port Albany in Western Australia, which was a site for shipment of gold exports and for transoceanic mail lines. In each instance, since the local state government lacked the resources or incentive to pay for fortifications on its own, being relatively poor, and since the sites provided a diffuse benefit to the continent as a whole, New South Wales and, to a lesser extent, Victoria paid a disproportionate share of the common costs (Millar 1969, 10; Donovan 1990, 64).

Following the first observable implication of my theory, there is little theoretical grounding for an expectation that nonexcludable goods can lead states to federate. Free-riding or, at most, cooperation via an alliance would be a more likely outcome. The problem of free-riding highlights one of the shortcomings of existing arguments about the origins of federations (e.g., Riker 1975). For example, one of the premises of the Alesina and Spolaore (2003, chap. 1) model of state size is that states expand in order to internalize externalities—in other words, to turn foreign free-riders into taxpaying citizens. Without a practical coercive option, however, this outcome is unlikely, since by definition free-riders benefit from their free ride.

New South Wales and Victoria

Federations form when potentially vulnerable states value cooperation but perceive that cooperation will lead them to invest more than their larger partners in relationship-specific assets. In 1890s Australia, Victoria was in exactly this position with respect to its more populous neighbor, New South Wales.

Initially, in the 1850s and '60s, the Australian states all exported primary goods, agriculture products and minerals, to Europe and North America. They were relatively open to trade with one another, economic policy being coordinated through ad hoc conferences. But despite this openness, trade was at relatively low levels, since their economies were not specialized and dealt mostly in overseas markets. New South Wales (home of Sydney), the largest and wealthiest, made its money exporting grain and wool. It had a weak preference for openness and cooperation, and for self-sufficiency (at least with respect to the other Australian states) if it could not get regional openness. Its parliament continually displayed a lack of interest in any serious proposals for federation or any other form of political integration (Wise 1909).

Victoria (home of Melbourne) likewise exported primary goods and preferred tacit cooperation—at least at first: within the state there was little interest in federation during the first decade of self-rule (Garran 1933). After Victoria's 1864 election, though, its position began to change. Starting then, its governments pursued tariff protection for industrial development (Turner 1904, 114–15); this protectionist coalition cemented its hold on power in 1872; and variants of it governed in the state through 1901 (Macfie 1893). New South Wales, in contrast, maintained a steady free-trade policy throughout, with only minor interruptions of rule by a protectionist coalition (Hiscox 2002, 119). Likewise, New Zealand governments consistently proclaimed a free-trade policy (Douglas 1909, 194–99). The other states fell between these extremes, with South Australia an intermediate case (Reeves 1899; Clark 1908b).

Figure 3.2 illustrates the difference between New South Wales and Victoria. The vertical axis is the average tariff rate, defined as a ratio of customs revenue over the total value of imports. The solid line is the tariff rate for Victoria; the dashed line is for New South Wales. Elections produced a short-lived protectionist coalition in New South Wales in the early 1890s, but at other times the state was consistently more open to trade than Victoria, and the difference only increased over time.

Starting in the mid-1860s, Victoria's leaders sought market integration with New South Wales in order to gain access to its large population of consumers. In particular, Victorians perceived gains from specialization, since while Melbourne was industrializing behind tariff walls, Sydney was remaining primarily a port city for agricultural trade. If Victoria could

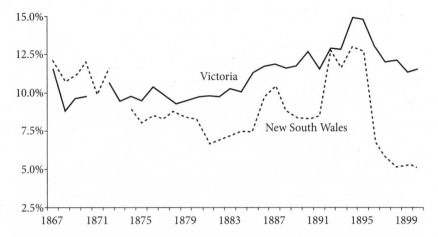

Figure 3.2 Average tariff rates in Victoria and New South Wales

have access to the New South Wales market, it could expand its industrial production.

Market integration would be profitable for Victoria, however, only if the common market could be protected from imports of manufactured European goods. If New South Wales opened its market and agreed to a customs union, then Victorians invested in an industrial expansion, and then New South Wales left the customs union, Melbourne would be saddled with an enormous overcapacity of uncompetitive industries. This position of vulnerability frightened Victorian leaders. In their memoirs (Westgarth 1887; Duffy 1890) and public speeches (Willoughby 1891; Macfie 1893) they referred to this dilemma: they hoped to promote industrial development but felt New South Wales was an untrustworthy partner (Allin and Anderson 1929).[5]

Negotiations over a customs union between Victoria and New South Wales failed, even though the local chambers of commerce in both Sydney and Melbourne supported a common market (Hirst 2000). The governing

---

[5] Members of regional preferential trade agreements are often motivated by the impulse to provide a large, captive market for infant industries. Mercosur, in Latin America, was at least partly a tool to protect regional manufacturers (such as Brazil's construction equipment producers) from competition from more industrialized countries by granting them privileged access to a large regional market (Mattli 1999), and some of the appeal to France of European integration in the 1950s was that it would give French farmers a larger, captive market (Moravcsik 1998). The point here is that these captive markets actually have to be captive (without an easy exit option).

coalition of New South Wales was led by the Free Trade Party, oriented (as the name implies) toward open market access. Henry Parkes (leader of the Free Traders and premier for much of the 1880s) adopted as his government's negotiating position that New South Wales would not accept an agreement that restricted its freedom of action; thus any common external tariff that the common market adopted as part of the original negotiations would be subject to a downward revision later. He viewed this stance as reasonable, since any potential revision would be voluntary by all parties, and any state could secede from the agreement if it disliked the outcome (Duckworth 1899; Galloway 1899; Allin 1907; Clark 1908b). Given this impasse, no agreement was reached even as the leaders of all the states in the region expressed support for one in principle. In 1888, New South Wales and Victoria ended decades of fruitless negotiations over a customs union.

Although Victoria preferred federation to self-sufficiency to IO, before 1889 New South Wales preferred IO to self-sufficiency to federation, and no deal was reached. The situation seemed to change in 1889, when Henry Parkes, the leader of the free-trade coalition in New South Wales, relented and agreed to a federal constitutional convention. His governing coalition promptly fell apart, however: he was abandoned by Sydney financiers who served as intermediaries in trade between New South Wales and Europe and therefore benefited from global trade and who would consequently be harmed by a high common external tariff. There followed a three-year period of rule in New South Wales by a protectionist coalition that took advantage of the split within the Free Traders (Knightly 2000, 55; Travers 2000).

Once the free-trade coalition returned to power, and following another period of internal debate, Sydney advocated federation despite misgivings. In the interim, the growth of potential markets in Australia had begun to make access to those markets nearly as appealing as the overseas markets New South Wales would lose by federating. The free-trade leaders would have ideally preferred a customs union but noted that "there are some people who suggest that we can have Intercolonial Freetrade without Federation; they must be very sanguine and unpractical. Ever since 1873...attempts have been made by the various colonies to enter into customs treaties with each other, &c., &c., all of which have ended in entire and dismal failure, although they were confined to a few articles of colonial production" (Baker 1897b, 7).

Given the lack of an alternative, private groups such as the New South Wales Chamber of Commerce reluctantly changed their views and backed federation (Martin 1964, 223).

This narrative so far shows evidence for the first five observable implications of my theory. Desires for an excludable good led to the development of the union, since market access was something the states could offer selectively—the first implication. The second implication, that federation is not the result of consensus, is clearly the case here, as the governing coalition of the largest state, New South Wales, preferred a customs union via a treaty. This also shows the third implication, that N prefers an international organization; market integration would not have led New South Wales to invest heavily in relationship-specific economic assets, since the structure of its agricultural production would not have changed, whether it was selling grain primarily to regional or world markets. Conversely, Victoria was in a potentially vulnerable position (state V), leading it to prefer a federation—as it did, confirming the fourth implication. Finally, per the fifth implication, the leaders of New South Wales attempted to elicit regional economic investments from Victoria without the ratification of a binding political agreement, while Victoria attempted to elicit a political commitment from New South Wales first.

Victoria Holds Out

In this holding-out contest the leaders of Victoria, as well as of the other smaller states in the region which had been pushing federation (chiefly South Australia and Tasmania), understood that having a federal constitution would go a long way to resolving their fears about the economic union. South Australia, like Victoria, would have made large relationship-specific investments in the event of market integration by reallocating labor from wheat production (in which New South Wales had a comparative advantage) to more specialized agricultural production, mostly grapes. A newspaper there captured the unique appeal of federation over a customs union when it explained that the federation would bring about a common market independent of the "good will or caprice" of their neighbors. Federation, which would make it more difficult for New South Wales to change course, provided insurance that states could get a common market they could trust (Norris 1975, 18–19, 28).

When Henry Parkes in 1881 proposed the organization that eventually became the Federal Council, the Victorians knew that it was not what they had been hoping for. Nevertheless, Victoria and the smaller states (but not New South Wales) joined the organization anyway, with the idea that they would eventually be able to use it as the first step in a process of federal unification (Deakin 1895).

For the first three meetings, each state sent two delegates to the Federal Council, delegates representing the government (that is, the party or factions that held the ministry) of each colony. Starting in 1889, however, each colony sent five delegates in order to include members of the opposition. Throughout, the council was organized with a rotating chair. (This arrangement is somewhat similar to that of the contemporary European Union, where a council of ministers acts as delegates from the member states and makes decisions in specific issue areas as agents of the state parliaments.) Australian supporters of the Federal Council, at the time, argued that the council was a uniquely Australian institution that was particularly well suited to the local political environment. Victorian Premier Alfred Deakin claimed that he saw the Federal Council as a success but recognized that without New South Wales as a member and without a comprehensive agreement on trade, its use was limited (Deakin and La Nauze 1963). Most observers were critical, comparing it to the early U.S. Articles of Confederation and noting that the whole point of the agreement in the first place was to bring Sydney into a common market (Garran 1897, 115).

Within New South Wales, the Free Trade Party was divided over the value of entering into a common market with the other states. Although nearly everyone in the party supported an Australian free-trade area, nearly everyone also supported a policy of free trade (with a uniform tariff for revenue only) with respect to the rest of the world. For the Victorians a free-trade area by itself was useless; they wanted a customs union, in which the states would adopt a common external tariff to keep out manufactured goods from Europe and North America. As a result, New South Wales had to choose: it could have free trade with the region but high barriers to imports from the rest of the world, or low barriers to imports from the rest of the world but high barriers to the goods it sent regionally. Its attempts to have both, by trying to get Victoria to agree to a common market that left Sydney able to control its own external policy, were nonstarters.

In late 1889, eight years after New South Wales pulled out of the negotiations over the Federal Council, Premier Henry Parkes made a reelection speech at a political banquet in the small farming town of Tenterfield in which for the first time he advocated an Australian federation. Newspapers in Victoria and South Australia were suspicious of his sincerity, since he had shifted positions on relations before by proposing and then abandoning the council. It was also unclear whether he would be able to deliver in any case, for not only was his party on the verge of losing to the Protectionists, who advocated barriers to both regional and global trade, but Parkes was fighting for control of the Free Trade Party with his rival

George Reid, who supported pursuing world markets and giving up on regional integration. Theories about Parkes's motives were varied: that he might have been trying to undercut the effectiveness of the Federal Council (Deakin and La Nauze 1963), wanted to distract attention from Reid (Travers 2000), or was drunk from having overindulged at the banquet (Knightly 2000, 55). Free Trade members of the New South Wales parliament said, at least in retrospect, that they understood Parkes's speech as a move to try to capture support from the urban interest groups (exemplified by the Sydney Chamber of Commerce) which would stand to gain from Australian economic integration (Reid 1917; Piddington 1929). Reid's antifederal stance was an attempt to win over the rest of the party.

Parkes's party won the 1889 elections, and Parkes was returned as premier. He followed through on his campaign promise, and over the next eighteen months delegates met at several conferences and drafted a federal constitution. By the end of 1891 the delegates had produced a proposal that was, with few differences, the one that the states actually adopted on January 1, 1901.[6] The bill then went to the six states for ratification. Although some of the state parliaments considered it, the other five all waited for New South Wales to ratify the plan before they took final action.

New South Wales, however, did not ratify the bill. In October 1891 the Free-Traders, badly splintered, lost power and were replaced by a Protectionist government, which lasted until 1894 and during its tenure kept federation off the agenda. In 1894 the Free Trade Party took power again, this time under the leadership of George Reid, who replaced Parkes by running on an antifederal platform and served as premier until late 1899.[7] In the early years of his administration he did everything in his power to keep federation off the agenda, which led federalists in Sydney and Melbourne to devise a plan to circumvent Reid. First, each of the six states would popularly elect ten delegates to attend a federal convention. If the convention produced a federal constitution, then the constitution bill would go directly to the voters in each state for approval by referendum, bypassing state parliaments.

---

[6] At the end of the 1890–91 series of conferences, the New Zealand government decided not to pursue membership in the federation, although it (unsuccessfully) sought language in the final draft that would have allowed it to join later on the same terms as the other states.

[7] After losing power, the eighty-year-old Parkes moved to the political margins, married his twenty-three-year-old mistress, and died in 1896.

By this time, with Parkes out of the way, Reid's control over the party was secure, and he began to move in the direction of favoring federation. His majority Free Trade Party was still divided, and the profederal faction was not large enough to pass the necessary laws by itself (and the party system was not yet strong enough that the leadership could make a bill a confidence vote), so Reid drew support from a small profederal faction of the otherwise antifederal Protectionists in order to gain passage of legislation to implement the series of referendums around the new proposal for a federal convention. After nearly a year of negotiations, New South Wales, South Australia, Tasmania, and Victoria elected delegates and sent them to a final convention, where they produced a bill modeled on the 1891 proposal.

In 1898 the same four states held referenda. Reid, facing an election and leading a party that continued to be divided on federation, faced a dilemma. New rivals were beginning to challenge him for the party leadership, taking the position that he had been too willing to make concessions on external trade policy to the other states—these insurgents were challenging him on essentially the same issue that he had used earlier to win power from Parkes. In a bind, Reid gave the federation proposal only a tepid endorsement before the referendum by conceding that federation would likely be, on balance, bad for New South Wales, and although he personally would vote in favor of it, he concluded that people might just as well vote against as for it. Confused journalists nicknamed him "Yes-No Reid."

The referendum of 1898 had mixed results. The bill got a majority of those voting in the four states: New South Wales, South Australia, Tasmania, and Victoria. However, the New South Wales parliament in 1896 had attached a condition to the act allowing the referendum, stipulating that for adoption the "yes" vote for the constitution would have to be either a majority of those voting or at least 80,000, whichever was higher. As it happened, there were fewer than 72,000 "yes" votes and slightly over 66,000 "no" votes (of 308,000 registered voters), so the bill failed, and the parliament dissolved for new elections in which federation was the primary issue.

Reid returned as premier with a reduced majority that was dependent on support from the profederal faction of the Protectionists (who by now had formed their own party, called the Federalists). Reid convened a final convention and persuaded the other states to accept several changes to the proposed constitution to make the product more favorable to New South Wales. In 1899 the new constitution passed in a referendum in five states—the original four plus Queensland—and the "yes" votes in New South Wales passed the threshold of 80,000 after Reid campaigned vigorously in favor of it. Western Australia, the sixth state, approved the bill by referendum in 1900, and the federation began on January 1, 1901.

The struggle between Parkes and Reid and Reid's later campaign strategy provide indirect evidence that Victoria's strategy of holding out for a federal commitment from New South Wales may have made the difference in getting Sydney to accept federation. Regional market integration, either through tacit cooperation or through a weak regional institution, would have been the preferred outcome for all the members of the Free Trade Party in New South Wales, but Victoria, through its unwillingness to put itself in an exposed position, effectively took that option off the table. This result provides further evidence for the fifth observable implication of the theory, that vulnerable states withhold investments in cooperation until after nonvulnerable states commit to federal institutions. It was only several years after the implementation of the new federal government that effective trade barriers came down and Australia began to move toward becoming a completely integrated market (Irwin 2006).

New South Wales, New Zealand, and the Structure of Federation

By the middle of the 1880s, New South Wales and New Zealand were in similar situations: both states had effectively established lucrative markets for exported primary products. For New Zealand in particular, this development had been surprising. Early on after the advent of self-government, New Zealand was as economically integrated with the other states as New South Wales was. Through the 1870s, however, the New Zealand economy gradually diverged from the others. Trade across the Tasman Sea (between New Zealand and the east coast of Australia) did not grow as fast as commerce with Europe.

In 1882, some shipping lines introduced refrigerated freight transport, which allowed New Zealand to export meat directly to Europe's growing middle class and revitalized the state's pastoral regions. Even had the Australian market been completely open, New Zealand would not have been able to engage in any production that more effectively capitalized on its comparative advantage (Galloway 1899; Sinclair 1970). In 1898, New Zealand exporters sent 2,700,000 frozen sheep to Britain, representing two-thirds of total British mutton imports. The trade generated demand for other industries, and much of New Zealand's economic growth over the

two decades following 1882 was popularly attributed to related developments as new firms made investments in freezing works, communications
networks with British and other European markets, and shipping facilities
and drydocks for long-distance merchant ships (Irvine and Alpers 1902,
364–8).

By the 1890s, New Zealand was sending a lower percentage of its exports to the other Australasian colonies than any of the others were. Still,
federation was controversial. Although ranchers and the new industries
that served long-distance trade opposed it, there was support for federation among grain farmers and exporters of forest products who could
have benefited in principle from trade with arid Australia and who feared
being excluded from the Australian market (Sinclair 1986a; 1987). The
strong balance of interests, however, favored staying out (Reeves 1901).
Figure 3.3 shows total regional trade (exports and imports to and from
the six other Australasian states) as a proportion of all trade (all exports
and imports).

Within both New South Wales and New Zealand, light manufacturing
industries had supported protectionist policies in the past. These groups
opposed federation, fearing that it would increase competition with manufacturers from Victoria. In New South Wales, agricultural interests that

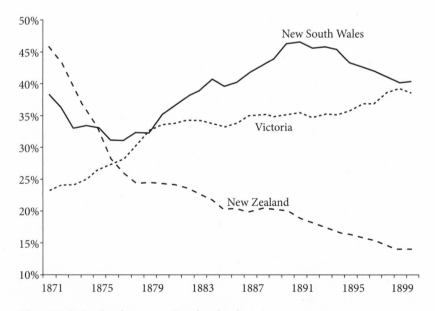

Figure 3.3 Regional trade as proportion of total trade

exported regionally supported federation, but other traditional free-traders included groups that depended on exports to Europe. These tended to oppose federation, at least before the mid-1890s. Although free-trade groups in New South Wales were divided, in New Zealand, where most of the traditional free-traders were in the business of exporting to Europe, both protectionists and the majority of free-traders opposed federation.

In that sense, New Zealand illustrates a counterfactual case to New South Wales. Had Sydney not moved to a position where the benefits from regional integration outweighed the potential losses from losing autonomy (and had Sydney not recognized that it was never going to get economic integration on its own terms, as an IO), the relationship between North South Wales and the rest of Australia would very likely have unfolded just as the relationship between New Zealand and Australia has, involving periodic economic cooperation but political independence.

At the early constitutional conventions in the beginning of the 1890s, when New Zealand was a full participant in the negotiations and most participants still believed New Zealand was seriously considering joining the federation, there was a conflict over the terms of its potential entry. New South Wales hoped to persuade New Zealand to join the federation, whereas Victoria designed procedural hurdles.[8]

Conventional wisdom predicted that in the hypothetical federal parliament, New Zealand's representatives, like those from New South Wales, would be more inclined to favor open trade with the rest of the world than would representatives from the other states (Reeves 1899; Wise 1909). Without New Zealand, Sydney's representatives would be in a distinct minority, and would either have to endorse substantially higher tariffs than they would otherwise prefer or be relegated to the opposition (Griffith 1896b; Robertson 1897; Barton 1901; Allin 1918).

Victoria's strategy can be interpreted in two ways. Straightforwardly, it was a way of keeping Sydney's free-trade preferences from gaining too much traction in a then hypothetical future Australian parliament. This interpretation is unsatisfying, though, since it is puzzling that Victoria went to the effort to take on this contentious issue when it could have advanced the same end of reducing the overall influence of New South Wales in other ways. For example, by the end of the 1890–91 conventions there

---

[8] Sydney sought to include a constitutional provision that New Zealand could join at a later date on the same terms as the other states: e.g., with seats in the two houses of parliament apportioned in the same way. Victoria won, instead, a provision that any new state would be admitted only on terms to be set by parliament.

was general agreement about the composition of the lower house of parliament: seats would be apportioned to the states on the basis of population—and New South Wales had the most residents. In principle, though, seats could have been distributed in a way that reduced that advantage by making fixed apportionments (Baker 1891). Alternatively, Victoria could have made efforts to reduce the influence of the lower house—apportioned by population in which New South Wales had an advantage—and to increase the influence of the upper house, with six senators from each state. Yet Victoria did not push either of these options.

A more compelling interpretation of Victoria's strategy was that it was, in fact, happy to have New South Wales send all its ablest politicians to the Australian parliament and to let them play an influential role in making policy for the federation. Getting Sydney's political elite invested in a national government was, after all, the entire point. Victoria's aim was simply to prevent any chance of the emergence of a free-trade majority coalition. The New South Wales political elite would rule Australia, but to do it they would have to rely on Protectionists in the parliament for their majority.

When voters in New South Wales rejected the first constitution and Reid reopened negotiations, representatives from Victoria quickly agreed to a proposal to increase the influence of the lower house at the expense of the upper house; this change had the largest proportional beneficial effect on New South Wales.[9] They also agreed to specify, for the first time, that the federal capital would be located in a federal district within the territory of New South Wales but at least 100 miles from Sydney. Reid expected the capital city to provide some economic benefit and was careful to hint that the site chosen would be to the south of Sydney, near the border with Victoria. The pastoral towns in this region otherwise opposed federation, but that promise may have swung some referendum votes (Hewett 1969).

The sixth observable implication of my theory is that when federal unions come about, the need for contrived symmetry leads nonvulnerable states to invest more than vulnerable states in the new federal institutions. In order to join the federation, Victoria and the other smaller states had to adapt economically. New South Wales, however, more than any

[9] The change gave some precedence to the lower house in the case of a deadlock between the lower and upper houses. The framers placed a great deal of importance on the tie-breaking procedure, since they anticipated that differing modes of election would lead to frequent disagreements between the two houses (Beach 1899; Barton 1901; Warden 1992, 151).

other state, had to adapt politically. Its leading politicians, unlike those from the other states, had to pivot upon entering national politics and endorse a protectionist tariff. George Reid, a committed free-trader in the Gladstonian tradition while premier of New South Wales, quickly became a fervent protectionist once in the Australian parliament—a change that he justified as a response to the new reality that federation had "settled" the tariff question (Reid 1917) but one that coincidentally allowed him to become prime minister of the federation after a decent interval (Crisp and Hart 1990). The capital region (Canberra) created an economic boom for the towns to the south of Sydney, which to this day remain dependent on the presence of the capital for their economic activity.

Federation, then, was a tool for getting New South Wales to commit to economic cooperation. Absent political institutions, it would have easily agreed to a customs union but would never have been able to refrain from pursuing its own economic interests by reopening to world markets. By tying Sydney's leaders to Australian parliamentary institutions, Victoria managed to tie New South Wales to Australia.

4

POLITICAL IDENTITY IN AUSTRALIA
AND NEW ZEALAND

Previously, I argued that my theory can account for the union of the Australian states without New Zealand, and in doing so I addressed an alternative explanation relating to demands for common security. Another potential alternative explanation for political union relates to social identity. Some Australian historians have recently argued that the Australian federation formed out of a shared sense of identity, and some international relations scholars have recently argued that shifts in political identity can lead to national integration or disintegration.

This alternative argument posits that states merge when citizens first imagine themselves to be part of a group of people with whom they can identify. Members in such an affective community have a common regard for their mutual well-being. Regardless of what policy outcomes they desire or material gains they calculate they can receive as individuals, members of a community value political union intrinsically, as an end in itself. A further, Kantian version of this argument predicts that liberal societies may be especially likely to draw together.

Australia should be an easy case for theories of political identity, since, unlike the other federal unions that emerged around the same time (Canada, India, South Africa) or at other times (Switzerland, the United States, Malaysia), the Australian states had a similar colonial heritage, a common language, similar legal systems, common economic organizations, and a common liberal political ideology.

Australia is also a useful case because, since the federation proceeded within democratic systems, the motives of different leaders and interest groups on both sides of the federation debate are observable. Various potential motives for federation are easy to distinguish because the differences in policy preferences among Australians from different regions mostly had to do with trade policy rather than with class or ethnicity, meaning that the influences of these different kinds of heterogeneity can be observed separately (that is, there was not an ethnic division of labor).

Evidence from the process of Australian federation strongly suggests that identity factors by themselves are insufficient to account for the federation. The separation of New Zealand, the electoral strategies of political parties in New South Wales, and divisions in the New South Wales parliament all could, in principle, have provided evidence for identity factors but instead show that economic considerations were paramount. I conclude, however, that Australian symbols and narratives of Australian identity that political elites used at the time, and the background conditions that made appeals to a nascent Australian idea plausible, may have played an important intervening role in cementing a union, even though the structural reasons for the union were themselves materialistic and nonideological.

I proceed in three sections. First I set out some general expectations about the role of identity and discuss the ways some scholars suggest political identity influenced the Australian federal movement. Second, I present an overview of the Australian federal process and conduct three tests designed to reveal whether economic motives or identity drove the federation. Third, I conclude with some observations about identity as a possible intervening factor in federal unions.

Identity and Union

Intuition suggests that political identity might in some way matter for decisions that states make to merge. Common identity, especially shared political values, may lead to willingness or even desire to live together in a state, whether as a means to some other end ("we who are so alike should share a government because we would get along well") or as an end in itself ("it is appropriate that we who are so alike should share a government"). The difficulty for analysis is twofold. First, patterns of political identity are often clear only once they have manifested themselves in political action, which can lead to post hoc measurements. Especially since both elites and other citizens have motivated biases to imagine that their states represent mythic, long-standing communities, there is a danger of overestimating the inevitability of existing states (Spruyt 1994). Second, it is not clear, in advance, what kinds of shared ideas of community can lead to the growth of states, and what kinds would be satisfied with forms of political recognition short of states. If shared identity can account for both federations (Wendt 2003) and international organizations (Adler 1997), then identity alone (just like potential gains from cooperation) cannot fully account for either outcome.

All forms of identity, even ethnicity, are to some extent constructed. But even common ethnicity is neither necessary nor sufficient for state amalgamation—as Latin America and India illustrate. Still, identities are sticky, and constructing new ones takes time and effort. To the extent that political identities are slow to evolve—or at least more resistant to sudden changes over time than are national borders—there is some theoretical basis in the existing literature for supposing that the sizes and shapes of states, and their tendency to be willing to join in federal unions, respond to identity rather than the other way around. After reviewing possible identity-based arguments about federation generally, I discuss their application to Australia.

Community

Scholars of international relations are familiar with the propositions that states and their leaders respond to social conventions, especially when they understand themselves to belong to communities of peers with whom they share common values. Part of the way members of a community define themselves is by referring to a set of shared characteristics that mark insiders. Scholars going back to Immanuel Kant have suggested that political liberalism, both because it is a convenient marker and also because of its ideological content, may be a trait especially likely to lead to community development.[1] Karl Deutsch (1968) argued that states sharing liberal social and political values might form "pluralistic security communities," and recent works in constructivist and sociological schools in international relations have picked up this theme (Adler 1997). The hypothesis is

[1] Jackson (2006) describes communities of states and the process by which a group of states as insiders can develop a definition of themselves that excludes others, although some argue that exclusion is not a necessary part of cosmopolitan liberal communities (Abizadeh 2005). Etzioni (1965) applies a version of this framework to the question of national unification; I discuss his treatment of the West Indies Federation in Chapter 6.

that when states share a common liberal political culture, they may each come to internalize the material interests of the others. That is, the states (Wendt 1999, 215–16), their leaders (Risse-Kappen 1995, 34–35), or their societies generally (Deutsch 1968) will redefine their conceptions of themselves to include the larger community of like-minded states, so that the idea of "we" expands to include more than just the home state. This may correspond to the Kantian notion of a peaceful, liberal federation (Doyle 1986b, 1158).

Political integration does not necessarily follow from shared liberalism. Many current identity-based arguments in international relations, for example, suggest that there is nothing about international politics that makes it incompatible with shared political identity. In Alexander Wendt's formulation, anarchy is whatever states make of it (1992). Even in anarchy, states and the people who live in them are perfectly capable of internalizing one another's expectations to the "third degree," where norms of community shape the identities of the actors themselves (Wendt 1999, 254, 273). Although growing feelings of inclusiveness may change the international behavior of states (Finnemore 2003), they do not necessarily lead to changes in the essential character of those states (decisions by one state to merge voluntarily with another, for instance).

Scholars of political development tend to be skeptical of claims that the sizes and borders of states emerged because of a preexisting common political identity. The nation-building project, in which elites or societies look back into their history and create myths of national identity in order to foster an imagined community, typically follows (rather than precedes) the development of the state as a political institution (Anderson 1983). In societies generally, postcolonial ones in particular, it is unusual for coherent national identities to precede the formation of states, although the past is later reimagined to make it seem that way (Emerson 1960, 114–119; Rustow 1967, 127–28; Pye 1971), especially in settler states such as the United States and Australia (Spillman 1996, 155).

An alternative view within a constructivist framework is that a liberal community of states would be incomplete without formal political integration, so that community therefore does impel federation. In a later argument, Wendt posits that the innate desire for political recognition will lead states to merge (2003). Here, the argument is not that a prior common political identity leads states to seek an expression of that identity through a political merger; rather, it is that states, like people, seek to be acknowledged as members of a community. Being admitted into a club not only confers status but also serves as a marker that validates a state as being a member of an in-group.[2]

Australian Identity

Australian historical scholarship has traditionally focused on two potential causal forces behind federation: economic and identity motives. At first, studies of federation privileged economic arguments. The leaders of the member states of the initial federation described their motives at the time, and later in their memoirs, as being related to economics. In particular, they saw federation as a means to establish a common market and viewed a federal government as necessary to keep the internal market intact (Griffith 1896b, 4; Baker 1897b, 7; Reid 1917; Deakin and La Nauze 1963). Many historians have backed up this interpretation by, for example, showing that the major private interest groups behind federation were business lobbies that supported expansion of the market (Martin 1964, 223–24; Martin 1969; Norris 1969; La Nauze 1972) and that the voting districts that sent profederation members to the state parliaments were those that would benefit economically from market integration, whereas those that sent antifederation members were those that would lose out (Norris 1975, 18–19, 28).

More recently, other historians have focused on the role of identity and argue that Australians in the late 1800s developed a political identity that included a common and distinctive Australian component (Blainey 1964). The basis of this common identity was civic rather than ethnic.[3] Recent scholarship specifically shows that late nineteenth-century Australasian political identity was uniquely and self-consciously liberal, as the states embarked on campaigns of progressive political expansion. For example, New Zealand and South Australia were the first two political jurisdictions in the world to extend mass suffrage to women, and female suffrage came close to passing in some of the other states prior to federation. The states also pioneered such early progressive-era reforms as the alternative ballot, the secret ballot, manhood suffrage, payment of members of parliament, industrial regulation, centralized electoral roles, and liberalized

---

[2] Wendt's critics include some constructivists who reject the premise that states, like people, seek external recognition or validation (Lomas 2005; Shannon 2005).

[3] Australia was ethnically and religiously divided by West European standards, with a large Irish minority, and lacked the ethnic base for common identity of European states in the same period (French 1978).

divorce laws (Irving 1999, 35, 38–39, 43; Craven 2001; Nethercote 2001; Sawer 2001; Ward 2001). These political reforms were, according to this view, something in which the British settler societies in the region took great pride (Dixson 1999).

Although the identity-based historical scholarship does not specifically engage contemporary constructivist or sociological theories in international relations, the connection is clear: a shared liberal political identity that preceded federation led the Australian states to remake their anarchic system into one more consistent with that identity. The two most important recent Australian scholarly works on federation, by John Hirst (2000) and Helen Irving (1999), argue that civic, liberal political identity defined a self-identified political community and led to federation. They conclude that the economic motives identified by a previous generation of scholars as causal were at most secondary.

The identity argument for federation is that before Australians formed a federation they had to imagine an idea of a national community. Hirst concludes that in Australia, "where there was no pressing need for federation, national sentiment was the precondition for union" (2000, 271). Irving (1999) argues that this national sentiment came from an elite-driven project of liberal social and political reform. Federation was a utopian social experiment, along the same lines as the other reforms of the 1890s. William Pember Reeves, New Zealand's first national historian, in his 1902 *State Experiments in Australia and New Zealand,* discussed women's suffrage, labor reforms, old age pensions, ballot access, and the like alongside federation, explicitly linking federation to a creative and distinctly liberal political energy.

The identity argument, that the federation movement in the 1890s was the manifestation of a shared political and civic identity, requires that a politically relevant and distinctive Australian identity (or at least plausible grounds for elites to claim such an identity) came first. Australian historians, however, have traditionally argued that such a common identity or "we-feeling" did not then exist. The conventional interpretation is that Australians did not develop a common civic identity until after World War I at the earliest (Moore 1910, 53; Clark 1963, 1980). Indeed, observers at the time of federation noted that Australia specifically lacked a common political identity and frame of reference (Griffith 1896a, 28).

In the debates leading up to the federation bill, social and cultural associations were mostly silent or divided on federation. The most active group that did not have a specifically economic base (that is, besides trade unions, manufacturers' associations, and chambers of commerce)

was the Australian Natives Association (referring not to Aborigines but to
people of European ancestry who had been born in the colonies), but it
was a substantial and active force in only two of the states and only later
than 1893, well after the movement for federation had already begun to
form (Reeves 1902).

To the extent that Australians *had* developed political identities, these
were centered on their state governments rather than on the region as a
whole. This focus is not particularly strange, since "Australia" at the time was
a remote abstraction, whereas New South Wales, Victoria, and the others
all had functioning governments with established institutions such that the
important decisions governing people's lives came from their state parliaments. Each state defined the geographic scope of the political community that actually mattered, teaching people to think in provincial terms
(Lewis 1976). The populations of Sydney (Shortus 1973) and Melbourne
(Thompson 1974) each celebrated different local holidays, pursued popular foreign policies with different values, and thought of the other as alien.
Throughout the prefederal period the states' separate cricket teams competed with other national teams on an independent basis (Mandle 1973).

The liberal progressive element in Australian politics at the time—
and the way in which some modern historians have linked the choice for
federation to this regional shift in how people (or at least political and
social elites) thought about the proper relationship between individuals
and the state—suggests that an investigation of the identity politics of
the Australian federation is therefore warranted as a way to explore the
relationship between market motives and identity as forces that may lead
states to federate.

Tests of Australian Identity

This section presents three tests of economic and identity motives that
focus on the process that led to the federation, rather than on the outcome
itself. I examine New Zealand's decision to stay out of the union, the way
in which political parties used federation as a strategic issue designed to
expand their constituency, and the divisions over federation within and
across political parties in the New South Wales parliament.

These tests of whether the Australian states federated because of economic goals or identity have several virtues. First, they provide clear expectations. In the New Zealand test, if the Australian states merged because
of a shared identity, and New Zealand chose to stay out of the merger, then
it must be that New Zealanders claimed a different national identity. Both

the identity and economic characteristics of Australians and New Zealanders can be observed and compared. The partisan strategy test is similarly clear. If political parties that were trying to appeal to an economically defined constituency used federation as an issue on which to win an election, then this is evidence for an economic motive. If parties that were trying to burnish their political liberalism credentials pushed federation as a way to create a brand name for themselves, then this is evidence for an identity basis. Finally, if the same people who voted for federation were also those who consistently voted for regional trade agreements, then federation was likely a tool to achieve market gains, whereas if the same people who voted for federation were also those who campaigned for other liberal reforms, then federation was likely part of the larger progressive liberal agenda.

A second virtue is that these tests are independent of each other. Although idiosyncratic factors might produce a misleading result in one of them, if all three tests point in the same direction, it is unlikely to be a coincidence. Third, the tests all involve observations of decisions in which well-informed political elites had incentives to reveal their true beliefs and expectations. Whether to join Australia or not was a momentous decision for New Zealand's leaders, and the question of whether and how to use federation as an electoral issue made or destroyed the political careers of Sydney's leading politicians, concentrating the minds of the region's cleverest political strategists.

New Zealand

In Chapter 3 I argued that the growth of New Zealand's trade ties with Europe and North America led it to stay out of a regional federation that would have limited its ability to trade on world markets. Identity considerations cannot account for New Zealand's decision. An "Australasian" identity claim was no less plausible in New Zealand than in any of the other states, and local political identity was no more ingrained.

Throughout the nineteenth century, the popular press as well as official documents and school textbooks referred to New Zealand along with what would become the Australian states as the seven Australasian states. Several labor unions were unified across the seven colonies, including those for miners, shippers, and wool shearers, and they observed common work stoppages (as they do today). Some religious organizations, including the large and influential Methodist Church, were unified across the Tasman Sea (the body of water between New Zealand and the Australian mainland, about as wide as the east-west width of the mainland itself), while those unions and churches that were divided across the Tasman tended to be divided within the Australian mainland as well. Passenger traffic was heavy. In 1895 the crossing was faster and less expensive than a trip from one side of Australia to the other—it took four days and cost one day's salary for a professional—and New Zealand and the mainland states were among the most popular holiday destinations for each other's tourists. One-third of all migrants to New Zealand came from Australia. In 1896 Australian newspapers made up 45 percent of all newspapers sent to New Zealand by mail; throughout the 1880s and 1890s the *Melbourne Australasian,* the *Sydney Bulletin,* and the *Sydney Mail* were competitive in New Zealand and devoted considerable space to New Zealand news in order to keep up subscriptions—creating, as a side-effect, an Australian citizenry that was highly informed about and affectively connected with New Zealanders. In short, even New Zealanders did not think of New Zealand as being distinct and did not develop a distinct national identity until after 1901 (Arnold 1970; Sinclair 1970; Arnold 1981, 356; Sinclair 1986b; Arnold 1987). In one of the first comparative studies of early nationalisms, Richard Jebb (1905) summarized his findings that New Zealanders had no distinctly national sentiment one way or the other but had evaluated the possibility for federation on purely commercial terms; he also asserted that his conclusions concurred with the conventional wisdom among scholars generally.

The same liberalism that captured Australians, according to identity theorists, also captured New Zealanders. Reeves referred in his 1902 title to state experiments in both Australia and New Zealand, and he attributed New Zealand's desire to stay out to only economic interests (1901). Irving (1999) acknowledges that New Zealand had exactly the same political spirit of innovation and liberal advancement as the other states (43, 121), but she never provides a reason why this spirit did not lead it to join the federation. Hirst (2000, 222) writes, "The fundamental reason why there was so little interest in federation was that New Zealanders did not think of themselves as Australians," but he never explains why they did not, even though a claim for a distinct New Zealand identity was no more plausible than a claim for any other state's distinct identity would have been.

Partisan Strategies

The way political parties strategically used federation as an issue to advance their electoral fortunes can reveal whether they perceived federation as being more about identity or more about economics. The decision as to whether or not to form the federation was closest in the state of New South

Wales, where the dominant party—Free Trade—at first chose in the 1890s to emphasize federation, then backed away from the issue, and then chose to push it again. Throughout, the party was torn between two competing strategic ideas. One group wanted to focus primarily on trade issues; the other wanted to broaden the party's appeal by pursuing an agenda of progressive reforms. Given the state of political competition in New South Wales, many party leaders believed they would be unable to pursue both effectively.

The record of these partisan strategists is clear: the federation idea flourished when the faction that believed the party's future lay in pursuing trade policy had the upper hand, and stagnated when the liberal reform faction controlled the party—suggesting that the party leaders saw federation as part of trade policy rather than as part of a liberal political project.

New South Wales began its independent political existence in the 1850s, but it did not develop a modern party system until the middle to late 1880s. Henry Parkes is typically credited with founding the two-party system that lasted through the federation period by dividing the parliament along free-trade and protectionist lines and by taking the lead of the free-traders. He also tried, most often unsuccessfully, to associate his party with liberal causes. As leader of the Free Trade Party, he championed governmental reforms to curb corruption and to expand free public education; he was also a public advocate of land reform and a progressive income tax. He was able to achieve most of these reforms but failed to capture the liberal label for the party; many of his reforms in fact divided his party, whereas many Protectionists joined him in the social agenda (Crisp and Hart 1990, 4; Travers 2000). The Free Traders lost seats in 1889, but Parkes remained in office until 1891 with a narrow governing majority while he pushed the federalist agenda. Partly as a result of Parkes's advocacy, federation politics grew in public salience throughout the 1890s, and a variety of organizations took positions on the issue. The New South Wales Chamber of Commerce began grudgingly to back federation, retreating from its earlier insistence on a simple free-trade area (Martin 1964, 223).

In August 1894, the Free Trade Party took power again under the leadership of George Reid, the devoted Free-Trader who had inherited a deeply divided coalition (Galloway 1899) and had opposed the 1891 federation bill opportunistically as a way to differentiate himself from Parkes (Deakin and La Nauze 1963). Reid kept power until losing it to a series of Protectionist governments in September 1899—by which time federation was assured (Hughes and Graham 1968).

Reid's rise to control of the party represented, at the time, a victory for the faction that sought to expand its base by supporting liberal reforms.

His supporters felt that Parkes had expended political capital in 1889–91 by pushing federation at the expense of reform and liberalization, and that Parkes's attempts at progressive reform (as when he moved for a study on female suffrage near the end of his term) were unconvincing. So, in 1894 Reid came into office with an agenda that focused entirely on liberal social and political programs such as electoral and civil service reforms and suffrage expansion.

During his first two years, when Reid was working feverishly on progressive electoral, civil service, budgeting, and economic reforms to capture the mantle of liberalism, he made no moves toward federation. As a result, the issue stagnated, opening a schism within the party, as some Free Traders thought that this strategy would weaken the party by alienating its economically motivated constituents. These were led by Bernhard Wise, who in 1898 would conspire to weaken Reid by making a deal with the "Federalists," a small group of profederal Protectionists. Reid's initial indifference in federation at a time when he was actively pursuing the label of a progressive liberal demonstrates that, at least in his mind, liberalism and federation were not linked (Wise 1909; Reid 1917; Piddington 1929; Crisp and Hart 1990).

Later, in 1896, Reid recognized the threat to his leadership from the core free-trade faction. He then changed tactics and began to move the party back to its free-trade origins by championing revenue reform, shifting from tariffs to property taxes as a primary means of government financing. (New South Wales had, until then, a uniform tariff for revenue.) From 1894 until 1896 Reid had ignored calls for revenue reform; it was only following the challenge from the free-traders that he revived the issue.

At the same time, he moved on federation for the first time since becoming premier. He backed the proposal, in 1896, to elect representatives directly to a federal convention to write a constitution that would then go directly to a referendum, and he expended much of his capital in fighting off most of the amendments Protectionists added to the enabling legislation that would have sabotaged the process. With support from the premier and a newly reunited Free Trade Party, voters approved federation in the second of two referendums in 1899, the voting generally consistent with the economic interests at stake in regional market integration (Norris 1975, 26–29).[4]

---

[4] The electoral districts voters used in the federal referendum were not the same as the districts in later federal elections, and state electoral districts were redrawn within a few years, making any systematic quantitative comparison of voting difficult.

Reid and members of both factions of his party all acted as though they considered the federation issue to be about trade and not about the liberal political reform agenda. Although they clearly thought that many voters in New South Wales favored furthering the liberal progressive project, these politicians did not think that delivering on federation was an effective way to demonstrate their own progressive credentials.

Divisions in Parliament

As an additional test of whether federation was driven by economics or identity, I use voting patterns in the New South Wales Assembly (the lower house of parliament) from 1894 to 1896. The New South Wales Assembly in this period had two specific characteristics that make it ideal for this analysis. First, the parliament considered many diverse issues over which there was considerable difference of opinion, including female suffrage, voter qualifications, labor wage bargaining, trade, defense spending, and federation.

Second, the New South Wales parliamentary decisions on federation had high stakes. Individually, they turned out to be more crucial to the shape of Australia today than any other single set of state parliamentary decisions. In 1896 the parliament set the rules for its referendum on the federal constitution. Rather than allowing the referendum to pass on a simple majority, as the other states did, a New South Wales parliamentary coalition skeptical of federation set the rule that the minimum number of "yes" votes had to be either a majority or 80,000, whichever was higher. As it happened, there were 71,595 yes votes on the first attempt, in 1898, and 107,420 on the second attempt, in 1899. (The 80,000 figure had been a compromise; opponents of federation initially sought a 120,000 threshold, and 80,000 was the lowest that Reid was able to get.)

For the period from August 30, 1894, through December 19, 1895, 563 assembly divisions on issues other than federation were recorded in the New South Wales Hansard (the legislative record). For each one, there is a record of the choice of each of the 149 MPs in the assembly at that time: yes, no, or abstain. Each member thus produced a history of votes that can yield clues about his preferred set of policies.

I use W-NOMINATE to derive an estimate of each member's ideal point (Poole and Rosenthal 1997).[5] "Ideal" or "ideal point" refers to the specific

---

[5] The procedure depends on estimating individual ideal points based on each member's voting pattern in relation to every other member's voting pattern. In a pure Westminster system, all members of a party always vote the same way in every division,

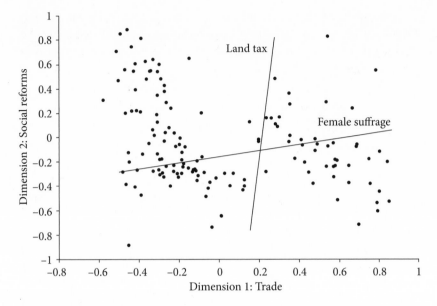

Figure 4.1 Sample Cutting Lines, 1894–95 NSW Assembly

bundle of government policies that a person prefers above all others. For example, George Reid's ideal point was a liberal program that included the expansion of the franchise to women and a free-trade program that included significant reductions in tariffs, with a shift to land and progressive income taxes as means of raising revenue. The technique takes a history of positions on various yes/no questions and produces a spatial map of the relationships—that is, positions and relative distances—among the ideal points of different members.

Figure 4.1 shows ideal points in two dimensions for the 149 members. Each of the 563 divisions produces a cutting line that divides the chamber, such that members on one side of the line vote yes and on the other side of the line vote no. Of all of the individual votes in this sample, 88.2 percent are correctly classified in two dimensions; that is, for any given member voting in any given division, there is an 88.2 percent chance that the two-dimensional map correctly "predicts" his choice. (This accuracy rate is comparable to results in studies of the U.S. Congress.) Although W-NOMINATE can create a preference map in any number of dimensions,

so there is no diversity and, hence, the type of estimation I use is impossible. Australian parties during the mid-1890s were still relatively weak, however, so the expressed ideal points of the assembly member are quite diverse.

I chose two for substantive reasons: as I show below, the two dimensions the technique reveals are related to the two underlying political conflicts, trade and progressive reform, that Australian scholars highlight (Crisp and Hart 1990).[6]

The next step is to identify the dimensions that the procedure recovers. The first dimension, on the horizontal axis, explains most of the sources of difference. The substantive issues the members were voting on show that this dimension represents economic conflict, primarily the differences between Free Traders (on the left) and Protectionists (on the right). The further to the left a member is, the more radical a free-trade proposal he will support; the further to the right a member is, the more radical a protectionist proposal he will support. Of the fifty most nearly vertical cutting lines, twenty-nine directly concern Reid's program of scaling back the tariff and replacing it with a land and income tax. The next largest group is on procedural issues; these presumably each had substantive policy issues behind them, but the hidden agendas are not recorded. The vertical cutting line labeled "Land Tax" represents the division on the third and final reading of the land tax bill on June 20, 1895—it would have replaced tariffs as a revenue source with property tax. This division is representative of most of the other divisions on economic and especially tariff issues; it divides the Free Traders, on the left side of the graph, from the Protectionists, on the right.

The second dimension, on the vertical axis, corresponds to issues of liberal progressive reform. There are slightly over seventy divisions with cutting lines that are almost exactly horizontal (that is, in which a member's vote could be entirely attributed to his position on the vertical dimension and in which his position on the horizontal dimension does not provide any information with which to make a better prediction of how he would vote). Of these, none concerned revenue measures or related to the tariff. Slightly more than half concerned government spending on administrative offices, and the third largest group directly concerned civil service reforms. (Both of these may have been directed at perceived corruption; advocates of many of these bills, motions, and amendments spoke in the assembly about the menace of American-style graft accompanying the spoils system of distributing salaried government offices.) The next largest group had to do with labor regulation, such as limitations

---

[6] Adding a third dimension improved the correct classification rate by less than 1 percent, and this third dimension was not a recognizable policy dimension.

on the number of hours contracted laborers could work and rules for a government agency that mediated labor disputes. Three of the divisions were about female suffrage, including one crucial division that postponed consideration of extending the franchise indefinitely. Two more dealt with electoral reforms generally. Only three divisions addressed overall military spending, and all three have a nearly horizontal cutting line. The rest of the bills in this group were varied: two concerned legislator pay, two concerned working conditions in mines, and the rest were procedural matters. In general, they seem to fall mostly into the category of political and social reforms.[7] These issues correspond to the liberal innovations that identity theorists (Sawer 2001) identify as central to the then emerging Australian basis of civic nationalism.

The horizontal cutting line in figure 4.1 is from a division from September 18, 1894 on a procedural measure to prevent female franchise from coming to parliamentary consideration. (It was actually the proponents of franchise expansion who engineered the move to prevent its consideration, since they knew that they did not have the votes to pass the reform at the time. Opponents of expansion voted against the measure and in favor of bringing the issue directly to consideration in order to defeat it.) This division broadly represents many of the other divisions that I have labeled "political and social reform" and divides the chamber along the vertical dimension—between the more reformist "top" of the graph and the more conservative "bottom." This reconstruction of the political map of New South Wales is consistent with that of other scholars, who in qualitative work have found that the primary difference of opinion was over tariffs and that there was also a strong conflict over reform (Loveday and Martin 1966; Hughes and Graham 1968; Hewett 1969; Norris 1975; Loveday, Martin, and Parker 1977; Crisp 1979; Crisp and Hart 1990).

To keep the initial measures of policy preferences distinct from federation, I do not include any divisions that directly concerned federation in the initial sample of divisions. In addition, in order to keep the distinction between the underlying preferences on nonfederation issues and the preferences specifically on federation as clear as possible, I apply the

---

[7] This dimension is as much about labor reforms as it is about political identity. William Morris Hughes was an early Labor leader; he shows up on the upper-left side of the figure, consistent with L. Finlay Crisp's placement (1990). Labor reforms and broader political reforms seem to have been related generally, though, with members of the early labor party supporting suffrage expansion, and so on, as the cutting lines on these issues reveal.

preference map I derive from the history of divisions in 1894–95 to divisions over federation from a later parliament. Specifically, I apply the spatial map to a series of divisions over federation that occurred in 1896. In other words, how did members' initial stance on the two basic issues of the day, trade and reform, correlate with their later position on federation? Are the cutting lines for divisions on federation more nearly horizontal, like a division on political and social reform, or more nearly vertical, like a division on trade?

Federation is much more like an economic than a reform issue. Figure 4.2 shows a key division on the referendum bill taken on October 29, 1896: a "yes" vote is to allow the assembly to continue amending the referendum bill. This was a ploy to stall for time while opponents of federation, led by William Lyne, tried to secure support for raising further the threshold of voters necessary to approve the federation bill in the referendum (this is my interpretation based on the floor debates and my reading of Deakin and La Nauze 1963, 87; see also Piddington 1929; Wise 1909). The assembly defeated the measure.

The angle of the cutting line is representative of the other votes on federation during 1896 (as well as in the earlier 1894–95 period). Regardless of the origins of any particular issue—that is, whether the particular

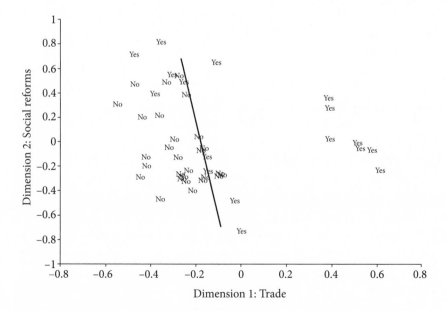

Figure 4.2 Federation Referendum Vote, October 29, 1896, New South Wales Assembly

division on federation is in response to a proposal by the government, to a private bill, or to a floor amendment—the pattern is quite stable: the cutting line is almost vertical, albeit with a slight angle. In all these votes the revealed proponents of federation were generally on the lower left side of the line, the opponents generally on the upper right.

Conclusion

Australia came together because the states wanted a common market, but Victoria did not trust New South Wales to refrain from renegotiating a customs union once it had begun. Federation was not a byproduct of Australia's liberal progressive politics. New Zealand's decision to stay out of the union, the Free Trade Party's linking of federation with economic rather than identity issues, and the divisions within the New South Wales parliament all provide evidence against an alternative explanation rooted in a preexisting political community.

Still, even though the evidence suggests that political entrepreneurs who engineered the federation and the ordinary citizens who voted for it were mostly motivated by economic considerations, they sometimes described the project in terms of an inclusive community and appropriated symbols of a common, imagined Australian nationalism (see, e.g., Gross 1948). This addition of a heroic gloss to what was otherwise a mundane commercial arrangement was probably more than just rhetorical self-indulgence or a strategy for inspiring votes. For leaders in New South Wales, putting an identity spin on the agreement may have been a way to demonstrate willingness to invest in the new federal union with a change in national identity. If they could show Victoria that citizens of New South Wales were willing to identify themselves as citizens of Australia, then Victoria and the other states would be less concerned about their asymmetrical vulnerability.[8]

In his studies of political communities, David Laitin (1986, 1998, 2007) argues that there is a relationship between elites and masses, and between the affective desires people have for a sense of belonging to a unique community and the material benefits that can come from membership in

[8] The conclusions about national identity and federation that I draw in this section are necessarily inductive arguments based on my observation of the political process in one instance of federation, and this section should not be taken as a test of a theory. Still, the consistency between my conclusions and at least some existing theories about national identity and state formation is reassuring.

communities defined in a particular way. For example, he describes the process by which people living in Catalonia might move between thinking of themselves as Catalans or as Spaniards (Laitin 2007, 36–47) as a tipping game involving the languages people teach their children. People wish their children to be able to communicate easily with their peers, understand the same in-jokes, and experience the same literature; such cultural capital is valuable both for its own sake and as a means to further status and prosperity within a community. Parents will teach their children Catalan if they believe that most *other* parents will teach *their* children Catalan, whereas parents will teach their children Castilian (Spanish) if they believe that most *other* parents will teach *their* children Castilian.[9]

This social background, where parents seek to bring up their children in the same culture as (they believe) most other parents, is the setting for a contest among political and cultural elites who have interests in defining a political community in particular ways. Catalan-speaking poets and local industrialists might be better off if the community were defined as Catalan, since that would increase demand for Catalan poetry and (to the extent that community division leads to market segmentation) Catalan manufactured goods. Castilian poets and merchants have the opposite preferences. Each side will try to create the perception that its narrative of community is the more widely shared in order to create the self-fulfilling prophecy of a common convergence on a language community. This kind of social interaction, where entrepreneurs try to manipulate groups into coordinating their choices in a certain way, can apply to a variety of other contexts, ranging from residential housing segregation to the diffusion of standards and regulations (Schelling 1978).

Laitin describes the problem in terms of coordinating on languages, but the same logic applies to coordination on political identity. Identity, like language, is reproduced by masses of individuals and includes the shared narratives that people tell about their history and the ways they define appropriate social behavior. People investing in a particular national identity are influenced by their perceptions of the national identities of the people around them with whom they would like, whether consciously or not, to identify (Dowley and Silver 2000; Bloodgood 2007). Elites keen to manipulate identity, either to maintain or to erode a distinct community, can use narratives about history or behavior to influence the direction of

---

[9] Laitin formalizes the argument in a study of language politics in Ghana (1994). On the origins of Spanish identity, see Bollen and Medrano (1998).

the self-fulfilling prophecy. School textbooks that emphasize a distinct (or common) national history, flags displayed in civic contexts such as law courts, and civic holidays can all contribute to a particular common conjecture that citizens apply in defining their political communities.

Elites in New South Wales, then, who began using an Australian flag and describing their motivations in terms of an Australian—rather than a New South Welsh—community were beginning the process of orienting their citizens toward a federal government. Exiting the federation later would mean having to disentangle those terms again, a potentially costly project; as Laitin notes, once a community has tipped in one direction, moving it back can be costly and difficult even if it is not impossible (Laitin 1994).

Hirst (2000) argues that it was only by contemplating federation with the mainland that New Zealand "discovered" its own national distinctiveness. Although that national distinctiveness may have been present all along, it is more likely that a plausible cultural narrative could have been constructed for either inclusion or exclusion in Australasia but that the near-unanimous consensus against federation among New Zealand's political elite resulted in few, if any, conflicting identity narratives for people to process. In South Australia, probably the most culturally distinct of the mainland states (since it had not been founded by convicts), a unified elite in favor of federation may have played a similar role in triggering an Australian identity cascade.

My argument that the states merged for economic reasons does not necessarily imply that national sentiment or an expanding political community were irrelevant to the process. Rather, the discovery of a shared political community among Australians, but not New Zealanders, may have been part of the mechanism that leaders used to solve the problem of how to integrate their markets in a way they could all have confidence in, by tying national sentiment to particular institutions of cooperation. In practice, the Australian federalists did not neatly separate their motives and tools into logics of consequences and appropriateness; they used all the tools they had at their disposal in order to close the deal. One observer quotes a Tasmanian federalist who was explaining the case for federation while touring southern Tasmanian orchards:

> "Gentlemen," he would say, "if you vote for the Bill you will found a great and glorious nation under the bright Southern Cross, and meat will be cheaper; and you will live to see the Australian race dominate the Southern seas, and you will have a market for both potatoes and

apples; and your sons shall reap the grand heritage of nationhood, and if Sir William Lyne does come back to power in Sydney he can never do you one pennyworth of harm." This, delivered in one level sentence, invariably won high applause; and, indeed, as a farmer remarked to one who derided the quaintness of the mixture, "It was a dam good speech; every word of it was true." (Wise 1909, 356)

5

COERCION AND UNION IN ARGENTINA AND GERMANY

Most of the paradigmatic cases of federation, including Australia's, did not involve threats of violence, but in some cases coercion did play a role, as in the unifications of Argentina and Germany. From the 1820s through the 1860s, Buenos Aires tried using a combination of threats and assurances to compel three states (the *litoral* states of the former Spanish Viceroyalty) to join in an economic and military union. From the 1850s through the early 1870s, Prussia similarly tried to maneuver several smaller, German-speaking neighbors into joining it. Both Buenos Aires and Prussia had commitment problems—their smaller neighbors were fearful of being exploited if they agreed to economic or diplomatic mergers—but both needed the cooperation of these neighbors in order to achieve broader economic and security goals. Neither state, at least at first, was able to establish a credible commitment that it would act with self-restraint and respect the interests of its new partners. Nevertheless, both larger states eventually arranged federal unification agreements in at least some instances, Buenos Aires after 1860 and Prussia in 1871.

Federation was not inevitable in either case. Alternatives such as conquest or loose cooperation seemed, at the time, the more likely outcome. Given the variety of ways states can arrange cooperation, why did Argentina and Germany unify into federations when they might instead have developed into international organizations?

William Riker's theory of the origins of federations begins with the assumption that there are security gains for states acting together. States form a federal bargain when they "seek to meet an external military or diplomatic threat or to expand militarily or diplomatically without the distraction of conquering their potential partners" (1987, 3). This argument assumes that if a strong state (for example, Prussia) wants to enlist the aid of a neighbor (for example, Bavaria), the two states have only three possible arrangements that they can live under: either each one remains independent and self-sufficient, or the larger conquers the smaller, or the two join in a federal union. In Riker's view, the states federate if Prussia is capable of conquering Bavaria and would be willing to do so rather than accept independence, *and* if both Prussia and Bavaria would be better off by reaching a federal agreement as an alternative to conquest.

Riker's theory, however, does not resolve the puzzle of federal unions, because the states have another alternative: they could form a military alliance and pool their resources through an international organization. Federations are costlier to form and impose more restraints on a strong state's freedom of action. The Soviet Union established the Warsaw Pact, for example, rather than incorporating its junior partners into a federal union. The puzzle in this chapter is why Prussia and Buenos Aires ultimately chose to coerce their neighbors into forming federations instead of international organizations.

The logic of contrived symmetry adds value to an understanding of cases involving coercion, for three reasons. First, states bargain with each other over how to structure cooperation, but they do so with the understanding that the bargaining does not end once they agree on an institution. Either a federal union or an international organization is simply a device that states use to structure their future bargaining over division of the gains from cooperation. States try to strike a deal when they believe either that the deal itself will give them more bargaining power in the future than they would have had otherwise *or* that a deal will make cooperation possible when states would otherwise not be able to reach an agreement.

Second, conquest is costly, and violence can have unpredictable results; attempts at conquest do not always succeed. If they did, then any attempt would lead to integration and a division of gains that would be favorable for the conquering state and unfavorable for the conquered state, meaning that a potentially conquerable state would never have an incentive to hold out for a better offer when presented with an ultimatum.

Suppose that two states, one that would not be exposed to relationship-specific investments in cooperation (N) and one that would (V), are discussing economic or military integration, and they both understand that N, in the absence of an agreement, will make an attempt to conquer V. Facing a likely military defeat, V still has some bargaining leverage, since it can make things easier for N by agreeing voluntarily to a deal. The more that cooperation would require disproportionate investments in relationship-specific assets, the more willing V would be to resist occupation, and the more leverage it would have to credibly demand a greater institutional bond (a federation instead of an international organization) as the price of accepting N's demands for integration.

Third, stronger states have the ability and incentive to try to change the outside options of weaker states, in order to make them more willing to accept negotiated integration. N will try to lead V to make a relationship-specific investment before N commits to an institution that would give it (N) an incentive to act with restraint. Once V's investment is made, and sunk, it can no longer credibly hold out for any sort of institutional commitment from N. In cases where N has the military capacity to take unilateral action, such as in Argentina and Germany, one expects to find it trying to build dependence in its partners. Where these attempts succeed, integration will take place more on N's terms (international organization or a loose alliance); where they fail, integration will take place more on V's terms (more institutionalized and federal, with N paying a large upfront investment).

At the end of Chapter 2 I presented six observable implications of my theory: (1) the motives for states to form federations involve excludable goods; (2) federations are never the first choice of all member states; (3) leaders of nonvulnerable states, those that would have few relationship-specific investments in cooperation, prefer international organizations or ad hoc arrangements; (4) leaders of vulnerable states, with large relationship-specific investments in cooperation, prefer to cooperate via a federation; (5) vulnerable states resist cooperating until after federal institutions are in place; and (6) nonvulnerable states joining a federation will invest more heavily in federal institutions by, among other things, making more substantial changes to their party systems. In this chapter I test these propositions in two cases: Argentina leading up to the federal union in 1862, and Germany leading up to the federal expansion in 1871.

These cases test important implications of the theory but are useful and interesting as a basis of comparison for other potential contemporary cases as well. Negotiations over reunification between mainland China and Taiwan, for example, or over a confederal arrangement for a future Iraq, may take place under the threat of conquest. The PRC and Taiwan are in a situation where the more powerful state desires some form of union but the more potentially vulnerable state is afraid that political dependence will put it at risk once a union is implemented. Taiwan, like the Argentine *litoral* and the smaller German states, ideally prefers that unification—if it happens at all—come with a strong set of institutions that would raise the costs to the mainland of exiting or renegotiating the agreement.[1]

The cases of Argentina and Germany are also methodologically useful because, within each one, there is variation in bargaining power and outside options. Buenos Aires tried threats and inducements for over thirty years without convincing the *litoral* states of Corrientes, Entre Ríos, and Santa Fe to unify with it—until after a series of events changed the bargaining power among the states. Prussia made offers to various German states to join in a federal system. I focus on two powerful states that engaged in prolonged negotiations: in 1866, Saxony refused a unification agreement (and was eventually defeated in a war); in 1871 Bavaria accepted an agreement without fighting.

Argentina

The Spanish Empire in South America began to collapse in 1810 with a series of antiimperial revolts prompted by a decline in Spain's military and economic power. On the eve of independence, the territory of modern Argentina was under the jurisdiction of the Viceroyalty of the River Plate, a Spanish regional division, centered on a key strategic waterway, that included all of present-day Argentina, Uruguay, Paraguay, and parts of Bolivia and Peru. The Plate, formed by the convergence of the Paraná and Uruguay Rivers, is only 180 miles long but widens from 31 miles across to 136 miles where it empties into the Atlantic. Buenos Aires stands on the south bank of the Plate, near a bend where the river is 26 miles wide at the narrowest point.

Although the hinterland to the west of Buenos Aires contained extremely poor farmland, the area to the north and northwest, the *litoral,* had rich pasture, and the states there had developed large and lucrative cattle ranching enterprises by the end of the eighteenth century. A system of inland rivers connected the *litoral* to the Atlantic through the Plate. This location made Buenos Aires the major port city of South America by 1800, facilitating trade between the South American interior and Europe.

By the end of the war with Spain in 1820, the states of the Viceroyalty were de facto independent, and it was by no means certain that Argentina would end up as one unified state; indeed, Bolivia, Peru, Paraguay,

---

[1] For more on the parallels between the PRC-Taiwan negotiations over reunification and these case studies in this chapter, see Kastner and Rector (2008).

and Uruguay all eventually became independent, and it would have been difficult to predict that today's Argentine provinces would eventually be united (Criscenti 1961, 367). All the provinces had met in 1811 without reaching any agreements, leading the more distant provinces in Upper Peru and Bolivia to establish independence. Another meeting in 1819 which included Paraguay and Uruguay ended with thirteen of the fourteen participants rejecting the final draft—a proposal from Buenos Aires for a unitary state. Buenos Aires responded by raising an army and making an incursion into Santa Fe, the first *litoral* province to the northwest. Santa Fe joined in a temporary alliance with the other two *litoral* states, Entre Ríos and Corrientes, and defeated the invading army.

With the war for independence over and the provinces in a military stalemate, a political order began to emerge among the provinces of the Plate River region. After ten years of virtual independence during the war and the rejection of the 1819 constitution, outside observers began to think of the provinces as separate states (Criscenti 1961, 384; McLean 1995, 8) or "virtually sovereign entities" (Hamnett 1997, 323). Each had its own constitution, military, and customs houses, and in the popular political dialogue people took "nation" to mean the local province rather than the Viceroyalty as a whole (Criscenti 1961, 370, 386). The borders between states began to shift, and parts of the old intendancy of Buenos Aries broke off to form other states. "As the provinces began to behave as nations rather than as provinces, Buenos Aires was compelled to conclude semipolitical and semi-international pacts with provinces determined to preserve their sovereignty and their exercise of national functions" (Criscenti 1961, 389).

The rest of this section on Argentina proceeds in four parts. First, a historical overview of the relations among the major states is followed by, second, the problem of cooperation over trade routes. Third, I show how my theory can account for the strategic decisions the states made during the crucial years following 1845. Fourth, I summarize the observable implications of the theory by arguing that the states with more to lose from further integration sought an institution that would make exit costly for the one state (Buenos Aires) that otherwise had less to lose, and that even though the bargaining process involved violence, the strategic logic was the same as in Australia.

Overview

Following the failed constitutional convention in 1819, another meeting in 1821 also ended in failure when Buenos Aires insisted on the establishment of a unitary state that it would control. In 1822, Buenos Aires and the *litoral* states signed an alliance agreement they called the Pact of the Quadrilateral. In it, Buenos Aires, Corrientes, Entre Ríos, and Santa Fe agreed to two things: first, free navigation through the Plate River, a concession essentially allowing goods from the *litoral* states to pass to Europe untaxed; second, as a concession to Buenos Aires, a diplomatic and military alliance against Spain and Brazil which committed the states to come to each other's aid without merging their military organizations.

The growing military threat from Brazil, which had prompted Buenos Aires to make the navigation concession in exchange for an alliance commitment, revolved around the future of what is now Uruguay. Uruguay had been originally colonized by Portuguese merchants who used their position along the north side of the Plate River to pass contraband from *litoral* cattle ranchers (and Upper Peruvian silver miners), using Portuguese ports to circumvent the harbor taxes charged by Buenos Aires. The Spanish fought back to preserve their monopoly on trade routes from the interior by founding the city of Montevideo and eventually incorporating all of modern-day Uruguay into the Viceroyalty in 1776. Local forces from Montevideo coordinated with other regional armies in the wars of independence, starting in 1810, and its leaders participated in early discussion of regional confederation with Buenos Aires and other provinces in the unstable decade that followed. In 1820, Portuguese forces from Brazil seized Montevideo, but Buenos Aires placed a high priority on winning it back.

At yet another constitutional convention lasting from 1824 to 1826, Buenos Aires sought to enlist the help of the other provinces for military preparations against Brazil. A war for control of Uruguay broke out between Buenos Aires and Brazil in 1825. Corrientes, Entre Ríos, and Santa Fe all had militaries that could have helped in the conflict, but these states rejected the appeals of Buenos Aires for help and instead made separate diplomatic overtures to Brazil. The war ended in 1828 when Britain used its commercial influence to mediate a solution that established Uruguay as an independent buffer state (Seckinger 1976). With the constitutional project effectively over, Santa Fe formally nullified any relationship with Buenos Aires; Corrientes and Entre Ríos signed a bilateral military alliance against Buenos Aires (Criscenti 1961, 400); and the three *litoral* states each formally declared independence (Rock 1985, 97; Vale 2000).[2]

---

[2] Under pressure from Buenos Aires, no European government formally recognized any of these states as independent.

After the political breakdown in the 1820s, the provinces entered a period of trade wars. Buenos Aires heavily taxed goods from the *litoral* which were loaded on ships in its port bound for Europe. Buenos Aires' control over outgoing trade routes was, however, far from perfect; the provinces had two outside options. First, they could load goods onto oceangoing vessels at the port of Rosario, a city in Entre Ríos along the Paraná (Rock 1985, 116). This option was reasonably cost-effective, since goods could travel by water, but it had two drawbacks. The first was that since shipments could not stop in Buenos Aires to change vessels, they would have to cross the ocean in the smaller ships that could pass through the lower Paraná, which made crossing the Atlantic costlier and riskier. The second drawback was that Buenos Aires made intermittent attempts to blockade the Plate River, so there was some chance that ships from Rosario would be stopped and forced to dock in Buenos Aires to pay transshipment taxes. For the most part, however, the Plate was so wide and Buenos Aries' control of the surrounding territory so weak that ships still had a high chance of making it through.

The second option for the *litoral* states was to ship cargo by land to Montevideo (Uruguay). There, cargo could be loaded directly onto larger transatlantic ships, avoiding the Paraná and Plate Rivers entirely. This option also had two drawbacks. First, the overland route to Montevideo crossed difficult terrain, making the trip costly. Second, Buenos Aires made consistent efforts to blockade Montevideo's port, so that even cargo leaving from there was not certain to get through. Montevideo's position on the Atlantic beyond the mouth of the Plate, however, made enforcement of any blockade difficult, and French and British naval vessels were often present and deterred attempts by Buenos Aires to enforce its blockade (Brown 1979, 206).

Military competition with Brazil and with France complicated the efforts of Buenos Aires to channel all regional trade through its port. In 1838, France began a blockade of Buenos Aires that lasted until 1840, and open war broke out between Buenos Aires and France from 1839 to 1841. (The proximate cause was a dispute over commercial rights; it was settled through British mediation.) During the war, the port of Buenos Aires was virtually closed to commercial traffic; further, the war rendered any blockade of Montevideo entirely ineffective, so through 1841 the *litoral* provinces had unimpeded access to Europe through Uruguay (Brown 1979, 215).

The war with France had an important effect on Buenos Aires. Juan Manuel de Rosas, its dictator from 1829 until 1852, successfully mobilized Buenos Aires for war far beyond previous levels. He created a standing army, which he then funded directly from the proceeds of large cattle ranches that he seized from political opponents accused of conspiring with France. The French blockade drove many local merchants out of business and triggered high local inflation, allowing Rosas to consolidate power even further. His military dictatorship therefore emerged from the war far more powerful that it had been originally (Rock 1985, 110).

Beginning in 1841, Rosas began using his larger navy to establish a permanent blockade of Montevideo, to which the French and British fleets acquiesced. The blockade was eventually supplemented with a long-term siege by land armies, which cut off the flow of goods to Montevideo entirely. The *litoral* states continued, however, to be able to send cargo down the Paraná River and past Buenos Aires on the Plate River, at least at night—until 1845, when the Buenos Aires army was finally powerful enough to establish fortifications along the Paraná at the town of Vuelta de Obligado. These included a system of controls along a narrow stretch of the river where it could be closed by a chain at night and where ships could be easily intercepted by day (Rock 1985, 111). Thus, by 1845, the *litoral* had been closed off from any alternative trade routes; from then on, all trade with Europe would have to pass through Buenos Aires.

This new regime ended the previous equilibrium in which de facto independent states maintained their autonomy after Buenos Aires tried, and failed, to maneuver the *litoral* states into supporting its military struggles against Brazil and France. When Buenos Aires established Paraná River controls in 1845, creating for the first time a virtually complete blockade of all exports from Corrientes, Entre Ríos, and Santa Fe to Europe, France and Britain initially objected. In 1847, however, they relented in the face of Buenos Aires' growing local naval power and accepted its monopoly on trade from the interior.

Once Buenos Aires had established control of all trade routes, the *litoral* states still had a choice about what to do: they could agree to political reunification with the city, or they could remain independent. The drawback to reunification had always been that Buenos Aires would have influence over commercial policy and would reduce the other states' ability in striking trade deals on their own. After 1845, however, the question was moot, since Buenos Aires had control over the river anyway: it might use its position from within a confederation to extract taxes on shipping but would be able to do that just as easily without a confederation.

Trade Routes

The key change in 1845 was Buenos Aires' establishment of control of all trade routes leading from the *litoral* to Europe, but control of trade routes was not, by itself, enough to lead the states to join in a federation. The contrary view, that trade routes do determine the shape of national borders, comes from David Friedman (1977). His theory posits that political jurisdictions will tend to expand to encompass the entire length of a trade route and a network of parallel trade routes. That is, there are economies of scale in the taxation of trade, and these scale economies are greatest as the size of a state grows to the size and shape of an entire trade network.

To see why this is so, consider a route that connects two cities. If the route passes through multiple political jurisdictions, then each one has an incentive to tax trade through its territory and will set a tax rate to maximize its individual income. But in a classic tragedy of the commons, the route becomes overtaxed, trade declines, and the states as a group collect less revenue. If one political jurisdiction controls the entire route, however, it can set a tax rate that raises revenue to the optimal level; hence, political entrepreneurs have an incentive to expand the size of a state, through either peaceful amalgamation or conquest, until it encompasses the entire route.

Similarly, revenue collection is inefficient if two or more states control parallel trade routes. Each state competitively lowers its tariffs, leading to a lower amount of tax revenue than could otherwise be sustained. Leaders thus have an incentive to eliminate competing trade routes by taking them over.

This basic model, along with some extensions (Blum and Dudley 1991; Wittman 1991; Artzrouni and Komlos 1996; Kaufman 1997; Ellingsen 1998; Josselin and Marciano 1999), assumes that states act independently. Friedman, in fact, specifically defines a state as "the largest political unit within which tax policy is effectively coordinated" (1977, 61). This class of theory, then, does not really address the motives behind state formation. Rather, it addresses the motives behind policy coordination and assumes that policy coordination is possible only at the level of the state.

Consider trade between Entre Ríos and Europe. Before 1845, there were three parallel routes: the Plate River with a stop in Buenos Aires to change from rivergoing to oceangoing vessels (technologically, the most efficient route); the Plate River without a stop in Buenos Aires; and overland to the port of Montevideo. After 1845, the second two routes had been eliminated, and only the first route, which passed through two different states, remained. Even so, the nature of the Argentine federation did not follow directly from the shape of the trade route alone; trade routes, by themselves, cannot account for political integration.

Suppose that the port of Buenos Aires is a necessary stop along the way—the situation after 1845. Friedman's theory suggests that as long as Entre Ríos and Buenos Aires are separate political jurisdictions, they will overtax the trade route, because each will have a choice between taking its agreed-upon share of the jointly optimal tax, which is lower, and the individually maximizing tax, which is higher, and each will therefore choose the higher tax. That choice will drive down the level of trade, and both states will therefore collect less than the total possible revenue.

This strategic situation between these two states is a classic prisoners' dilemma. Actors playing this game once will tend to defect—to overtax the trade route—resulting in an inefficient outcome. However, if the players interact with each other repeatedly, and expect to continue to interact well into the future, they will tend to cooperate. Establishing a pattern of co-operation conditioned on the other side's cooperating can make each side better off in the long run than it would be by reaping the benefits of defecting in the short run (Axelrod 1984). All that is necessary is for the two states to agree in advance how to divide the revenue between them and, given the relatively transparent nature of harbor taxes and the repeated interactions, even the "cheap talk" of a prior agreement is sufficient, in principle, to sustain cooperation. As I noted in the Introduction, an extremely large literature in international relations theory demonstrates that states can, over the long run, coordinate on sustained cooperation even in anarchy. Friedman (1977) and others provide an important starting point for a theory of federation by showing that joint gains can arise from economic geography, but these gains are not enough to account for states' cooperation via federations instead of customs unions or alliances.

Strategies

The political conflict over confederation did not end in 1845, of course, but the events of 1845 changed the terms of the negotiations by creating a new economic threat to the states in the interior. The *litoral* states were quickly unified in an alliance led by the largest of them, Entre Ríos, which, like all the *litoral* provinces, was ruled by a coalition of aristocratic cattle ranchers. Led by Governor Justo José de Urquiza, the largest landowner, these ranchers depended on access to European markets for their exports, and the consolidation of control over trade routes by Buenos Aires was an economic threat to them. The prospect of transit taxes on goods was the most important political economy issue facing the ruling coalition, and it gave these landowners a compelling incentive to organize (Walford 1939; Bunkley 1950; Whigham 1988).

Urquiza began by raising a military force locally; he then negotiated agreements with the other *litoral* states. The resulting Triple Alliance among Corrientes, Entre Ríos, and Santa Fe agreed both on giving Urquiza operational command over the combined militaries of the three provinces and on a framework for negotiating with Buenos Aries about the shape of a confederation that would limit its influence over trade on the river, although the three states agreed among themselves that some concessions to Buenos Aires would be acceptable. After several years of raising an army and engaging forces from Buenos Aires in several minor battles northwest of the Plate, in 1851 Urquiza allied with Brazil and Uruguay. Rosas, still in power in Buenos Aires, abandoned his siege of Montevideo and retreated to the outskirts of Buenos Aires. Urquiza claimed victory and entered Buenos Aires in February 1852, while Rosas escaped to England and lived the rest of his life in exile. The actual fighting, however, was limited in scale. Most historians note that the key battle was determined more by massive defections from Rosas's army, after Urquiza had negotiated a complicated power-sharing arrangement with several of Rosas's generals, foreshadowing the constitution that followed (Halperín Donghi 1972; Bethell 1993).

Having outmaneuvered Rosas, the *litoral* states next moved to bring Buenos Aires into an arrangement that they hoped would give them the benefits of economic cooperation with the powerful city (access to its port, in principle the most efficient way to reach European markets) while also protecting them from extortion. Urquiza called a constitutional convention among all of the Argentine states, which produced a constitution that made Paraná, the capital of Entre Ríos, the Argentine capital. Thus began a seven-year "confederation" period (Angueira 1989). The central government in Paraná used the period of calm to begin a series of infrastructure improvements—including not only some railroads that gave the interior easy access to Buenos Aires but also others that allowed freight to bypass that city in favor of other ports.

Urquiza never had complete military control over Buenos Aires, however, and the new regime never successfully brought its plans to completion (Goodwin 1977). The city resisted a government that its citizens perceived as dominated by outsiders, and in 1859 a three-year war broke out. As in the war that preceded the creation of the confederation, the combatants relied more on military and political maneuvering than on actual fighting.

It began when Buenos Aries, with a reorganized army, renegotiated the terms of the confederation and began the process of consolidating control over the provinces (Burr 1955, 47). Fighting was sparse and the eventual bargain was designed to make it seem as though Buenos Aires had won a battle near its outskirts, although whether in fact a battle took place is a matter of conjecture (Bunkley 1950; Moreno 1965). Following negotiations, Buenos Aires joined the confederation under the terms of the 1853 constitution with some modifications: they established a central bank, codified Argentina as a federation, and made Buenos Aires the national capital city.

International Organization and Federation

Economic cooperation among the Argentine states would have allowed them to capitalize on their comparative advantage in cattle on world markets by using the most efficient trade route available to them. The conflict among the states was not over whether they should trade with the outside world but rather over how the gains from trade would be divided: the *litoral* states ideally preferred to keep the surpluses for themselves; Buenos Aires ideally preferred to keep a large share for itself. In principle, any division among the states would have been sustainable.

With the only possible trade route connecting the *litoral* states to Europe being controlled by Buenos Aires, however, any investments landowners in the *litoral* made in more production would have been specific to the relationship with Buenos Aires; that is, their value would have depended on the extent to which Buenos Aires cooperated with the landowners' home states. But cooperation would not have led Buenos Aires to invest in relationship-specific assets to nearly the same extent. Since its port facilities were already in place and once the land around the river (valuable for other uses in any case) had been acquired, controlling the flow of river traffic required a miniscule initial investment in chains and customs houses.

The outside options for the *litoral* differed before and after 1845. Before 1845, a lack of cooperation with Buenos Aires made trade with Europe more expensive, but not prohibitively so. With a strong outside option, the *litoral* had little incentive to cooperate at all, preferring instead free use of the alternative routes (bypassing Buenos Aires). States form federations only when the gains they can get through cooperation are excludable— the first implication of my theory—so the *litoral* lack of interest in any form of union is unsurprising.

After 1845, however, that only one route was available to the *litoral* and that using it required Buenos Aires' consent created a classic case of unequal potential dependence (as described in Chapter 1). Cooperation over the trade route would lead the *litoral* to make investments in the interior, which would increase Buenos Aires' bargaining leverage. Although Rosas had from time to time claimed political jurisdiction over parts of the *litoral*, he had until then made little effort to enforce those claims. With potential economic linkages, however, the interior states could not be certain that Rosas, or later rulers of Buenos Aires, would refrain from using economic leverage to compel future political concessions from the interior.

The changes in 1845 had another consequence as well: when Buenos Aires constructed river controls and blockaded the alternative routes via Montevideo or the Plate River), it made *existing,* rather than just future, economic investments in the interior relationship-specific, since assets would now generate wealth only if ships could get to Europe, which they could do only with the cooperation of Buenos Aires. The city's ploy was to change the *litoral's* calculations from being about potential future investments—in which case caution about future diminished bargaining power would lead the states to resist integration—to being about gains over a status quo in which relationship-specific investments had already been sunk, in which case cooperation on Buenos Aires' terms would be the logical choice. In other words, Buenos Aires tried to ensure that the *litoral* states' investments in the route were made up front, before any constitutional settlement, whereas the *litoral* resisted making such investments until after a settlement. These efforts provide evidence for the fifth implication of the theory, that N tries to get V to invest in cooperation without an institutional framework in place, whereas V resists.

As the second, third, and fourth implications of the theory predict, the *litoral* states and Buenos Aires disagreed about how to proceed. Given the new status quo—high joint gains and high specificity for the interior states but low specificity for Buenos Aires—the *litoral* states preferred some sort of federal system that would use institutions to restrain the city. They also would have been at least as well off by changing outside options back to what they had been before 1845 by denying Buenos Aires the ability to exercise a monopoly on river trade.

General Urquiza tried both. First, he used a series of alliances and military maneuvers to seize Buenos Aires' points of control along the Paraná River and to end the blockade around Montevideo. Second, he established a set of institutions over Buenos Aires, the government of the confederation, to try to prevent it from making another attempt. The federation they established had some, but not all, of the characteristics of one designed to extract a political bond from Buenos Aires—the sixth observable implication. The federal congress drew a large number of representatives from Buenos Aires (because of its population), but majority and supermajority requirements gave them incentives to form coalitions with representatives from other regions in order to accomplish anything (Moreno 1965). Furthermore, the capital was outside of the territory of Buenos Aires; thus it was difficult for physical investments made in the capital region by politicians from Buenos Aires to have any value should the federal agreement fail. The limited tasks the federal government took on, however, and its failure to conclude any of them, ultimately rendered investments in the federal government next to useless anyway.

At least part of the problem was that elites in Buenos Aires viewed the confederation as a temporary aberration, something they accepted while they husbanded their resources and waited their chance to mobilize to demand a revision of the agreement. Their choices were also what the theory would predict. Crucially, once Buenos Aires had recovered from the losses it had sustained in 1851–52, it did not seek a wholesale revision of the existing order, either by conquering the other states outright or by ending all institutional cooperation. Rather, it accepted that it was more likely to get value from the *litoral* by cooperation than by conquest, and that cooperation would be more forthcoming if it was structured by a federal agreement.

The concessions Buenos Aires won by the end of 1861 might seem almost absurdly trivial—the national bank, the location of the capital—but were in fact important institutions that influenced how the states would have expected to bargain over trade revenue in the future. In effect, the final settlement had all the states investing in a federal institution; Buenos Aires less so than its partners had originally hoped but as much as they could have reasonably expected, given its military advantage and its interest in controlling the river.

Germany

The Congress of Vienna at the end of the Napoleonic Wars in 1815 established thirty-nine German states, including the two largest, Prussia and Austria; these thirty-nine were unified that year in the Confederation, a mutual defense pact. The Confederation as an entity had some formal ability to sign treaties with foreign states, but its member states retained the ability to conduct foreign relations as well, entering into or breaking alliances with outsiders. There were permanent institutions, but delegates voted as representatives of state governments rather than as individuals or members of political parties (Koch 1984).

By 1834, Prussia had engineered the creation of the Zollverein, a separate grouping, a customs union that grew by 1842 to include twenty-eight of the thirty-nine states. By Prussian design, it did not include Austria. Like those of the Confederation, member states had the ability to veto decisions made by the group as a whole, although in practice Prussia dominated it. Now an economic union as well as a defensive alliance, the Prussian sphere of influence entailed a greater degree of military and economic integration than scholars typically associate with international agreements (Forsyth 1981, 168). Still, the state governments remained institutionally separate, and the governing institutions of the region, rather than forming a new, distinct layer, were intergovernmental and entailed less political integration than, for example, the European Coal and Steel Community (Hallerberg and Weber 2002, 5).

At a constitutional assembly in Frankfurt in 1848, during a period of struggle between democratic movements and monarchs, a group of elected representatives proposed a federal constitution featuring a lower house with directly elected representatives and an upper house of delegates from the states. Although their goal was to institutionalize representative government at the expense of monarchs, the institutions they proposed also had the characteristics of the kind of federal bond that would contrive symmetry between a less dependent state (Prussia) and its more dependent junior partners. This federal constitution was ratified by twenty-eight of the smaller German states, but none of the larger states (including Prussia) approved it (Hallerberg and Weber 2002).

Within the Confederation, Prussia and Austria struggled for supremacy, and Prussia provoked war with Austria in 1866. After Prussia's victory, it grouped the smaller German states into two organizations: the new North German Confederation (the *Norddeutscher Bund*), replacing the previous Confederation, and a reconstituted Zollverein. The North German Confederation was a military organization with a substantial, directly elected set of federal assemblies—in other words, a federation as I define it (Hudson 1891). One historian described the shift from the old to the new confederation as representing an even more substantial deepening of political integration than the change in America from the Articles of Confederation to the Philadelphia Constitution (Smith 1923, 40). The new confederation included only the northern states, so the next two largest German states after Prussia, Austria and Bavaria, were not members. The second-largest member was Saxony, which had allied with Austria in the 1866 war but had been overrun by Prussia. The second institution, the new Zollverein, was also more politically integrated than in the past, with a representative assembly that actively made trade policy and international agreements.

Prussia, seeking to preserve its own security and independence from other regional powers such as France, as well as to protect the large common market it felt was necessary to support its late industrial development, continued to move to absorb the other German states as well, finally negotiating the entry of Bavaria and the rest of the southern states in 1871, just before the outbreak of Prussia's war with France.

Like Buenos Aires with the *litoral,* Prussia could claim that it was pursuing a reunification of territories that had, in the past, been unified. Prussia's political leaders styled themselves a second German Reich, heir to the first, medieval Reich, although that earlier German system had been a very loose, decentralized arrangement (Conradt 2005). Also like Buenos Aires, Prussia deployed threats and assurances in its attempt to induce the other states to join it without violence.

One key difference between Germany and Argentina was that the Argentine states were economically independent, and the federal constitution was the eventual tool that Buenos Aires used in order to create an economic union. The German economic union already existed prior to federation, however, so Prussia had no need of a federal constitution to induce it. Economic integration had been an intended consequence of the customs union from the beginning but was dramatically deepened, in an unintended way, by the completion in the mid-nineteenth century of rail networks that reduced transport costs to low levels (Lee 1988). Prussia's goals in forming the federation were not directly economic but strategic; its leaders desired the advantages that would come from a unified German diplomatic policy.

States, in principle, can act together to pursue common security goals, without forming a federal government, via a military or diplomatic alliance. Member states of NATO or the European Union, for example, often cooperate not just in preparing to use their militaries defensively to a common purpose (the mutual defense aspect of a security agreement) but also in formulating a common strategy. These two issues are distinct. The member states of the European Union, for example, have separate processes for military and diplomatic cooperation, with joint diplomacy falling under the Directorate of External Affairs. The European Commission plays an increasingly important role in international relations and has a representative at the G8 summit (Bache and George 2006, 279).

Diplomatic cooperation is fundamentally different from military cooperation; it typically involves a greater degree of joint action, because it
requires states to follow a common agenda even in peacetime.

Given its position in Europe between rival powers, and with a growing
economic and military base that made it a potential rival to other great
powers, Prussia's diplomatic objectives were extremely important to its
leaders. Prussia's fundamental aim was to pursue wealth and independence
by ensuring that it would be safe from predation by other nearby powers,
namely France and Russia. To achieve its goals, Prussia required the active
diplomatic cooperation of its German neighbors. Otto von Bismarck, who
became the minister-president of Prussia in 1862 and dominated German
politics throughout the period of unification, was particularly concerned
that France might be able to maneuver itself into a diplomatic alliance
with Saxony or Bavaria, setting the latter up as a buffer to contain Prussia
in its bid for security and diplomatic leverage over its rivals. Keeping the
smaller German states apart from France and in Prussia's camp would
give Bismarck the leverage he needed in Europe to achieve all his other
grand strategic objectives, from negotiating favorable trade agreements to
securing his territorial claims.

Diplomatic cooperation can, in principle, be achieved through ad hoc
cooperation, without any institutional basis. For the states in question,
though, noninstitutionalized diplomatic cooperation would have posed a
commitment problem because diplomatic cooperation itself would have
worsened the outside options for the smaller German states by more than
it would have worsened them for Prussia. Given its position in the European balance of power, Prussia, a rising power, did not have the realistic option of allying with France, regardless of what it did. The smaller
German states, buffers between France and Prussia but each too small to
affect the balance of power by itself, did have the option of allying with
either of the great powers or of remaining independent of both. Once a
state does ally with a major power, its future options become more limited, since leaving one camp and joining the other is risky at best (Fazal
2004, 321); even though alliances are fluid in principle, in practice, allying
with one side can be dangerous for an individual state, especially when the
regional order is bipolar (Waltz 1979). Within a potential diplomatic alliance between Prussia and its smaller neighbors, therefore, outside options
and thus bargaining power generally would decline more rapidly for the
smaller states than for Prussia. Consequently, the smaller states had reason
to be concerned that giving up their outside options would put them in a
position to be exploited by Prussia. Prussia and its potential partners faced

a common dilemma: how to make diplomatic cooperation credibly better for all of them than the status quo.

This section proceeds in three parts. First, I discuss the Prussian relationship with Saxony leading up to the formation of the North German Confederation in 1866. Second, I consider Prussia and Bavaria through 1871, both because they are important for their own sakes—as the largest northern and southern states—and because they illustrate Prussia's general strategy as well as highlight an important puzzle: why Prussia sought political integration by incorporating Saxony and Bavaria into a federal union rather than by using its coercive potential to control them by less institutionalized means. I address this puzzle in the third section where I relate Prussia's goals, and in particular Bismarck's, to the available options and argue that the threat of sustained resistance from the German states led Prussia to accept a federal constitution that required from it a heavy initial investment. Because the smaller, more potentially vulnerable states had at least some ability to hold out for an institutional commitment, the origins of Germany's federal institutions after 1871 are consistent with my theory.

Saxony

By 1866, other than Prussia itself, Saxony was the strongest of the North German states, with a large economy and a growing population. It had been one of the first German states to industrialize and by the 1860s had one of the most advanced economies in continental Europe (Flockerzie 1991). Its economy gave it considerable influence, although it lacked a large standing army, and its military power generally lagged behind Prussia's even in proportion to its population. Saxony also had a geographic problem: immediately to the southwest of Prussia, the two states shared a long border. Over the previous fifty years, Prussia had been making increasingly insistent claims to Saxon territory as it carried on its project of unifying the German states. Because of Prussia's long-term intentions, Saxony's leaders were extremely wary of their growing dependence on Prussian and Prussian-controlled markets.

From the beginning, Saxony had been a member of the Zollverein, the customs union that linked it and most of the rest of the German states to Prussia. The advantages of membership were twofold. First, it established the German states as a common market, which meant that the smaller states all had the same ability to produce at a higher level than they would have had otherwise, taking advantage of scale economies. Second, it allowed the states to negotiate as a unit with foreign governments over reciprocal trade access, giving them as a collective more leverage than they would have had as individuals.[3]

Although they benefited economically, Saxon leaders were generally resistant to deepening trade and looked with alarm at rising trade between Saxony and Prussia. Several authors have noted Saxony's growing economic dependence on Prussia in the years leading up to the 1866 war, and Saxony's refusal to join the proposed North German Confederation voluntarily prior to 1866 has generally been attributed to its fears of growing economic dependence (Bazillon 1990; Carr 1991).

Furthermore, small states that joined the customs union gave up the ability to raise customs revenue independently. Leaving the union and going back to raising money self-sufficiently, however, required being able to put a large administrative apparatus into place, something that would have been painfully costly for Prussia but prohibitively costly for the smaller states. Switching to direct taxes would have undermined the bases of the political regimes and was therefore unthinkable (Ziblatt 2006, 48).

The growth of dependence is by itself, however, insufficient to account for Saxon resistance, for two reasons. First, the potential loss of Saxon bargaining leverage was at least partly offset by the growth of Prussian dependence on Saxony. Unlike the dominant states of New South Wales in the Australian case and Buenos Aires in the Argentine one, Prussia actually did have substantial relationship-specific investments at stake, with Saxony and other northern and southern German states as well. Chambers of commerce in the industrializing Prussian cities of Cologne, Düsseldorf, and Frankfurt all submitted appeals to the Prussian government in the 1860s to ensure that they would have unimpeded access to the southern cities that absorbed their exports under a common protective tariff (Ziblatt 2006, 40).

Second, what matters for the strategic choices that a state makes about cooperation is not how appealing or unappealing its outside option is in the abstract; rather, what matters is the extent to which any one particular agreement to deepen cooperation would uniquely change the state's outside option. Saxony was already economically dependent upon the Zollverein, and although further political integration might have resulted in its becoming even more deeply entwined with Prussia, this change would

---

[3] Britain, for example, had several rounds of trade agreements with Prussia and therefore by extension with the Zollverein generally. Trade treaties with Britain applied to all British possessions, so the Zollverein states had most-favored-nation status with the whole of the British Empire (Porritt 1922).

have been only incremental at most. The damage—loss of bargaining leverage due to unequal trade dependence—was already done.

Saxony's leaders valued the economic development and wealth that regional trade generated but were fearful of Prussia's potential to use its military and economic influence to undermine Saxony's position. For a long time, they relied on the security strategy of playing Austria and Prussia off against each other. Although they did not trust either of the two largest German states, they believed that the second-largest was less a threat—and it was further away—and so in a classic balance of power ploy, they generally allied with Austria (Friedjung 1935).

In early 1866, Prussia issued Saxony an ultimatum, demanding that it disarm and adopt a position of neutrality in the conflict between Prussia and Austria. Prussia also demanded that Saxony accept a series of changes that Prussia had proposed to the confederation agreement governing the German states—in effect demanding that Saxony join a federation. The events leading up to the ultimatum were complex: Bismarck, seeking to provoke a crisis with Austria, had led Prussia into invading the smaller German state of Holstein. When Austria mobilized for war and attempted to rally its allies against Prussia, Prussia demanded that Saxony (and two other states, Hanover and Hesse-Cassel) renounce Austria and join the new confederation (Robertson 1918, 203; Smith 1923, 35).

Prussia's proposal was for a federal parliament that would direct foreign and military policy. Although such a parliament would be dominated by Prussia, it would by no means have been a complete Prussian instrument, since the smaller states would have disproportionate influence and would, in principle, be able to block Prussian actions. Still, Prussia's influence in the parliament would have been substantial, and in any case it was not clear to observers at the time that Prussia's commitment to bind itself to the federal parliament was sincere (Albrecht-Carrie 1958).

Prussia's proposed confederation was troubling to Saxony for another reason as well. Bismarck, by now the diplomatic and military leader of Prussia, proposed that the federal parliament be popularly elected. Bismarck had been impressed with Napoleon's use of mass suffrage in France to circumvent the wishes of the urban elite and gain support by tapping into French mass nationalism in order to boost his power. Reasoning that he could do the same with a growing sense of German nationalism among the population as a whole, Bismarck hoped that using a parliament would cut out the traditional aristocratic rulers of the states and consolidate his control. Making universal suffrage part of his appeal also gained him some support from liberal reformers in the other states (Friedjung 1935, 120; Weichlein 2000).

The ultimatum from Prussia put Saxony in a difficult position. Prussia could easily defeat Saxony in a war of conquest. (That the Prussian army eventually did conquer Saxony in a matter of days was no surprise; Saxony's army did not even attempt to resist the invasion directly, instead retreating to join with Austrian forces in the hope of making an eventual counterattack.) If Saxony accepted the agreement, it would find itself with much reduced military and diplomatic freedom and would likely thereby lose control of its domestic autonomy as well. For the elite Saxon leadership the prospects were even worse, since they would see their power undermined by mass elections.

Holding-out kept alive the possibility that Saxony would receive military and diplomatic support from Austria. Although Austria would eventually be defeated by Prussia, Saxony of course did not know this at the time; it therefore recognized that its best chance for outside help to enhance its leverage with Prussia was for Austria to win the war, or at least fight to a stalemate. There was even the possibility of support from France, which was wary of Prussian consolidation and sought to keep Saxony alive as a buffer state (Albrecht-Carrie 1958; Fazal 2004). If Saxony accepted the deal, however, it would lose the ability to negotiate independently with outside states for support. The terms of the Prussian offer forbade an independent military and foreign policy and Prussia was unlikely, once in control, to interpret the agreement loosely in Saxony's favor.

War broke out between Prussia and Saxony in 1866, when Saxony refused the offer of federation. Like the nearly bloodless wars that ended the Argentine campaigns a decade earlier, the conquest of Saxony was more a matter of military maneuvers than of actual combat. Under the command of Prince Albert (who would later become the king of Saxony under the terms of the negotiated settlement that ended the war several months later), the Saxon army ceded all of Saxony to Prussia and fell back into Bohemia, where it joined with Austrian forces. The Saxons then fought several battles against the Prussians until the end of the war, when they were incorporated into the new North German army. Albert retained his post as leader of the Twelfth Army (composed of Saxons but under the command of the Prussian general staff), which fought on the Prussian side in 1870 (Albrecht-Carrie 1958). The war, then, was not so much between Saxony and Prussia as between a free-floating Saxon military apparatus and the Prussian army.

After the war, Bismarck initially pursued a policy of directly annexing the territories of the smaller states and by some accounts would have preferred to directly annex Saxon territory as well, eliminating the separate governments (Robertson 1918, 209; Eyck 1950, 125; Pflanze 1963, 309). However, he eventually settled on a different approach that maintained the separate existence of the Saxon state and folded it into the confederation.

Daniel Ziblatt argues that Bismarck actually preferred a federal system to annexation. Although Prussia could easily have conquered Saxony, it refrained from doing so, not merely because Prussia sought to reassure France (Pflanze 1963) and Austria (Eyck 1950) about its limited ambitions after the war but also because the existing Saxon state presented Bismarck with an opportunity. Ziblatt shows (2006, 121–27) that the presence of working political and economic institutions in the German states gave Prussia potential partners. By forging a compromise with these states, Bismarck could achieve his objectives without either frightening France and Austria or risking the social and political instability that would come from entirely replacing and rebuilding a governing apparatus in Saxony. Ziblatt's argument (which, like mine, begins with the assumption that national leaders can choose any of a variety of possible solutions to structuring their relationship) can account for why both Prussia and Saxony preferred the federal compromise to outright annexation.

Prussia bought Saxon cooperation by granting concessions, such as representation in the national parliament and some institutional restraints to Prussian action. Although the Saxon military had lost control of Saxon territory in the war, it could in principle have kept fighting (even after its defeat in the battle at Königgrätz). Prussian assurances that the Saxons would be able to keep their own military leaders and monarch made the negotiated settlement, and continued cooperation with the Prussians afterward, more palatable. The choice of a political settlement instead of a campaign of eradication is consistent with the way historians generally understand Bismarck's view that the German states would, in the long run, be ungovernable through coercion alone (Feuchtwanger 2002, 163). It is, on the other hand, surprising in the context of state consolidation generally, since most violent civil wars end with the military defeat of one side rather than a negotiated settlement (Walter 2002).

Before 1866, Saxony had jealously guarded its diplomatic independence, because its leaders felt that their ability to make and break ties with Prussia, Austria, and France gave them the leverage they needed to protect all their other interests. As a result, Saxony had rejected all of Prussia's previous attempts to bring it into a diplomatic alliance even as it accepted Prussia's economic and military overtures.

In 1866 when Prussia again offered a diplomatic union, there were two differences from earlier proposals: the offer came as an ultimatum with the threat of war as an alternative, and, unlike previous proposals for diplomatic integration via the existing quasi-international institutions, the new offer came with a promise of a federal institution. The latter difference is puzzling. Bismarck had been, by most accounts, a Prussian nationalist who used both domestic and foreign policy to advance the goal of preserving and extending the Prussian monarchy; for example, he had opposed the Frankfurt plan for German federation on the grounds that it would have reduced the power and influence of Prussia and by extension its king (Gall 1986). His decision to move toward a federal solution was taken over the grumbling of the Prussian military establishment, which strongly preferred to handle Saxony directly, without intervening institutions. The federal constitution embodied in the confederation agreement, however, put institutionalized limits on Prussia. Not only did it preserve the state governments; it actually gave them a say in federal policy—more than would have been necessary simply to preserve them as agents capable of administering a region on behalf of a federal principal. The puzzle is why Prussia did not push for an alternative potential organization, either a purely hierarchical or a more decentralized one, which would have left it with a freer hand.

Bavaria

After the 1866 Prussian-Austrian war, Bavaria had a standing army of 100,000 men and a rapidly developing industrial base. Having escaped the war with its independence intact, Bavaria recognized that its best remaining hope for an outside security guarantor was France. Diplomatic correspondence indicates Bismarck's clear recognition that Prussian expansion was triggering a coalition between France and Bavaria (Ziblatt 2006, 124) which would have undermined everything that Bismarck had worked to achieve. He therefore set out to cement diplomatic cooperation with Bavaria, hoping at a minimum, to keep Bavarian military and resources out of the French camp (Bismarck and Butler 1899, 39).

Bavaria was still substantially weaker than Prussia, and so any diplomatic cooperation between the two would be grossly unequal. Bavaria's strategy was to play Prussia and France against each other; even if it never actually exercised the option, the possibility that it could leave Prussia's orbit and find security through a relationship with France gave Bavaria the exit option it needed in order to reduce Prussia's leverage over it. Integrating its military and diplomatic functions with Prussia—through either an alliance, a federation, annexation, or any other kind of partnership—would seriously erode Bavaria's position.

Countering, again, the advice of the general staff, Bismarck declined to mount a direct move against Bavaria, either by immediately issuing an ultimatum to merge its diplomatic identity with the new federation or by making a military move (Lerman 2004, 139). Instead, he patiently waited until he had engineered two things: first, an offer for Bavaria to join as a member of a federal union and, second, a situation designed to make Bavaria more willing to accept the deal. The offer itself was quite generous. Bismarck had taken advantage of Saxony's entry into the North German Confederation as a way to showcase Prussia's restraint with its German federal partner states. The preservation of the Saxon monarchy and military, and the general respect that Prussia showed for Saxon territory, gave credibility to Bismarck's promises.

The particular concessions Prussia offered in the negotiations over federation actually preserved some of Bavaria's independent foreign policy, giving it more of an outside option. Under the guise of a cultural exception, since Bavaria was predominantly Catholic, whereas the northern states were predominantly Protestant, Bavaria retained an independent diplomatic representative in the Vatican (Mitchell 1979), thus creating independent diplomatic representation with every other state that had ties to the Vatican as well (notably France, Italy, and Spain). Bavaria would in principle still be able to secure at least quasi-formal security agreements with these other states (Windell 1970).

Prussia's only diplomatic representation under the proposed system, by contrast, would be through the federal foreign ministry, ultimately accountable to the emperor and parliament. These, of course, reflected Prussian interests more than they did the interests of any other one member state. But Prussia would be unable to dominate them unilaterally and would have to forge at least some kind of coalition with smaller states.

The federal proposal included a number of other concessions to Bavaria as well. Some took the form of informal guarantees that Bavarians would have a share of some federal ministries and military posts (Robertson 1918, 283; Eyck 1950, 174); others took the form of direct payment to the Bavarian royal family (Stern 1977, 77).

The physical geography of Germany also helped to mitigate to some extent the degree to which Bavaria would face disproportionately high economic costs (as opposed to political or military costs) if leaving an arrangement. The key was not so much Bavaria's physical distance from Prussia as the fact that Bavaria's position on the periphery of the Zollverein gave it direct access to foreign markets—newly growing Italy and, by extension, French ports on the Mediterranean—without having to pass through Prussian-controlled territory—and kept direct lines open to the new Italian state. As a consequence, although closer ties to Prussia worsened Bavaria's outside option in political and military terms, its economic outside option remained tolerable.

The second part of Bismarck's strategy was to change the regional political situation to reduce the outside options that Bavaria would have had anyway. By taking preemptive steps to remove even the option of allying with Austria or France, Bismarck assured that Bavaria would have less to lose by accepting any kind of offer. Austria had now been decisively defeated and was no longer a source of outside support for the smaller German states.

The potential for meaningful support from France had also diminished. Although war with France had not originally been Bismarck's goal, he came to see it as the only way to force Bavaria to choose between Prussia and France (Feuchtwanger 2002, 159). By maneuvering Bavaria into the war on Prussia's side, Bismarck helped solidify the Bavarian case for joining the federation, since any Bavarian threat to abandon Prussia and join with France would no longer be credible (Eyck 1950, 135). In any case, Prussia was generally expected to win regardless of whether or not it had the support of Bavaria (Albrecht-Carrie 1958).

Bavaria's leaders faced a choice: accept Bismarck's offer, or reject it. Accepting the offer would reduce their bargaining leverage with Prussia; however, rejecting the offer would reduce their bargaining leverage even more. Bavaria voluntarily joined the federation in 1871.

Joining with Prussia was a difficult decision for the Bavarian political system and was extremely unpopular. In 1869, for example, the Lantag elections returned to power a party that opposed any closer relationship with Prussia, and public opinion had been moving in a generally anti-Prussian direction throughout the end of the 1860s (Lerman 2004, 140).

On balance, Bavaria benefited from the package of diplomatic integration and the side-payments it came with, but preferring an institutional arrangement that would bind Prussia, it negotiated actively to that end. Some historians (e.g., Eyck 1950, 174) argue that Bavaria's leaders preferred an alliance rather than a federation, but that argument conflates the issue areas subject to cooperation with the institutional form of cooperation. Bavaria wanted military cooperation (an "alliance") but was skeptical of the value of diplomatic cooperation in the abstract; most observers took "federation" to necessarily mean a diplomatic union. This difference, though, highlights the fact that Prussia and Bavaria were negotiating not just over *whether* to institutionalize cooperation but *how* to do so. Bavaria's actions are consistent with the theory: like Saxony, it was more vulnerable than Prussia and, like Saxony, preferred federal institutions as the price of diplomatic integration. Bismarck's choice for Prussia, however, opting for federation, is superficially puzzling.

Prussia

Prussian interests are not, by themselves, sufficient to explain why the period of German national integration unfolded as it did, but they are a necessary part of the explanation. The puzzle is why Bismarck cemented cooperation with the other German states via a federation when he could have done it in other ways. Both international organization and conquest were on the table.

Prussia and its junior partners prior to 1866 cooperated through two international organizations; these had actually been quite effective at both deterring France and Russia and also furthering regional economic integration. Most contemporary scholars, following Riker, take as a given that Bismarck's core objective was the political unification of Germany (Riker 1964). This assumption may be an anachronism, however; earlier biographies have Bismarck only reluctantly arriving at the conclusion that unification would serve his more basic interest in Prussian security (Eyck 1950). Either way, though, there is a puzzle, since maintaining the international organization was at least an option. Prussia was able to achieve nearly complete economic integration with the German states through a customs union, without having to share power via a sort of federal constitution.

The Prussian general staff, the military leaders who advised Bismarck but were ultimately subordinate to the civilian government, favored military force to conquer and directly govern the German states. They were not alone in this view but were joined in it by nationalists in the Prussian parliament. Ziblatt argues that Bismarck chose federation, instead of conquest, in order to use the existing German state governments to exercise effective local control, thereby saving Prussia the expense and inefficiency of governing the new territories directly. Conquest followed by a hierarchic relationship, however, does not necessarily imply the loss of the administrative capabilities of regional governments. Prussia could have conquered (or annexed) Saxony and Bavaria and ruled them through local governments, as many past and future empires have done (Cooley 2005). Indeed, several decades later Germany would quite effectively establish a hierarchy over occupied territories in World War II, using local regimes to carry out economic and administrative functions without giving those local regimes an institutionalized voice at the center and without putting institutional restraints on the center's prerogatives (Liberman 1996; Hollander 2006).

So why would states choose any one of these options instead of others? Conventional explanations are unconvincing. Riker (1975) argues that the German states merged because of external threats and opportunities, but this does not explain why Prussia opted for a federal union instead of an alliance or a hierarchy. Furthermore, that it was Bismarck himself who triggered the war with France as a means to compel Bavaria to join the federation reverses the causality of Riker's argument.

Daniel Ziblatt's theory can account for more. Given the choice between destroying the other states via conquest, directly governing their territories, or forming a federation with a common central government, Ziblatt (2006) shows that the presence of competent state governments made federation possible. His theory, however, cannot account for the larger question of alternatives. If the states had potentially valuable administrative apparatuses, then why wouldn't Prussia have been able to cooperate with them via an international organization, contracting out governance functions to junior partners in an alliance? Or, if Prussia's military advantage over the smaller states was so great, why didn't it establish effective control over the states but keep their administrative bodies intact?

Ziblatt begins his analysis by noting that Prussia had both a military and an economic motive for extending its reach over the other German states (2006, 5). He therefore takes it as given, following Riker, that Prussia was the "state-making core" of Germany. That is, Prussia valued political integration as an end in itself—or at least as a means to a higher end that could be achieved only through integration into a state, which is effectively the same thing. Riker and Ziblatt then trace out the implications of the presence of a state like Prussia that valued state building above all else.

From a broader perspective, though, the assumption is troubling. Ziblatt argues that building a federation is less costly than building a new state from scratch. But it is still an enormous effort. Prussia, in particular, did not have a surplus of military or economic resources that would allow it to pursue unnecessary projects; rather, its leaders saw it as being tightly constrained. Furthermore, assuming at the outset that Prussia desired to form a German state risks mixing preferences with outcomes. Knowing that Prussia eventually did unify Germany, we may be tempted to take it for granted that German unification was Prussia's destiny all along.

Riker and Ziblatt argue that the origins of the German federation rest with the interests of the member states in benefiting from a united economy and common security, coupled with the threats that Prussia deployed in order to coerce a union. Ziblatt further shows that Prussia was able to economize on its threats to compel the federation by combining them with assurances that the new member states would be treated well. Prussia's concessions to Saxony after 1866 demonstrated to Bavaria in 1871 that it would be able to join a union with at least some faith in Prussia's intentions to live up to any promises of local autonomy and authority within the federal government.

Prussia's strategy was to use institutions—a federal constitution that put real restraints on Prussia—as well as its reputation in order to make cooperation more appealing to the smaller German states. Threats of conquest and assurances of institutional protections are not incompatible tools; Prussia was able to use both threats and assurances credibly because it had a demonstrated interest in diplomatic integration and an interest in maintaining the kind of military and economic cooperation it had benefited from during the earlier period of the Zollverein and the Confederation.

The smaller states had the ability to make the process of integration difficult and costly for Prussia, even if they could not stop it altogether. Their ability to raise the costs to Prussia, either by fighting to the death or by denying Prussia the use of their state administrative apparatuses, gave them bargaining leverage during the negotiations over federation. Just as the smaller Australian states were able to turn around the extortion that New South Wales, by its very size, implicitly threatened them with, demanding that New South Wales agree to a federal constitution as the price of integration, the smaller German states were likewise able to hold up national integration. Their leverage was not as great as that enjoyed by Melbourne (which could have stopped integration entirely, rather than just slow it down or make it more costly), but it was still enough, logically, to give Prussia an incentive to accommodate them.

Conclusion

Even where violence is a possibility, states still have an incentive to forge federal agreements when potentially vulnerable states can hold out for institutional concessions from their less vulnerable potential partners. Of the six observable implications of my theory that I noted at the end of the second chapter, several can be directly tested with evidence from the origins of Argentina and Germany.

The first potential implication was that federations form when the member states have the potential to benefit jointly from an excludable good. In the Argentine case, the states had the potential to benefit jointly from a trade route that allowed them to ship cattle from the interior to Europe via the port city of Buenos Aires. The mechanics of the river route, with the cities arrayed in a line and the mouth of the river eventually falling under Buenos Aires' control, were such that access to it was excludable after 1845, when the federation formed, but not before. Likewise, the diplomatic cooperation that the German states (or at least Prussia) sought was also excludable, in that uncooperative states could be left out of a united front, and that Prussia itself could have been excluded if the smaller states had continued their traditional diplomatic strategies of playing the great powers against each other. Excludability makes free-riding impossible, meaning that states can achieve the gains from policy coordination only if they actually cooperate with one another.

The cases also very clearly demonstrate the second implication, that any federation is never the result of consensus and that at least some of the members would have ideally been better off with some other arrangement (that is, if that other arrangement had been politically feasible). Both the *litoral* states and the smaller German states preferred more institutional checks on Buenos Aires and Prussia, whereas leaders in each of the larger states ideally preferred to be unconstrained (although Bismarck, recognizing the benefits of negotiation, accepted the value of compromise).

The third and fourth implications concern relationship-specific assets. The investments that the *litoral* states made in the Plate River trade route, and the options of allying with France or Austria that the German states relinquished, meant that they were made more vulnerable by joining in cooperation than by staying out. Cooperation therefore would have exposed them to the risk of being exploited. The *litoral* and small German states were both highly reluctant to join in any sort of agreement with Buenos Aires and Prussia and only proposed or accepted agreements that included federal guarantees.

These cases find mixed evidence for the sixth observable implication, that federal institutions will be designed to contrive symmetry by imposing more exit costs on nonvulnerable states than on vulnerable states. Ending up with constitutions giving disproportionate representation in the legislative branch to the smaller states forced both Buenos Aires and Prussia to govern through coalitions. It was not clear at the time, however, that it definitely produced more constraints for Buenos Aires and Prussia than for the other members—especially since each national capital was established in the largest city of the dominant state. Still, though, the constitutions created at least some new constraints on these major states, giving them some value to the smaller states and creating more institutional guarantees than the small states might have had if Buenos Aires and Prussia had simply conquered their partners.

The cases also show evidence for the fifth implication, that nonvulnerable states will try to lead vulnerable states into making relationship-specific investments before any institutions for cooperation are agreed upon. The *litoral* states resisted economic integration with Buenos Aires at least partly because they did not need access to that city's port in order to carry on trade with the outside. To worsen their outside options, then, Buenos Aires expanded its military so that it would able to cut off alternative routes. Likewise, Prussia mounted an effective diplomatic campaign to isolate the other German states from other potential partners. Both Buenos Aires and Prussia tried to arrange (by committing to a trade route for the Argentines and by committing to an alliance for the Germans) that their potential partners would invest heavily in relationship-specific assets first, before any institutional agreement was reached. The stronger, less potentially vulnerable states understood that once their junior partners' relationship-specific investments were already sunk, they would no longer be in a position to resist credibly even an agreement that left them with few institutional protections.

This chapter began with a puzzle: federations create constraints on powerful states that international organizations do not, so why would a powerful country ever coerce a weaker neighbor to join in a federal union when it could instead coerce the weaker neighbor to join an international organization? Weaker states can hold out for federations instead of international organizations when they are able to threaten resistance unless they get the institutional guarantees they seek. The cases of Argentina and Germany demonstrate that states can use institutions to cope with threatening powers, and that federal unions can be a constructive solutions even in situations where rival states are prone to mistrust.

6

THE UNRAVELING OF EAST AFRICA
AND THE CARIBBEAN

In the decade leading up to decolonization in East Africa and the Caribbean, nationalist leaders were unanimous and vocal in their support for forming regional federations. Proposed constitutions were drawn up; parties won elections on the basis of their support for political integration; and constitutional drafting conventions were held. In each region, the large state that would have benefited from integration without itself becoming economically tied to regional partners—Kenya and Jamaica—as well as the other states that would have become more dependent on cooperation, all seemed willing in principle to commit to ambitious timetables for ratification. Yet despite this unanimity and seeming support, neither the East African nor West Indian federal unions took root. Furthermore, in both instances, once the federation movement failed, the states grew apart and eschewed cooperation generally by developing separate military and security strategies and keeping their markets closed to one another. This seeming paradox, that countries on the verge of federating would be, within a few years, so divided, is precisely what my theory predicts: states with unequal potential investments in relationship-specific assets can face commitment problems that make cooperation impossible unless they enter into a federation.

The previous three chapters provided support for the theory by examining evidence from the processes by which Australia, Argentina, and Germany coalesced into federations. Here, I turn to failed federations in East Africa and the Caribbean to look for evidence from the process of failure with which to test the theory.

My argument about these two cases is straightforward. Large inequalities in potential dependence across members made the less developed and the smaller states unwilling to join a common market unless they could do so with a strong institution protecting them from the risk that their less potentially dependent partners, Kenya and Jamaica, would later claim a larger share of the benefits. Although they would both have benefited from regional cooperation, neither Kenya nor Jamaica would have benefited enough to outweigh the start-up costs of establishing a real federation. In the metaphor of posting a bond, the states were willing to post only a small one. In both cases, the unraveling began when one state opted out of the proposal, leading to a chain reaction when the remaining states were more unbalanced then they had been before. The remaining potentially dependent states faced a situation in which the smaller number of them would require even tighter institutions to restrain the remaining less dependent states, making a federal agreement even less likely.

These cases can test the other implications about states' preferences over whether to cooperate via a federal union or an international organization. They are particularly useful in demonstrating the importance of potential relationship-specific investments to whether states prefer federal unions or IOs: two states, Tanganyika and Trinidad, actually changed their positions midway through the process, from supporting a federation to supporting an international organization. These changes in position corresponded to changes in their individual circumstances, rather than ideology, identity, or the broader security environment.

This chapter discusses the East African Federation—a proposed union of Kenya, Tanganyika, Uganda, and Zanzibar—and then considers the Federation of the West Indies—a group of ten Caribbean political units, including Jamaica, Trinidad and Tobago, and Barbados. I conclude by noting how the process by which these federations unraveled provides additional evidence for my theory.

East Africa

The borders of Kenya, Tanganyika, Uganda, and Zanzibar were set by European powers during the period of colonization in the second half of the nineteenth century. By the time of their independence from Britain, the four colonies had each had at least sixty years of history as modern territorial units, with local civil servants and an African political elite. During the period of nationalist movements before independence and the years immediately afterward, both of Kenya's major parties consistently supported federation, provided that it would be on their terms, and Tanganyika's dominant party strongly advocated regional federation. Internal division in Uganda led its governing coalition to change from support to opposition in 1964; without Uganda, Tanganyika soon retreated, and plans for federation collapsed. By the end of 1964 it became clear that those three states would remain independent, and by the end of the decade they had broken off nearly all forms of cooperation and had begun to pursue extreme forms of self-sufficiency.

The initial push for federation happened during a time when there was a strong consensus among elites that regional economic integration could, in principle, help the leaders achieve their developmental goals by increasing the amount of foreign investment capital the states would be able to attract. These gains, however, involved relationship-specific assets. Foreign investment in the region was expected to be concentrated around Nairobi because of its advantage in both education and transportation; nationalist leaders proposed a system of tax redistribution by which Kenya would pay Tanganyika and Uganda out of the subsequent revenues. But this unequal industrial growth (which would be oriented toward exporting goods from the region) not only would create a regional dependence on Kenyan industry but also raise the potential benefits to Kenya of exiting an agreement.

If the reason for the failure had to do with the difficulty of creating an agreement that would bind Kenya to cooperate with the others by raising its exit costs to the point where it would be unable to renegotiate the agreement once it took effect, then this would be evidence for the theory I described in Chapter 2. Other sources of failure, having to do with security concerns, nationalism, or ethnicity, would not support the theory. I find little evidence that these other potential concerns played a role, and two pieces of evidence that do support the theory: the evolution of Uganda's negotiating position, and Tanganyika's response.

I proceed in four parts. First, I present an overview of the political history of the region around the crucial years (1961–63) of decolonization and federal negotiations. Second, I consider and dismiss the roles of security, ethnicity, and pan-Africanist ideology, since they can account neither for the initial interest in federation nor the subsequent collapse. Third, I detail how the commercial interests of the governing coalitions made it so that there would have been large and unequal relationship-specific investments in cooperation, which led to Uganda's decision to stay out. Fourth, I show how Uganda's decision led to Tanganyika's choice to pursue a separate development plan and a quasi-federal merger with Zanzibar.

Overview

Uganda is a landlocked state along the coast of Lake Victoria. Kenya, to the east, borders the Indian Ocean and extends north to its shared borders with Somalia and the Sudan. South of Kenya and southeast of Uganda is Tanganyika; the island of Zanzibar lies off the coast near the major city, Dar es Salaam.

Prior to European political colonization, the fertile farmland around Lake Victoria sustained several local states. Among these was the Kingdom of the Buganda, a highly centralized state with a large population but a relatively small territory, led by a hereditary king, the "Kabaka," with whom early British and German traders negotiated agreements. British influence in the region grew until the Kabaka, in the 1890s, agreed to a protectorate while retaining autonomy over domestic affairs. Britain established Uganda's borders to include additional territory that it administered directly. Kenya, which Britain also directly ruled, absorbed European settlers who established modern farms, but this wealthy white population also attracted early industrial development around Nairobi making it a regional magnet for manufacturing and services. Tanganyika passed from German to British control after World War I.

So, Kenya, Tanganyika, and Uganda all had centralized governments exercising control within the borders set in the 1890s. Although all the territories had colonial parliaments, they had very little real authority until, beginning in the 1950s with Tanganyika, Britain began to transfer control over some limited functions to the local legislatures. But these were always circumscribed by British executive authority until 1960. African influence was larger in the civil service, where the colonial authorities had extensively trained and promoted local officials.

Tanganyika became independent in December 1961, followed by Uganda in October 1962, and Kenya and Zanzibar both in December 1963. During the 1950s, as locally elected parliaments gradually took on more significance, the nationalist anticolonial movements had remade themselves as political parties organized around winning local elections. The leaders of the nationalist independence movements formed the local political elites that took over upon decolonization. In Tanganyika this was the Tanganyika African National Union (TANU), whose leader, Julius Nyerere, led negotiations for independence and upon independence became the first president of Tanganyika as a one-party state. In Kenya, Jomo Kenyatta's Kenya African National Union (KANU) was consistently the largest party and had absorbed its local rivals by the achievement of independence. In

Uganda, Milton Obote's Uganda Peoples' Congress (UPC) competed with several regional parties and did not achieve a parliamentary majority by itself until the late 1960s; its two major rivals were the Democratic Party (DP), an opposition party spread throughout Uganda, and the Kabaka Yekka ("the King Forever") Party that dominated the Buganda region. TANU, KANU, and the UPC shared a common ideology they called African Socialism, arguing for state control of some economic sectors with an active role for the state in promoting development.

In June 1960, Nyerere put East African federation at the top of the political agenda by publicly proclaiming it as a goal. His argument was that federation would bring the benefits of development and integration while preserving the independence of the region from the great powers; thus he couched the move to federate in nationalist terms (Nye 1965; Rothchild 1968).[1]

Beginning with this announcement, TANU, KANU, and UPC leaders (and later, leaders from Zanzibar) met regularly over the next four years to negotiate the details of the proposed federation. In June 1963, once Tanganyika and Uganda were independent and it was clear that Kenyatta would soon lead an independent Kenya, the three leaders held a meeting in Nairobi to discuss the federation proposals that had been privately circulated and revised at lower levels. They issued a joint statement indicating their intent to form a Federation of East Africa by the end of the year.

A working party to write a draft agreement met continually for the next year but never produced a proposal to be submitted for consideration by the states. The ultimate failure of the federation would have been difficult to predict at the time, since all three leaders campaigned on the issue, both together and separately, and KANU ministers acknowledged that they had gained support in the May election by explicitly promising to cede Kenyan sovereignty to a regional federation with its neighbors (Rothchild 1968, 81).[2]

---

[1] Kenya's European settlers had led a previous movement for regional federation among the three colonies after 1945 as a way to extend the disproportionate representation they enjoyed in the Kenyan parliament (Rothchild 1960, 18), like that of a similar federation between Rhodesia and Nyasaland. The African majority therefore at first associated federation with white settlers' schemes, but this attitude began to change once it became clear that black Africans would control Kenya.

[2] Outsiders took the commitment to federation seriously. For example, a 1963 report by a West German advisory commission on Tanganyika's financial system assumed that the states would federate and gave detailed technical advice on the governance of the (hypothetical) East African Federal Central Bank (Kimei 1987, 63).

Within several months of the Nairobi declaration, however, the movement for federation began to fall apart. A Ugandan minister stated that, given the state of negotiations, federation would be impossible by the end of the year and that the declaration's goal would not be met. Ugandan newspapers began to report that the negotiators were deadlocked over the role of the senate. Once Uganda began to equivocate, Kenyatta declared that Kenya would be willing to go ahead with Tanganyika, and Uganda could join later if it chose. Nyerere, in Tanganyika, delayed making a decision. The working group continued to negotiate, and Kenya became independent in December.

In January 1964 there was a series of militarily minor yet politically significant army mutinies in Kenya, Tanganyika, and Uganda. Enlisted soldiers in the regular armies mounted small insurrections on several bases, demanding higher pay and opportunities for promotion into the officer corps. The mutinies were quickly put down by a combination of local forces and British and Nigerian troops called in at the request of the national governments.

By March 1964, with little apparent progress on federation, Kenyatta, Nyerere, and Obote formally met and produced the Kampala Agreement, a framework for coordinating economic development in the three states without a federal government. The agreement pledged the states to find ways to develop industries in Tanganyika and Uganda to balance the relatively rapid industrial development taking place in Kenya. The states agreed on a system of industrial quotas and licensing that would encourage or require firms to move production to particular areas. This was partly in response to monetary pressures, since the states had a common currency but unequal rates of growth and no mechanism for making fiscal transfers. With the agreement, which presupposed central planning along African Socialist lines, the leaders hoped to maintain the common market without federating (Hazlewood 1975). The regional organization they created—EACSO, the East African Common Services Organization—was a policy coordination forum without strong enforcement or implementation mechanisms and with a small civil service staff that acted in an advisory capacity (Banfield 1965).

Ironically, the states became more economically integrated at the same time that they were moving apart politically (Nye 1968). This happened despite a failure of policy coordination, though, and was not an intended consequence of regional integration. Economic integration continued and intraregional trade expanded, largely driven by industrial development in Kenya. In response to growing regional integration, in mid-1964 Uganda withdrew from the common tourism organization, and Tanganyika began to put restrictions on labor and capital movements, to pull out of the common navy, and to push to dismantle the system of industrial licensing (Rothchild 1964).

In June 1965 the common currency ended when Tanzania (renamed after the merger of Tanganyika and Zanzibar) issued its own money. This led to further deterioration of cooperation on services. In 1967, EACSO was reformed as the East African Community but market barriers persisted, and the EAC was dissolved in 1977 when the Kenya-Tanzania border was closed (it reopened only in 1985).

Alternative Explanations

William Riker argues that the failure of the states to federate demonstrates his argument that common security threats are a necessary condition for states to form federations, and "no external or internal threat existed" (1975, 125). Riker's argument is unconvincing, though; the states did face both internal and regional security threats that were very real to the leaders at the time. Although internal threats did not necessarily call the independence of the states as units into question, they revealed to the leaders that their political institutions were more fragile than they might have thought. Given that state building was among the most pressing considerations leaders faced (Herbst 2000), the general expectation was that the army mutinies would revive the federal movement. Two political scientists wrote that "the short-lived crises in the East African armies in January 1964 brought the need for security and stability to the surface. It seems impossible that the discussion of closer association should not receive fresh impetus from these events" (Leys and Robson 1965, 5).

This internal threat, however, quickly passed when the states proved able to cooperate with each other and with outsiders to put down the challenge (Mazrui and Rothchild 1967; Tordoff 1967). Kenyatta, Nyerere, and Obote may have drawn the lesson from the mutinies that federation was in fact *un*necessary to ensure political stability, since even in a crisis they had been able to draw on mutual help to restore order.

A more serious set of concerns, at least for Kenya and Uganda, involved threats from regional neighbors. During the independence movement and throughout the early 1960s, Somalia made repeated claims on territory occupied by ethnic Somalis in Kenya's Northern Frontier District. In 1963, after a summit in Rome between nationalist parties in Kenya and Somalia failed to solve the problem, Kenya signed a military alliance with Ethiopia against Somalia. Defying expectations, Kenya did not join the 1963 defense pact between Tanganyika and Uganda, instead relying on its agreement with Ethiopia. The Kenya-Ethiopia alliance apparently continued to deter Somali revisionism, and the alliance remained strong even after political tensions induced by the 1974 Ethiopian Communist military coup (Orwa 1994, 303–12). Kenya and Uganda also shared a border with Sudan, which had an aggressive posture toward its southern neighbors, and both states established defensive fortifications along their Sudanese borders. Despite the common threat, however, they never engaged in any serious military cooperation directed at Sudan (Orwa 1994).

A second possible explanation has to do with identity, stemming from either ethnicity or political ideology. East Africa in the 1960s was in a period of considerable flux, since colonialism was being widely seen as illegitimate and, with the exception of the Kingdom of the Buganda, there were no surviving local indigenous institutions left in the region. The idea of a political unit called "East Africa" was no less real to Africans than the idea of political units called "Kenya" or "Uganda" (Leys and Robson 1965, 183). Without prior political identities, elites had a variety of ways they could have directed the development of national attachments.

Ethnic affiliations did not have a strong influence either for or against regional political integration. Ethnic identity claims did play an important role in state formation, especially in Kenya (Kahl 2000), but elites with ethnic bases would not have been able to manipulate government institutions one way or the other on regional integration issues. Kenya had some forty-two ethnic groups, with no one majority. Even the major groups were by themselves so small that no single "ethnic coalition" would have been able to hold power. KANU had a diverse base united around an economic program and included, for example, two ethnic groups traditionally hostile to each other, the Kikuyu and Luo communities. TANU in Tanganyika had a similarly heterogeneous base (Berg-Schlosser 1994, 249). The language of administration in all the major states was English; Kiswahili was the second most common language in Kenya and Tanganyika and was widely understood in Uganda, being one of the primary languages taught in schools prior to 1943 (Kabwegyere 1974, 218).

Joseph Nye (1965) studied the role of Pan-Africanist ideology in the failure of the states to form the East African Federation. Although nationalist leaders in the independence movements, led by Kwame Nkrumah of Ghana, made political unity among the African former colonial states a central part of their platform, after independence a rift developed within the movement. Nkrumah argued that the African states should all join a large federation together, and that regional cooperative arrangements of any sort (whether federations or looser organizations) would only undermine the push for continental unity. Julius Nyerere disagreed, publicly arguing that regional cooperation and federations would help the cause of African unity by demonstrating the feasibility of integration.

Nye (1965, 201) concluded that Pan-African ideas may have at most only indirectly influenced the language that leaders used in explaining their decisions. When material interests and ideology came into conflict, leaders followed their economic interests. Doing so was made easy for them, since the same ideology could justify a profederal (using Nyerere's logic) or antifederal (using Nkrumah's) position. For example, when Milton Obote in Uganda first campaigned for East African federation, he argued his case using Pan-African rhetoric. When he switched to opposing federation in late 1963, he once again explained his position in terms of Pan-Africanism.

Uganda and Relationship-Specific Assets

Neither military threats nor identity politics can entirely explain why East Africa's leaders initially advocated federation but then one by one dropped out. Nor can they explain why the leaders of Tanganyika and Zanzibar chose to federate with each other but then, along with Uganda, undermined the Kampala accord and other attempts at regional cooperation through an international organization.

The interests the leaders had in developing and extending local markets generally match the political outcomes in the way the theory I propose suggests. In Chapters 1 and 2 I argued that states will be inclined to form federations when their leaders benefit from cooperation but anticipate that economic or military integration will lead them to make unequal levels of relationship-specific investments. In East Africa, the new governments did in fact perceive benefits from market integration, although the potential direct gains were probably small, since the states had greater comparative advantages on world markets than regionally (Hazlewood 1975). Most accounts have stressed the view that market integration might have made the market seem more stable in the minds of potential foreign investors (Birch 1965, 14).

Kenya's leaders consistently supported federation in principle, and the various proposals received unqualified support from the governing KANU, which had explicitly campaigned on support for federation in the May 1963 national elections. The opposition Kenya African Democratic Union

(KADU) gave support that was more qualified; with a larger base in ethnic minorities outside of Nairobi, it maintained that local regions should retain autonomy under a federal system (Adar and Ngunyi 1994, 399).

Kenya's leaders and urban industrialists—including managers of state-owned enterprises, local manufacturing firms, and local agents of foreign investors—understood that any market resulting from federation would be protected and would therefore be a source of future profits. Industrial expansion would also, KANU hoped, help make good on promises to expand urban employment and increase tax revenue (Nye 1965).

Market integration meant more than just dismantling trade barriers, since all three governing coalitions engaged in some kind of central planning. For the system of industrial licensing and quotas—part of the overall effort to create local industry to substitute for imports—to have any chance of success in a common market, the states would have needed to coordinate their development plans to take regional effects into account. In practice, according to the prevailing economic doctrine, this meant encouraging firms in particular sectors (tobacco processing, bootmaking, and so on) to operate exclusively in only one of the three states in order to create balanced trade in the region while achieving the benefits of industrial scale.

Experience had demonstrated that economic integration, even before decolonization, benefited Kenya by attracting foreign investment in manufacturing and services around Nairobi. Once Nairobi had a developed service sector, it was yet more appealing as a location for further development. From 1961 until 1964, Kenya's regional trade balance had growing surpluses—while Tanganyika's and Uganda's had growing deficits (Birch 1965, 22; Hazlewood 1975, 57)—which created pressure on the common currency (Newman 1965). More important, nationalist ideology placed a premium on urban industrial development, and throughout TANU and the UPC there was a perception that the common market would result in Kenya's attracting foreign investment for industry that would otherwise have gone to Tanganyika or Uganda. These fears were reinforced by economic assessments that weighed the benefits of economic integration against the costs of trade diversion and protectionism and found that Kenya benefited the most from economic integration and Tanganyika benefited the least (Ghai 1965).

Federation meant that Kenya would have to finance some fiscal transfers to the other states or endure some distortions arising from industrial licensing that relocated firms to Tanganyika and Uganda. Even so, as long as Kenya had enough voice in the federal government to keep those transfers at a low level, the benefits to federation would outweigh the costs if federation meant guaranteed future access to the regional market. Throughout the early 1960s, then, there were constant tensions over how to redistribute the potential gains (Rothchild 1968, 120; Hazlewood 1975, 142). Proponents of federation saw federal fiscal transfers and central planning as the solution. The system of quotas envisioned by the Kampala Accord was an attempt to achieve the same goal through decentralized cooperation. As it happened, Kenyans widely understood the leftist backlashes in Uganda and Tanzania in 1967 and 1969 as products of the belief that Kenya was benefiting disproportionately (Gordon 1984).

As the leaders up to 1963 perceived the situation, economic integration would create very unequal relationship-specific investments for the states. The creation of a common market, they believed, would increase the total amount of foreign investment going into the region. But not only did they expect most of the extra investment to go to Nairobi; they also expected that integration would divert to Nairobi investment that would otherwise have gone to Dar es Salaam and Kampala. Tanganyika and Uganda would have received a net benefit from integration as long as Kenya participated in a system of redistribution. If cooperation ended, however, Kenya would be left with a larger industrial base than it would otherwise have had, and Tanganyika and Uganda would be left with industrial bases smaller than they otherwise would have been. So, cooperation would have led to Kenya's outside option getting better over time, and those of the other states getting worse.

The proximate reason the June 1963 push for federation did not lead to the adoption of a federal constitution by the end of the year was that the Ugandan delegates to the working group refused to compromise on several key issues, leading several government ministers to proclaim, first, that federation would not happen by the end of the year and, later in 1964, that Uganda would not join in any case. Although some early journalistic accounts attributed Uganda's decisions to the internal politics of bargaining between the UPC and the Buganda (Mazrui 1965; Okoth 1994, 364), the latter probably would not have blocked federation had it come to a vote. As early as June 1963, just after the Nairobi declaration, Obote and the Kabaka secretly agreed that federation would preserve Bugandan autonomy, and Kenyatta and Nyerere seemed willing to accept this unique status. The Kabaka's influence over the party guaranteed that the Bugandan parliament would no longer block federation (Nye 1965; Rothchild 1968, 88; Kabwegyere 1974, 238).

In fact, it was opposition from within the UPC itself that led Uganda to pull back from federation. Although Obote had originally favored federation for economic reasons (Nye 1965; Okoth 1994, 364), the surprising growth of Uganda's GDP and trade balance since independence convinced many UPC elites that they would be able to achieve their development goals without tying themselves to a larger market.

Entering into any agreement would have immediately created, for Uganda, the disadvantage of a declining bargaining position. Federal institutions that created a disproportionately high bond for Kenya might, in principle, have offset that disadvantage, but Uganda had little reason to believe that a sufficiently binding institution was possible. For one thing, Kenya was unwilling to relent on the composition of the legislature. Ugandan negotiators pushed for a greater role for the senate, in which representation would be by state and so would offset Kenya's population advantage (9 million to 6 million) in the lower house, where representation would be determined by raw population (Leys 1965; Rothchild 1968). A more subtle source of concern was the composition of the federal bureaucracy: if the civil service was oriented toward serving the urban industrial area around Nairobi, it would further enhance Kenya's exit option (rather than serve as a bond) and leave Uganda even worse off, since it would have missed the opportunity to develop its own institutional apparatus (Franck 1964).

Ultimately, Obote was not convinced that even the federal institutions Kenya seemed willing to accept would prevent an erosion of Ugandan interests over the long run. With real, but only moderate, potential benefits to federation, and a danger of long-term exploitation, Obote chose to pursue self-sufficiency, competing with Kenya for investment rather than tying itself to an uncertain partner.

Tanganyika

At the time of independence, Tanganyika's economy was oriented around primary production (mostly rubber and sisal, a fiber used in making twine). What little industry there was tended to concentrate on the processing of agricultural products for export. Early after independence the government enacted a set of import-substitution policies that led to growth in the manufacture of consumer goods, although these industries tended to be concentrated in a relatively small number of monopolistic sectors (Silver 1984). The economic benefits of joining a regional common market were always slim, but a common market would still have been of some help to the state's economy even before taking into account the possible gains from redistribution (Nye 1965). A common market would bring the benefits of a larger region for sales of some consumer goods and processed food. Most Tanganyikan industry, geared for export anyway, did not compete with imports from Kenya.

As with Uganda, the widespread perception among elites was that the common market with Kenya was leading to unequal levels of industrialization in the two states, with Tanganyika losing out. In the absence of some sort of revenue sharing, industrial concentration around Nairobi made the common market politically unsustainable for Dar es Salaam (Nixson 1973, 35). Unlike Uganda, though, Tanganyika had the same population as Kenya (Steinberg 1961) and could, in principle, have done just as well in a federal parliament. If TANU was willing to join a federation with Kenya and Uganda, why wasn't it willing to join a federation with just Kenya? Arguments based on Pan-African political identity or military threats cannot answer this puzzle.

The loss of Uganda weakened Tanganyika's bargaining position vis-à-vis Kenya. That is, Tanganyika and Uganda together could have offered Kenya a large enough market that Kenya would be willing to make at least some concessions in order to guarantee the market into the future; Kenya would have been willing to give up substantial control over the decision-making institutions of the federal government in order to get Uganda and Tanganyika to agree to follow through with their plans for market integration. (In the end, though, Kenyatta was unwilling to give up enough to reassure Obote). A higher bond for Kenya would be an unmitigated good for Tanganyika, even if it gave more influence to Uganda, since the point of federation was to make the system of fiscal transfers away from Kenya credible in the long run. The purpose was to make it difficult for Kenya to renegotiate the terms of a deal after it had started, and so all that mattered was the size of Kenya's initial investment. Without Uganda in the federation, however, Kenya would come closer to being able to dominate the federal government, since it would be able to credibly demand more representation at the constitutional bargaining table (because it would be getting less benefit from federating with just Tanganyika than with Tanganyika and Uganda). Taking out Uganda made the transfers away from Kenya less credible, reducing the appeal of federation to Tanganyika.

Once Uganda left, in negotiations between Tanganyika and Kenya both sides recognized the heightened stakes: if Kenya ever got even a slim working majority in the federal parliament, it could reduce or eliminate the transfers. In the working group meetings throughout 1964 and 1965 (by which time nearly all hope of reaching a compromise was gone) TANU pushed ever harder for advantages for its own interests and representation in a federal government, making it harder for Kenya to agree to any sort of political integration (Rothchild 1966, 285). The Kampala Agreement, a consolation prize for Tanganyika, promised some transfers, but the program quickly collapsed. Later, it was (the renamed) Tanzania itself that ended the residual traces of the common market and the common currency, because without transfers it could no longer sustain a political coalition in favor of continued integration (Hazlewood 1975, 64).

Tanganyika had originally been profederal because it understood that it and Uganda would be the vulnerable states in any system of economic cooperation (the third and fourth observable implications of the theory). With Uganda on its side in the federal parliament advocating for the continuation of transfers, even though Kenya would have a slight plurality and would likely be represented in the ministry, Tanganyika would be assured that Kenya's political system would be tied to the federation by a federal party system that would force Kenyans to forge ties with elites from the other states in order to maintain power. After Uganda left, however, that calculation became trickier. It was no longer clear that Kenya's elite would be forced to maintain ties to Tanganyikan parties, and there was therefore little reason for TANU to have confidence in the maintenance of the union.

The one successful instance of institution building was the decision, in April 1964, to merge Tanganyika and Zanzibar to form Tanzania. Tanganyika, poorer than Zanzibar and with thirty times the population, made a host of concessions in order to entice Zanzibar to integrate its political system into a federal government. Zanzibar got substantial overrepresentation in the parliament, the vice presidency of the new federal government, and the foreign ministry (Shivji 1990; Sadleir 1999, 275). The foreign ministry post was an actual position of authority; most sources attribute Tanzania's move toward alignment with the Communist countries in the late 1960s to the influence of Zanzibari elites in several key positions (Martin 1988, 56).

Zanzibar had become independent in December 1963 with a governing coalition between parties representing the Arab minority (the ZNP) and a moderate African splinter group (the ZPPP), with the more popular opposition party (the Afro-Shirazi Party, or ASP) in opposition thanks to extreme gerrymandering (Bailey 1973, 10). A violent uprising in January 1964 had brought the ASP to power, and it quickly sought support from TANU in order to maintain its hold (Ayany 1970; Clayton 1981, 112).

Zanzibar's primary export (besides goods from the mainland transshipped through the port of Zanzibar Town) was cloves, and there was very little other economic production on the island. So, although the economy would benefit from integration with the mainland insofar as it would have easier access to consumers, these benefits would be more than offset by the costs associated with entering into a protected market (Leys and Robson 1965, 202). For example, the previous ZNP/ZPPP government in 1962 had initially been interested in joining EACSO but had ultimately stayed out for fear of losing its control of trade policy; for the same reason it was skeptical of joining the East African Federation when negotiations began in 1963, although it did participate in the working group in order to keep the option open (Bailey 1973, 18).

Nyerere's interest in federating with Zanzibar was related to Tanganyika's traditional use of Zanzibar as a link in a trade network to South Asia and the Middle East. In particular, Arabs in Zanzibar had been crucial intermediaries for goods from the mainland entering world markets in the century before decolonization (Mpangala 1992), and this trade network provided Tanganyikan exporters with a valuable resource that would be difficult to replace if it were lost. Networks, including those based on ethnicity, have been shown to have important effects on trade patterns, especially in small developing economies like Tanganyika's (Gould 1994; Rauch 1999; Rauch and Watson 2004). As with federations generally, what drove this particular federation was the fear that dependence on this relationship-specific asset might someday be used against Tanganyika, which is why TANU went to some lengths to establish a binding agreement that preserved their access to trade networks on favorable terms (Tordoff 1967; Martin 1988; Sadleir 1999, 275).

The Caribbean

In January 1958, on the verge of independence from Britain, a group of twenty-four inhabited islands in the Caribbean, comprising ten political units, entered into the Federation of the West Indies. Jamaica was the most populous, followed by Trinidad and Tobago, and then Barbados. Other members included Antigua and Barbuda, St. Kitts and Nevis, Anguilla, Montserrat, Dominica, the Bahamas, the Caymans, St. Lucia, St. Vincent and the Grenadines, and Grenada. Jamaica supported federation in name only, consistently opposing moves to implement an actual federal system, and its voters by referendum seceded from the union in September 1961, leading to a chain reaction of secessions that ended with the abandonment of the project by the end of 1962.

Unlike the other cases I have considered, the West Indian federation was a British imperial project rather than a local one; the impetus for the union was a decision by colonial authorities in London that the islands would be more capable of effective self-government, and more likely to develop economically, if they pooled their resources. Unlike the Australian states in the 1890s, the West Indian islands through the federation period were mostly Crown colonies, with governments formally run by British appointees rather than by locally elected parliaments—although local parliaments did exist and were permitted control over most domestic affairs. Many of the main federalists—the people who made the initial proposals and lobbied hardest for them—were British, but at least some local groups expressed support. At the time, both local leaders and outsiders took the process seriously, and the conventional wisdom was that the project was likely to succeed (Proctor 1956).

The exogenous origins of the federation proposal can provide a novel way to test some of the implications of my theory. The reactions to the proposal of different groups on the islands can provide evidence for the ways state leaders and other social groups view federation and its alternatives. Even if the West Indian case by itself cannot be a complete test of the theory, given the British influence, the ability to observe reactions to the federation proposal makes the case a potentially interesting experiment.[3]

The unraveling of the federal proposal happened in two stages. First, after not quite three years of operation, Jamaica opted out of the federal union. Then, though the remaining states considered continuing as a federal union, eventually the project collapsed when the next largest island, Trinidad, changed its position and, following Jamaica, exited the union. After Trinidad left, the project came to an end. Two separate questions merit answers. First, why did Jamaica opt out despite the economic benefits that, in principle, federation could have brought? Second, why did Trinidad's leaders switch from supporting a strongly centralized federal union to opposing federation as soon as Jamaica opted out?

---

[3] Some observers downplay the British influence and argue that at least some of the energy behind the federal proposals was local in origin (Will 1991, 14; Hart 1998, 145), but this is a minority view (Etzioni 1965). Some nationalist politicians seemed to believe, at first, that federation would hasten complete political independence from Britain. At the time the islands began to achieve independence, however, a federation had not yet been implemented, so local leaders were then free to act on behalf of their genuine beliefs or expectations about federation without being influenced by how their choices would play in London (Springer 1962). British diplomats, both publicly and privately, maintained that they would not intervene in support of a federal government if the states chose not to implement one (MacLeod 1985).

I begin with an overview of the history, then discuss politics in Jamaica, and conclude by examining federation politics in Trinidad.

Overview

Spread out over an enormous area in the Caribbean Sea, the main population of the Federation of the West Indies was concentrated in just a few islands. Of the 3.1 million people total, just over 1.6 million lived in Jamaica and about 826,000 lived in Trinidad and Tobago (and over 95 percent of those on the island of Trinidad). Of the approximately 700,000 remaining, Barbados accounted for about 230,000, and no other island had more than 90,000.

British economic planners after World War II anticipated that the West Indian colonies would eventually become independent but were concerned that the new states would be too small to be economically viable. Following what they saw as the successes of federal integration in Australia and Canada, they suggested that regional federation in the Caribbean would lead to better growth through a larger common market and a better ability to coordinate development projects such as health and education infrastructure. In the 1950s, British governors-general in the region began working with local parties and elected assemblies to find acceptable terms for a federal compromise, in effect acting as intermediaries for bargaining among the future leaders of the soon-to-be independent states. To entice cooperation, British administrators quietly made it understood that political independence from the Empire would come faster if the states agreed to a federation than if they did not.

Once construction of a local constituency in favor of federation seemed possible, the British Parliament approved legislation in August 1956 establishing the policy of federal union for the islands. The act appointed a governor-general for the federation as a whole, who oversaw the implementation of the federal constitution in January 1958 and chose March 1958 for the first elections to the federal parliament.

Following other postcolonial federations, the federal parliament was bicameral. There would be ten provinces, of unequal size: Jamaica was one province with just over half the population of the federation; Trinidad and Tobago made up one province with just over half of the remainder; at the other extreme Montserrat was a province by itself with 0.4 percent of the population. Representation in the lower house was loosely based on population, modified to underrepresent Jamaica by giving it 17 of 45 seats and, to a lesser extent, Trinidad and Tobago by giving it 10 of the 45. Each province sent two senators to an upper house except for Montserrat, which sent only one.

The constitution had been designed to give national politicians incentives to invest their careers in federal politics, and so leaders were prohibited from holding elective office at both the state and the federal level simultaneously. The idea was that, as in other federal systems, the drive to organize parties around the goal of maintaining federal offices would serve as a mechanism to keep leaders engaged in the federal project. In the 1958 elections, however, Jamaica's main nationalist leaders did not run for federal office, indicating their unwillingness to invest in the federal institution. Although the federation existed on paper, then, a true federal system was never actually implemented.

Similarly, the federation never achieved the actual policy outputs British planners had hoped for. The islands' markets remained divided as Jamaica pursued its protectionist policies and continued to maintain high barriers on goods from the other islands, and at Trinidad's insistence the federation did not allow the free movement of people. Jamaica's protectionism was at the core of the development plans advocated by both its major political parties, and Trinidad's reluctance to open itself to local immigration stemmed from its oil wealth and relatively high standard of living. As a result, the only actual cooperation among the islands was the joint funding of a university and a small civil service staff to assist agricultural development.

Political power in Jamaica was closely divided between two parties, both espousing variants of socialism. Norman Manley's liberal nationalist People's National Party (PNP) made links with the middle and business classes while formally allying itself with the Social Democratic parties in Europe. William Bustamante, who like his cousin Manley had come from a privileged background, used his control of urban unions to organize a more populist socialist party called the Jamaican Labour Party (JPL). Although Manley did not run for a position in the federal parliament, he claimed to support federation as a matter of principle, and as the leader of the Jamaican government (effectively the prime minister) he continued to argue that federation would be good for Jamaica, although he made little headway. Bustamante made opposition to the federation the centerpiece of an electoral campaign, arguing that the benefits to integration would be slim and that Jamaica would be exploited economically by the poorer states that outnumbered it in the parliament. Manley attempted to outmaneuver Bustamante by calling a national referendum on federation, but 54 percent of the electorate voted against the federation in September

1961. Bustamante went on to win the following election and to lead Jamaica out of the federation and into independence (Hudson and Seyler 1989, 55).

Manley's vision of a West Indian federation was relatively limited; although profederal by Jamaican standards, he opposed the creation of a strong federal bureaucracy, did not himself run for federal office, and contested any proposals for actual economic integration. In effect, he supported federation in name only; his actual policy was in favor of an international organization. In Trinidad, however, the nationalist leader Eric Williams energetically campaigned for a strong central government that would bind the states and take an active role in economic integration and development planning. Like Jamaica, Trinidad was wealthier than the smaller islands—in this case because of oil resources, not the nascent industrial development that Jamaica had experienced. Williams's calls for a strong federal government as the most appropriate means of advancing regional development quickly turned after September 1961 to calls for a loose confederation. Without Jamaica, opinion in Trinidad shifted against being tied to eight poorer states, and the island (with Tobago) pursued independence alone.

After the formal end of federation in 1962, the states remained economically separate for most of the rest of the decade, although they maintained some functional policy cooperation on education, agriculture, and meteorological services via a regional international organization. It was not until the mid-1970s that the states made even a little headway in liberalizing trade (let alone other kinds of integration such as the free flow of people).

Amitai Etzioni's (1965) early work on political unification includes one of the few discussions of the West Indian federation in the context of broader theories of political unification. Etzioni argues, essentially, that the federation failed because it had everything going against it. The islands' economies would not have benefited from regional trade as much as from trade with North America and Europe, the diverse economies (with different levels of development concentrated in different sectors) gave the leaders of the states different interests, so that there was little sense of regional identity.[4]

---

[4] Etzioni (1965) also focuses on the nature of the federal constitution itself, and notes that the constitution failed because it did not give enough representation to Jamaica. This simply begs the question, though, of why the negotiators were unable to devise a constitution that would be able to both entice Jamaica into the federation

Etzioni's argument that the material benefits to political integration were slender is largely consistent with what other authors have argued (Lowenthal 1961; Lewis 2002). In other words, existing studies of the failure of the West Indian federation leave little to explain: British planners tried to maneuver their soon-to-be former colonies into a political union for which the costs outweighed the benefits, and nationalist leaders balked.

At another level, though, politics in Jamaica and Trinidad present some puzzles that allow additional tests of my theory. Tight electoral competition in Jamaica, with federation as a main issue that rival parties clashed over, suggests that at least some Jamaicans (such as Norman Manley) thought that federation even as it was proposed was in Jamaica's best interests. If just 5 percent of the voters had cast different ballots in 1961, this chapter would be about the origins of the successful West Indian federation. That two politicians calculating how best to win an election came up with different answers on whether to endorse or oppose federation suggests that the answer may not have been as clear at the time as it seems in retrospect. The particular political strategies of Manley and Bustamante, and the ways they understood their situations, may ultimately be better evidence about the conditions that lead some states to join federations while others stay out. The shift in Trinidad may be equally illuminating. Rather than just the result of its political process—a decision to resist continuation of the federal process with the remaining islands after Jamaica's referendum—considered in a vacuum, the shift from support of a strong institution to support of a weak institution can provide evidence for how leaders evaluate proposed mergers.

Jamaica

Racially distinct from metropolitan Britain, people in the West Indies by most accounts never developed a regional political community that preceded the moves toward federation in the 1950s. Jamaica was typical in that a traditional British political culture and political elite coexisted with more homegrown elements of a regional culture (such as food, music, and

---

and at the same time satisfy the smaller states. He also notes that the federation failed because leading politicians from Jamaica and Trinidad did not seek office at the federal level. However, decisions by some national parties not to invest in the federal government were the implementations of political decisions to stay out of the federation, not the causes of them.

popular literature). Norman Manley, like most of the middle-to-upper class, and most of the political elite, was educated in the traditional British style and had studied traditional British political economy subjects at Oxford-style schools. Political parties were organized in a Westminster system, and Imperial (later Commonwealth) partisans regularly traveled back and forth between Britain and the island, organizing parallel political structures (Lowenthal 1961, 69–73). To the extent that there was an emerging regional political identity, then, it was subsumed within a larger British worldview.

Jamaica's security situation in the late 1950s was uncertain, given its proximity to Cuba and to the prospects for internal subversion, whether inspired by the Cuban example or directly linked to the revolutionary movement. After the outbreak of World War II, Britain formally ceded responsibility for West Indian defense to the United States, which gave up its naval installations after the war; Britain formally resumed responsibility, even though its actual ability to provide for the defense of its possessions was limited. Still, although Cuban revolutionary groups were active in Jamaica (and in other islands in the Caribbean as well), Jamaica's leaders understood that the United States perceived an interest in preventing further Communist encroachments in the hemisphere as a way to contain Soviet power; as a result, security issues were never high on the political agenda in Jamaica (Hudson and Seyler 1989, 141).

The two dominant politicians in the 1950s and 60s were Manley (leading the PNP) and Bustamante (leading the JPL). Both organizations effectively organized across racial and class divides, and the parties converged in the independence period around similar economic policies, both emphasizing mild socialism and protectionism with state-led investment in industrialization. Among voters, partisanship became as important an organizing principle as anything else, although there were few programmatic differences between the two parties. One of those few differences, however, was foreign policy, including federation (Hudson and Seyler 1989, 123).

The material interests of different economic coalitions cannot alone explain why the PNP supported federation and the JPL opposed it. Both parties ran import-substitution policies and sought to build up local industries in order to win support from urban constituencies. The difference between the parties seems to have been in their beliefs about whether regional federation would enhance the industrialization agenda. Manley argued that federation would give Jamaican industries access to more state financing and, potentially, to more consumers (although he also advocated a federal system that would permit Jamaica to retain barriers to imports from the other member states). Bustamante argued the opposite, that federation would erode Jamaica's industrial investments and lead it to lose out in competition with Trinidad and the other islands (Lewis 2002, 13).

Jamaicans considering federation opposed market integration and rarely discussed security issues. Manley and profederal newspapers mostly defended federation as a means to achieve administrative gains: a larger state, drawing on a broader tax base and pooling the talents of elites throughout the region, would be more capable of making strategic investments in new and growing industries and better at achieving the newly independent states' ambitious goals for agricultural development.

Throughout, Manley (and also Bustamante prior to 1960, when he supported federation in principle) argued for a federal government that would be limited to coordinating industrial policy and agricultural services. These were the two issues that the major constituencies of both major parties (urban labor organizations and farmers) cared about. Whereas the agricultural services envisaged by the federal planners were diffuse public goods—most politicians at the time talked about state-sponsored research into developing farming techniques that would adapt green revolution technologies to the unique climate conditions of the Caribbean islands—industrial policy was an area in which the federal government would be making allocation decisions. The different islands would be in competition for federal development aid and for foreign investment licenses. Jamaica, as the largest member state with the largest economy and the potential to dominate those aspects of the federal bureaucracy that control distributions of divisible goods (as opposed to those agencies that provide public goods), would have found its bargaining position increasing with the other states increase over time, giving it the ability to exploit them in the long run.

The only potential check on this ability would have been strong federal institutions. Shortly after the formal ratification of the federal constitution, however—led by Bustamante's JPL, but quickly endorsed by Manley and the PNP—Jamaica's representatives in the federal parliament began seeking to make changes to the agreement which would limit federal powers generally, and those of taxation in particular, and increase Jamaica's representation in the parliament. Both changes were eventually accepted by the other states (Flanz 1968, 98).[5]

---

[5] The constitutional renegotiations were concluded well before the Jamaican referendum to withdraw from the federation; before leaving the federation, Jamaica got nearly all the revisions it had asked for (Springer 1962, 769).

Even before the referendum, neither Manley nor Bustamante made a serious effort to integrate his political organization into a broader West Indian political party, and neither ran for office at the federal level, even though it had been widely assumed before 1958 that Manley would be elected to the federal parliament and become the first prime minister of the new federation. In the absence of a serious contender from either Jamaica or Trinidad, that role went to Grantley Adams, who until then had been the premier of Barbados. Manley's decision not to pursue the office followed naturally from his limited view of the federation generally. The Jamaican referendum was, ultimately, only the final blow to a process that had already been moribund for lack of clear support from the Jamaican political establishment. Jamaica's reluctance was entirely as the theory would predict: the largest state, with little to risk from administrative integration with smaller, more potentially dependent states, was willing to implement an international treaty but extremely reluctant to consider a real federal union, absent substantial gains from integration.

Trinidad and Tobago

In September 1959 the government of Trinidad and Tobago published, under the name of Premier Eric Williams, a report titled *The Economics of Nationhood*. It was, in effect, an argument for a strong federal government for the West Indies. It noted the potential advantages to "centrally directed economic coordination" (6) and advocated a central government with the ability to levy direct taxes and make decisions about development projects without first having to negotiate with the provincial island governments on a case-by-case basis (Williams 1959; Springer 1962). The report, couched in terms of the interests of the region as a whole, explained how all the islands would benefit from integration and development in the long run—even those that would initially be taxed to finance the projects.

The report explained, in particular, the advantages of a regional common market. It noted that many of the islands were too small by themselves to be economically viable and that scale alone would make the region more prosperous.

This argument reflected the unified position of the Trinidadian political establishment, which was strongly profederal. The government of Eric Williams, the nationalist leader who dominated Trinidadian politics during the independence and federation periods, had come to power in the 1950s by organizing the political system along class and racial lines but had then advocated a development program similar to Manley's in

Jamaica: state-led industrialization. In 1956, for example, Williams staked a key election on his position that Trinidad was too small to be a serious country, and that only by achieving a larger size through federation would it be able to govern itself properly: "Federation is inescapable if the British Caribbean territories are to cease to parade themselves to the twentieth century world as eighteenth century anachronisms" (quoted in Springer 1962, 762).

Trinidad, unlike Jamaica, had oil, and even before the rise in oil prices in the 1970s, this resource gave the island economy access to inexpensive energy and to a steady stream of revenue that it could use to finance industrial development—in particular industrial development related not just to oil drilling but also to modern tanker and container shipping. By 1960, as a result, Trinidad had a denser industrial base than any of the other islands and a greater interest than any of them in forming a regional customs union that would have a common external tariff.

Williams's and Trinidad's view that the states should merge under a strong central government is consistent with the implication of the theory that those states with a greater potential level of relationship-specific investments in cooperation will prefer a stronger federal government. Trinidad, prior to the Jamaican referendum, behaved in exactly the same way as Victoria in the Australian case: it cheerfully agreed to let Jamaica have more representation in the federal parliament on the condition that the federal government be established with enough authority that its very presence would make it difficult for Jamaica to withdraw later.[6]

After Jamaica decided to abandon the federal project, the conventional wisdom in the region was that Trinidad and the remaining eight other states would proceed with the creation of the strong central government they had wanted all along (Flanz 1968, 102). A British diplomatic cable noted that "Eric Williams has always dislike[d] the present loose form of Federation which has been a condition of Jamaica belonging. The defection of Jamaica will give him the opportunity to press for the tighter form

[6] Springer (1962, 764) notes that it is strange that Trinidad so strongly supported a strong federal government, since it was already the most industrially developed island in the region and had a relatively high standard of living. His analysis, however, mixes the gains from cooperation with the exposure to relationship-specific investments. Absent cooperation (whether via a federation or an international organization), Trinidad would have been better off than Jamaica. The problem was that economic integration would have provided at least some benefits to the region that the states would have had to share, and integration without a federal institution would have eroded Trinidad's outside options more than Jamaica's.

of Federation which he has always advocated, with strong central powers over taxation, development, planning, etc." (MacLeod 1985, 93). Representatives from Barbados, which had also consistently supported a tighter federal institution, began meeting with Trinidadians, expecting general agreement on moving forward.

The conventional wisdom proved to be incorrect when Williams made it clear that Trinidad would not agree to a federation without Jamaica.[7] Popular histories have attributed his change of heart on federation to a variety of causes: among them, first, that nationalism within Trinidad had been growing so that a regional federation had become politically impossible, by coincidence at about the time of the Jamaican referendum (Springer 1962, 764); and, second, that Trinidad's economy had turned in several years of good performance, leading Williams to believe that regional integration would no longer be valuable as an alternative to openness to the rest of the world generally. The economic differences between Trinidad and the smaller potential members was particularly large, and newspapers in Trinidad began to speculate about the likelihood that it would be called upon to subsidize the poorer members if federation were to proceed (Meyerson, Seyler, and Hornbeck 1989, 172; Meighoo 2003, 57). Neither of these explanations is completely satisfying, however, since little evidence of Trinidadian nationalism as an impediment to federation was obvious at the time, and Trinidad would have been no more likely to have to subsidize the other islands without Jamaica in the group than with it. If anything, the loss of Jamaica would have put Trinidad in a better bargaining position both with the other states and with Britain, which had a commitment to provide development assistance to the poorer islands and would have made up any shortfall in Trinidad's contribution (MacLeod 1985).

At the time, Caribbean leaders simply concluded that Williams was no longer interested in regional economic integration. As a result, they were all surprised when, within two years, Trinidad had taken the lead in organizing the major islands (except for Jamaica) to make substantial progress toward a free-trade area, which was finally ratified in 1968 (Will 1991; Boxill 1993, 43). This development is not surprising in light of the theory: with a better exit option and less (or at least not more) exposure to relationship-

---

[7] After the referendum, Williams briefly proposed a unitary state for the region with Trinidad hosting the national capital and dominating the smaller states, but with the partial exception of Grenada, none of the other islands' leaders took his proposal seriously (Will 1991).

specific investments than its partners, Trinidad moved toward advocating cooperation via an IO rather than through a federation. The smaller states, unable to hold out credibly for a federal constitution they would have been unlikely to get from Trinidad anyway—and probably not inclined to in any case, given the low levels of relationship-specificity in which they would have invested—quickly agreed to an international institutional arrangement.

With Jamaica in the federation, Trinidad would have been relatively more vulnerable than its primary partner. With its smaller economy and population base, dependent on central planning decisions made by Jamaicans and orienting its local industrial development in line with the regional market, its outside option would have eroded over time while Jamaica's would not. Only a strong central government that tied Jamaica to the union would keep inter-island negotiations balanced; Trinidad (state V) supported federation, demonstrating the logic of the fourth implication of the theory (V prefers federation). With Jamaica out, however, Trinidad suddenly found itself in the position Jamaica had previously occupied (as state N). Trinidad had little interest in accepting constraints on its own ability to negotiate freely with the smaller islands, which in turn would be dependent on Trinidad and which continued to prefer a federal union. Trinidad's switch is therefore further evidence of the third observable implication of the theory (N prefers IO).

Conclusion

In the two decades after decolonization, on at least ten separate occasions, one or more African states that could have been independent advanced instead toward some sort of regional federation. The East African Federation and the federation of Tanganyika and Zanzibar were two. Four others succeeded in creating new states: in 1956 British Togoland voted in a plebiscite to join Ghana; in 1960 the British and Italian Somali colonies unified on independence; and in 1961 the northern region of British Cameroon voted to join Nigeria, while the southern region joined French Cameroon in a federation. The United Arab Republic of Egypt and Syria eventually failed, although it lasted for three and a half years. Three others that were negotiated but never adopted were between Senegal and what is now Mali; Ghana, Guinea, and Mali; and Egypt and Libya (Kurtz 1970; Bailey 1973, 110). Those regional groups that contemplated federation but ultimately chose to pursue independence generally failed to devise successful international cooperative agreements, just as the theory suggests.

The failure of the Federation of the West Indies initially led to the collapse of regional cooperation, but eventually Jamaica and Trinidad took the lead in developing several regional organizations, including, eventually, the Caribbean Community (CARICOM)—an IO that governs a reasonably integrated common market—as well as several specialized agencies that administer policy coordination on diverse subjects, including health and education. Formed in 1973 and including Jamaica, Trinidad and Tobago, and many of the smaller states, CARICOM has increasingly taken on more functions, including external economic relationships, and the member states (as of 2008) were in the process of adopting a common passport.

In both of the regions examined, failed (and occasionally successful) federal constitutions shaped the political geography that the next generation of leaders inherited; the question of why and how many of the proposals failed—a development that seemed to take many observers at the time by surprise—is therefore an important one in its own right. The process of failure also sheds light on the larger issue of why states sometimes federate.

Tanzania's decision to stay out of the federation after Uganda's exit, and Trinidad's similar decision after Jamaica's, raise questions that cannot be answered by traditional theories of federal integration. Existing theories posit that either there will be gains to cooperation or there won't, and that these gains alone can explain states' decisions. They therefore cannot account for why states may actively campaign for federation (against an international organization), given one set of potential members, and then turn around and actively campaign against federation (in favor of an IO), given a smaller subset.

In general, these two cases of failures show further evidence for several of the observable implications of my theory: federation is never the first choice of all members in a group, and those members with disproportionately high potential relationship-specific investments prefer federation to IO, while the others prefer an international organization as their first choice.

CONCLUSION

Federations are rooted in fear and mistrust. Unequal outside options from an alliance or customs union can lead some states to fear exploitation by their partners. Federal unions are born when vulnerable states demand political commitments, up front, from their potential partners as the price of their cooperation.

Since the 1964 publication of William Riker's book *Federalism: Origin, Operation, Significance,* the leading theory of federal origins has been that states merge when they have common security interests. The literature since Riker has, likewise, focused on the gains that states can achieve by joining together (Alesina and Spolaore 2003). This focus on the returns to scale, however, is unable to explain why states form federal unions instead of international organizations. The members of the European Union, the North Atlantic Treaty Organization, the Zollverein, and the Andean Community, for example, have achieved gains from economic or military integration without federating. Although some scholars (Ordeshook and Niou 1998) have speculated that federations might be more credible than alliances or other international organizations, and that therefore federations are more efficient solutions to cooperation problems, they have been unable to account for how states overcome their initial distrust to arrive at such a solution.

When cooperation entails relatively similar levels of relationship-specificity among potential partners, whether those levels are high or low, states can agree to cooperate without needing to devise institutions to bind them. They may choose to create institutions for other reasons, such as to promote transparency or to reduce transactions costs or to cultivate specialized expertise, but they will have no need to use institutions to make their mutual commitments more credible. Ad hoc cooperative arrangements or loose agreements to form alliances or customs unions will be enough. The more unequal the levels of specificity are, however, the more potentially vulnerable states will prefer to cooperate through a federation and the less they will value cooperating through a looser arrangement such as an ad hoc system or an IO. When they are unwilling to cooperate without a high commitment from their partners, and if cooperation can be shown to lead to valuable returns, vulnerable states may be able to extract a federal constitution from their partners in exchange for cooperation.

I did not test my theory by comparing all groups of states that formed federations with all groups of states that did not form federations and then showing that the former groups had more asymmetry in potential relationship-specific investments in cooperation. Such a research design would have been impractical and probably impossible, even in principle. Instead, I ended Chapter 2 with six testable implications of the theory:

1. The motives for states to form federations involve excludable goods.
2. Federations are never the first choice of all member states.
3. Leaders of nonvulnerable states, those that would have few relationship-specific investments in cooperation, prefer international organizations or ad hoc arrangements.
4. Leaders of vulnerable states, with large relationship-specific investments in cooperation, prefer to cooperate via a federation.
5. Vulnerable states resist cooperating until after federal institutions are in place.
6. Nonvulnerable states joining a federation will invest more heavily in federal institutions by, among other things, making more substantial changes to their party systems.

These implications are nontrivial, different from what prior theories would predict, and they are independent. The presence of successful federal unions that do not match these implications would be evidence against the theory.

I tested the six implications on five cases of successful and failed federations and found evidence to support the theory.

- *Australia.* Desiring a common market, Victoria and New South Wales were unable to agree to a customs union. Victorians feared that fixed industrial investments catering to the New South Wales market would act as hostages, allowing New South Wales to renegotiate an agreement later. Victoria held out for a federal constitution that would be costly for New South Wales to leave, reducing the latter's future bargaining advantage.

- *Argentina.* After 1845, the *litoral* states sought to expand trade with Europe but knew that doing so would make them dependent on a port controlled by Buenos Aires. A commercial treaty was unacceptable to them, since they believed that Buenos Aires would renegotiate the terms in its own favor once the *litoral* became dependent. So they used force to hold out for a federal constitution that would restrain the city.

- *Germany.* Prussia, Saxony, and Bavaria could have benefited jointly from a diplomatic union and a common foreign policy (provided that Prussia made side-payments to its junior partners), but for Saxony and Bavaria to give up the option of outside alliances would leave them dependent on Prussia. A federal constitution eventually gave Bavaria confidence that it could join a union while maintaining a level bargaining table with Prussia.

- *East Africa.* Nationalist leaders expected a large common market among Kenya, Tanganyika, and Uganda to enhance Western interest in investing in the region, but they were concerned that most investment would go to Kenya and that the other two states would grow dependent on transfer payments. Kenya was ultimately unwilling to commit to a strong central government, and Uganda backed out. Tanganyika, lacking the confidence that it alone would be able to restrain Kenya in a federal parliament, opted out as well.

- *West Indies.* When Britain proposed a federation, Jamaican leaders ultimately opted out. When Jamaica's departure changed Trinidad from a potentially vulnerable member to a nonpotentially vulnerable member, relative to the remaining members, Trinidad, supportive of federation when plans for regional union had included Jamaica, instead created an international organization.

Other historical cases I have not explored include the Swiss confederation, whose growth was related to the mistrust of the cantons for one another's willingness to refrain from forming outside alliances with nearby great powers (Stuart-Cansdell 1891; Lister 2001); the Malaysian federation, where economic and military concerns led nine Malay and three non-Malay states (Sabah, Sarawak, and Singapore) to merge in the presence of endemic mistrust over the future direction of federal policy (Hanna 1965); and the United States, in which, following the British withdrawal, the new states experimented with the loose Articles of Confederation before adopting the Constitution, following concerns about the potential disproportionate influence of Virginia (Deudney 1995; Dougherty 2001; Goldstein 2001). To test the theory more broadly, will require devising a research method that properly uses control cases, so that cases of federation can be contrasted with comparable cases of nonfederation—something I plan to address in future work.

The theory and evidence presented in this book have some important implications, both for the rise of potential contemporary federations and for studies in political science generally, which I describe here in turn.

Contemporary Issues

New federal unions are not formed every day, but potential federal processes are under way in several parts of the world. At least some people suggest that the European Union is evolving in the direction of a larger federation; there are discussions of unification or reunification between the People's Republic of China and Taiwan and between the two Koreas; federalism is often proposed as a stable solution in states such as Iraq which have the potential to break up; and, perhaps surprisingly, the question of world government via a global federation has recently received serious scholarly attention.

Europe

The European Union began after World War II as a compact among a group of states who sought to use economic integration as a way to foster growth and also as a way to make war less likely among the states. The founding members also faced a common threat from the Soviet Union.

In the early phase of integration in the immediate postwar period, European leaders proposed a set of agreements to form the Coal and Steel Community, the Defense Community, and the Political Community. The Coal and Steel Community (ECSC) was adopted and became the basis for further economic integration, whereas the Defense and Political Communities (EDC and EPC)—the latter planned as a two-chamber parliament with considerable powers of lawmaking and oversight (essentially a federation)—were abandoned (Moravcsik 1998). The main participants in the ECSC, France and Germany, were in relatively similar economic positions, so that integrating markets and economic planning for heavy industry would not put one of them in a more vulnerable position than the other. France's rejection of the EDC, however, was likely motivated by its position as having the most to lose from integration. If national militaries were separate, France would retain the most independently capable standing army on the continent. Military integration would have put French, German, Italian, and Benelux armies under a unified command, making it difficult for each of these countries to exercise military independence. Given the realities of the postwar order, however, Germany, Italy, and the Benelux states would have been unable to use their militaries to much independent purpose in any case; only France would have given up a substantial source of leverage. Furthermore, from the French perspective any potential gains from integration would have been low, given the American interest in deterring the primary security threat (the USSR) to the region. Neither the EDC nor the EPC (a mechanism that would have made exit even more costly) were sensible investments for France at the time.

Many early studies of European integration since the formation of the ECSC have focused on the strategies of the member states' governments. Scholars in the intergovernmentalist school (Hoffman 1964) argue that moves toward economic integration were strategic decisions by national leaders and influential interest groups. Continuing in this tradition, Andrew Moravcsik (1993) maintains that the decisions of the contemporary European Union are the product of policy coordination among the larger states. International institutions are tools to help the states coordinate their actions, promote transparency, and formalize and codify their commitments to each other (Moravcsik 1999).

An alternative view, sometimes called supranationalism, is that the national governments have lost control of policy. As interest groups within states become invested in existing EU rules, they demand more governance from the EU level than from national governments, taking effective control further away from member states (Stone Sweet and Sandholtz 1997). The institutional features of the Union as written by the member states themselves—such as supermajority voting requirements—make it difficult for member states to keep EU agencies in check, so divisions among and within states leave national governments with little effective control (Marks, Hooghe, and Blank 1996).

One implication of the contrived symmetry theory of federation, however, is that these intergovernmental and supranational ways of thinking about the EU do not necessarily contradict. As others have observed (e.g., Branch and Ohrgaard 1999), as long as member states have control of the larger constitutional process, it may be less important that they have lost effective control of day-to-day regulatory matters. Indeed, for the larger states to cede decisions to a new political layer may be the point: a mechanism that separates policymaking from the strict control of the dominant states can be a tool the larger states use to elicit deeper cooperation from their junior partners.

Some institutionalists, emphasizing the role of history, argue that even if national governments at one time intended to use supranational institutions as tools, long-run processes have led to those institutions being independent of their creators in unexpected ways (Pierson 1996). The European Court of Justice, for example, has successfully asserted authority—beyond what either its founders or the present member governments seem to have intended—by forming alliances with national court systems (Alter 1998). Others argue that particular EU decision-making institutions are less important than the growth of feelings of community among both ordinary citizens and elites who come to define their political identities in terms of the Union rather than the national states, and to redefine the locus of effective political authority from states to the EU through their use of transnational networks: both formal networks such as lobbying organizations, unions, and firms; and informal networks such as friendships and working connections among political and bureaucratic peers (Bache, George, and Rhodes 1996; Bache and Flinders 2004; Risse 2004). Both of these alternative views, focusing on historical institutional development and epistemic communities, may be able to explain some of the workings of the EU as practiced today but do not produce obvious answers to a larger question: is the EU evolving into a federal state?

Although European elites often use the language of federal institutions to describe their system of government (McKay 1999; Burgess 2000; McKay 2001; Verhofstadt 2005; Burgess and Vollaard 2006), the Union is not really federal in the classical sense. The unification of political parties across member states is a key attribute of federations, both according to existing theories of federation (Riker 1964, 129; Sawer 1969), as well as mine (Chapter 2). The member states today, who have been willing to integrate their national economies without a strong federal government, are not under the same pressures to federate that the Australians were, since the

Europeans have already achieved all the objectives the Australians sought without having to go through the costly process of devising a new set of governing institutions. In institutional terms (not policy outputs), the EU comes close to resembling the early Australian system of cooperation under the Federal Council. Although this system might risk eventually increasing disproportionately the influence of the largest states—Germany and, to a lesser extent, France—other members have not been willing to hold up integration until they could get a firmer guarantee.

This is not to say, however, that there have not been tensions. Concerns about the "democratic deficit" in Europe are especially strong among elites who fear their states may be most disadvantaged by intergovernmental bargaining (Moravcsik and Vachudova 2003; Moravcsik 2006). Although it may be too early to understand fully the recent failure of European constitutionalism (Slapin 2008, however, convincingly argues that it reflects the preferences of the larger members), it is possible to speculate that there may not have been much, if any, space for the major states to agree. Given that economic integration had already proceeded, it is not clear that other kinds of excludable goods (such as diplomatic integration) would provide enough gains to motivate European states not only to be willing to coordinate but also to be willing to pay the political costs of setting up a federal government in order to govern coordination.

In recent years the eastward expansion of the Union has led to a series of concerns over whether the EU can survive, now that there is even more economic diversity among the member states than before: members run the gamut from the core states (such as France), which are large, wealthy, and economically diversified, to newer members (such as Bulgaria and Romania) that are not. Still, differences in the structure and prosperity of national economies are no barrier to federal political integration. If anything, larger diversity of interests today may make state members more mistrustful of one another in the long run, a condition that could lead them to demand deeper levels of federal integration. Eastward expansion alone will not trigger more binding, federal institutions, however, because the economic integration of the East has already happened: no one side can credibly hold out any longer, because markets have already been largely merged, and many one-sided investments in relationship-specific investments have already taken place.

Security and diplomatic issues, however, may create conditions in the long run that make eastward expansion a stimulus for a more binding federal union. Consider, as an analogy, Bavaria, which gained from playing

France and Prussia against each other. Forging a firm diplomatic alliance with Prussia would have deprived Bavaria of its option to use the threat of allying with France as a tool to ensure its independence from Prussia. Since diplomatic integration caused it to lose an outside option it otherwise would have had, Bavaria needed a credible institutional guarantee—a federal constitution—in order to make integration less unpalatable. Some East European states such as Poland have had at least some success playing the United States and Western Europe against each other, and by investing in cooperation on Iraq and terrorism-related issues, they have kept alive the option of a general alignment with the United States. This gives them more leverage in their relationships with the rest of the EU, leverage they would lose if the EU were to develop into a diplomatic alliance.

It may be, then, that if core European states perceive benefits from incorporating the East into a diplomatic alliance, making a credible foreign policy arm of the EU, the only way they will have to entice East European holdouts who would fear their potential loss of influence in such a system will be a tighter federal bond. So, demands for a tight diplomatic alliance together with eastward expansion may together be sufficient to bring about a European federation.

Another possible set of holdouts that could bring about deeper political integration are on the other side of the continent. The United Kingdom, Denmark, and Sweden (EU members that have so far abstained from complete economic integration by rejecting the common currency) and Norway (a nonmember) are relatively wealthy states in which integration with Europe is a contentious issue. At least part of the reluctance in Britain and Norway is that their economies are not entirely synchronized with those of the other EU members. Britain is more economically tied to the United States, and Norway has independent oil reserves; both provide stable outside options for economic stability. While joining the Union and adopting the common currency would not remove these outside options entirely, they would make realizing the outside options more difficult, thereby reducing the leverage in the region of these states—which are therefore unlikely to join European institutions unless joining would come with some sort of mechanism to preserve their bargaining power vis-à-vis existing members.

In short, the theory suggests that unless dramatic shifts in geopolitics—such as a widening schism between the United States and Western Europe—substantially increase the potential benefits of a complete European diplomatic union, a United States of Europe is unlikely in the foreseeable future.

Chinese and Korean Unification

Within two pairs of de facto sovereign states, the People's Republic of China and Taiwan, and North and South Korea, substantial sentiment exists in principle for unification agreements that would resolve long-standing territorial claims. Thinking about federal agreements as tools to contrive symmetry can help clarify some of the issues involved with reunification, even if the motivations for reunification are identity-based and not related to material gains.

The PRC, in its "one country, two systems" proposal, has offered Taiwan a high level of autonomy within a unified state, which would in principle have characteristics verging on those of a confederation. Yet despite the PRC's apparent flexibility concerning Taiwan's status in a unified China, Taiwan clearly has not been receptive. Since the mid-1990s, for example, between 70 and 80 percent of the Taiwanese population has rejected Beijing's proposals; support for them has remained under 15 percent. Polls also show, however, that a majority of Taiwanese do not appear to be opposed to reunification in principle, and that over 60 percent would support reunification if the political, social, and economic disparity between mainland China and Taiwan were to lessen (Chu 2004; Niou 2004).

Clearly the problem is the PRC's credibility. Although it might initially promise Taiwan that economic, military, and diplomatic integration could proceed while maintaining significant internal autonomy for the island, this promise is not intrinsically credible. Taiwanese leaders understand that deeper integration would leave Taiwan with worse outside options in the future than it would have had otherwise, meaning that integration would put the island more at risk of opportunistic behavior by the mainland. Federal institutions and other mechanisms to contrive symmetry, mitigating the degree to which Taiwan's outside options would be worse with reunification than without, could ultimately make a deal more appealing to Taiwan. Some changes in the mainland, such as moves to include capitalists in the Communist Party as a way to give them a credible voice in governance (Dickson 2008), could be extended to Taiwanese business and political elites—although this move by itself would be insufficient to bind the PRC credibly to an agreement, given that Taiwanese interests would still be represented by a substantial minority in any possible leadership coalition.

Other mechanisms might be more effective. A reunification agreement that permitted Taiwan to maintain its alliance with the United States and its independent representation in international bodies such as the World

Trade Organization, or even permitted it to claim a seat in the United Nations as a region of China (modeled after the inclusion of the Ukraine and Belarus as UN members during the Soviet period), could increase Taiwan's confidence in its outside options, rendering it more willing to contemplate a reunification agreement that would be otherwise risky. Bavaria can serve as a historical analogue. Prussia offered Bavaria a set of institutional guarantees but also allowed it to maintain its ties to outside states through its independent representation at the Vatican (the European equivalent at the time of the United Nations). These measures facilitated German integration even in the presence of deep-seated mistrust (Kastner and Rector 2008).

The relationship between North and South Korea is also marked by mistrust, although, as the German and Argentine examples illustrate, this is not necessarily a barrier to political unification; leaders in Seoul, Pyongyang, and Washington are carefully considering alternative scenarios of voluntary confederation or a South Korean absorption of the North (Harrison 2002). Paradoxically, it may be that mistrust between the two Koreas actually *requires* that further economic integration take the form of some sort of federal union. The South's sunshine policy of using economic linkages in an effort to bring the North into a more cooperative posture over the long run (Kahler and Kastner 2006) may be limited to the extent that the North Korean leadership is sufficiently farsighted to understand the risk to its future autonomy, since growing economic ties will tend to enhance the bargaining leverage of the wealthy South at the expense of the North. Some level of political integration may be necessary in order to convince North Korea's rulers that South Korean promises to respect their interests will be met—unless a sudden collapse of the North Korean political economy renders its outside option so poor that its military leaders would be willing to accept even a bargain that did not provide them with long-run institutional protections (Pollack and Lee 1999).

Absent such a collapse, the potential for an agreement between the two Koreas may also be limited by normative considerations. For a federal agreement to contrive symmetry successfully, the leaders of the non-vulnerable state—in this case South Korea—must be willing to govern a federation in a way that separates them from their local constituents and makes them reliant on a coalition that includes political leaders from the vulnerable state—in this case the North. It is difficult, however, to imagine a party system in a democracy that could accommodate such a bizarre arrangement as a reliance on North Korea's Communist leaders, and they will be unwilling to agree to any federal agreement otherwise.[1] This impasse suggests that significant political change in North Korea is a precondition for either further economic integration or a political union.

Iraq and Post–Civil War States

Power-sharing agreements, regional federalism in particular, are often proposed as settlements to civil wars that threaten to break states into independent regions; in some cases these have been effective in helping warring parties preserve or reinstate national unity (Burgess and Pinder 2007). There is, however, a drawback to such agreements. Federal constitutions are agreements among the governing coalitions of states (or potential states) that seek to work together for some common purpose but need to have confidence that each will be able to defend its interests by bargaining effectively with one another over future issues as they arise. Federal systems are kept in place by party systems and other mechanisms that organize political activity at both the state and the federal level. These mechanisms have the intended effect of preserving the existence of the state-level political organizations as focal points of political activity. As a result, they may serve to perpetuate the political divisions that led to civil conflict in the first place. Several studies have shown that states that ended civil wars with power-sharing agreements such as federalism were more likely to restart those civil wars later than states that did not use power sharing as part of a settlement (Roeder 2007; Jung 2008). Power-sharing agreements may give political leaders incentives to mobilize citizens along ethnic or territorial lines, keeping in power those leaders who chose war in the first place (Roeder and Rothchild 2005) and inhibiting the development of national loyalties (Elkins and Sides 2007).

Even so, federal solutions may be the most plausible remaining alternative to ongoing violence. In situations where the parties to a conflict are unlikely to trust each other with the management of a unitary state, such as Iraq today (Byman and Pollack 2007), federal solutions may be able to instill confidence (Lake and Rothchild 2005), making them a preferred approach despite the long-run drawbacks.

---

[1] An outside guarantor, such as the PRC, which could serve as a North Korean ally even in a reunified Korea is problematic for the same reason.

Federal agreements do have an additional potential advantage: federations allow states to have confidence that they can work toward economic integration with their neighbors without having to fear that they will be subject to opportunism later. The more confidence local leaders have in federal power-sharing agreements, the more they will be willing to let other forms of integration proceed. Even within a unified state, a region fearful for its future bargaining power may seek to restrict trade by using hidden or cultural barriers (Helliwell 1996, for example, shows a provincial border effect on trade in Canada). To the extent that national economic integration may, over time, erode regional loyalties and also contribute to general prosperity, there may be an indirect benefit to federal union.

Effective governance in contemporary Iraq, following the 2003 U.S.-led intervention and despite the U.S. military successes in the troop surge of 2007–8, has been devolved on a de facto basis to three regions—Kurdish, Shia, and Sunni—with American policy moving toward the encouragement of a federal arrangement among them (Biden and Gelb 2006; Bouillon, Malone, and Rowswell 2007). As of late 2008, the reduction in violence over prior years has left the regions effectively autonomous in two respects. First, the Shia-dominated central government has faced little pressure to bring Sunnis into the governing coalition, as higher oil revenues, closer ties with Iran, and the security provided by the United States gives the Shia community space. As a consequence, the current government led by Prime Minister Nouri al-Maliki lost the Sunni Iraqi Accord Front. And the two largest Kurdish parties, the Patriotic Union of Kurdistan and the Kurdistan Democratic Party, have only remained in the Shia coalition in return for guarantees of effective regional autonomy (Katulis, Lynch, and Juul 2008). Second, the American strategy of arming the Sunni Awakening Councils against Al Qaeda in 2007 has led to a coalesced Sunni military power independent of an Iraqi national state (Simon 2008), so that the Shia central government has fought an escalating series of battles for territory both against the Sunni Awakening and the Kurdish Peshmerga, while at the same time preventing the latter two groups from integrating into the national military and police forces (Jones 2007). Kurdish and Sunni regions remain inwardly focused and self-policing. In short, Iraq is divided, with effective sovereignty exercised at the regional level (Katulis, Kahl, and Lynch 2008).

Although the Kurdish, Shia, and Sunni groups in Iraq are mutually suspicious, there are, in principle, large potential gains from cooperation on economic and security issues. Ongoing violence is costly, and all three groups face threats from outside groups including Al Qaeda—and, in some ways, from the United States as well, at least insofar as there is popular sentiment in all three regions against a continued U.S. military presence. National unification under a competent central government would bring the benefits of international recognition, including the ability to participate in regional economic arrangements and the ability to credibly negotiate oil exploration agreements with foreign multinational firms (uncertainty over who has the authority to authorize oil field development in the area around Kirkuk, for example, has delayed investments).

All else being equal, however, economic and security cooperation would almost certainly change the bargaining dynamics among the three regions to the benefit of the Shia. Even without access to oil in Kurdish regions, the Shia would have favorable outside options because they control the oil fields in the South and would have access to world markets via the Persian Gulf. They would also maintain close ties with neighboring Iran, and would be unlikely to lose their influence over the military and police and the city of Baghdad. Sunnis, however, would lose their independent military capability. If it were widely believed that the United States would be more likely to draw down its military presence sooner if the regions implement an effective regime of economic and security cooperation than if they do not—a logical supposition widely shared—then cooperation would mean than the Sunnis would also lose the tacit protection of the United States military. Although initially the Sunni Awakening was premised on the theory that it would accelerate the American withdrawal, the attitude of Sunni leaders seems to have shifted in favor of a continued American protection against the Shia national government (Kahl, Flournoy, and Brimley 2008; Katulis, Lynch, and Juul 2008). Integration would lead to a substantial increase in Sunni dependence on a central regime, and a much less increase in Shia dependence. The Sunnis are potentially vulnerable; the Shia are not.

The Kurdish region would also be in a worse bargaining position with the Shia, after the start of cooperation, although the losses would be likely to be less than for the Sunnis. The status quo for the Kurds, relative security and at least some economic investment, albeit with missed opportunities due to an uncertain international status and tensions with neighboring countries that are reluctant to accept a de facto Kurdish state, provides a sustainable outside option. Effective economic and military integration with the Shia, however, would remove their outside military option and their ability to negotiate oil contracts, meaning that future bargains (such as divisions of oil revenues) would be increasingly unfavorable from their perspective. The establishment of a competent central regime would also increase U.S. pressure on Kurds to work within an Iraqi political system, as American policymakers would be less inclined to cross Turkish, Iranian, and Syrian interests, since, presumably, the American willingness to protect de facto Kurdish independence is not an end in itself but is rather a product of the United States's poor assessment of the competence of the central Iraqi government.

Iraq's three regions therefore have the characteristics of groups of states that form federal unions: potential gains from cooperation but unequal levels of potential dependence. Effective military and economic cooperation is therefore unlikely without genuine political integration that binds political leaders in cross-regional parties. Regional leaders, in turn, will only choose to join such organizations when they see federation as preferable to independence (since Sunni and Kurdish fears of exploitation render a less-binding form of cooperation such as a loose alliance or confederation unworkable). This condition can only hold if there is a common belief that the American security presence is limited and has a definite end date that is not conditional on Iraqi political developments. Specifically, the Sunnis and Kurds must believe that the American security guarantee is not conditional on the pace of political integration at the center, and that the United States will stay or leave on its own timetable. Because the American security presence enhances Sunni and Kurdish outside options, and therefore their abilities to bargain with the Shia, it will be difficult for them to accept a deal that gives them some leverage at the center if a consequence of that deal is that they lose the leverage gained from the American commitment. The Shia must believe that recent security gains will only be maintained if they reach a political settlement with the other groups, and that the American military is about to withdraw regardless of whether or not a deal is struck.

World Government

The United States today stands in a position of global leadership, with the world's largest economy and military and a substantial lead in other assets such as technology and culture. Many of its relationships with other states are characterized by a seeming inequality in exit options. For example, the United States has a diverse economy with a relatively small exposure to international trade (compared with the other industrial democracies) and does not depend on market access to any one state for its prosperity, aside from a few suppliers of natural resources such as Saudi Arabia. Many of its partners, however, have much smaller economies that are heavily invested in producing for American markets. Furthermore, those states on which the United States is economically dependent, such as Saudi Arabia, are even more dependent on the United States in other ways, such as for security.

Not only are America's external relationships characterized by unequal levels of relationship-specific investments, but there are also large potential gains from cooperation. The integration, at least among wealthy countries, of markets for goods and capital has produced enormous gains generally, and the worldwide gains from further integration could be immense. In addition, cooperation in other policy areas—such as efforts to mitigate climate change or to interdict transnational terrorism—could, in principle, produce large payoffs.

The idea of world government has rarely been taken seriously in the study of international politics, but recently several scholars arguing from very different sets of assumptions have made serious predictions that the world as a whole is moving in the direction of a federal union. Dani Rodrik (2000) argues that complete economic integration is probably impossible without political integration, because states that seek the benefits of fully integrated common markets, including regulatory harmonization, will also seek to preserve their ability to have a say in what those regulations should be. The only way to have both results, he speculates, is to form a world federation, since economic integration without a federal government would produce involuntary harmonization through market pressures rather than through political choices.

Rodrik's argument is that there are economic gains from market integration, and that markets can be fully integrated only via political integration. He predicts that states and leaders will eventually settle on a system in which they can make decisions about common-market policies in a way that generally reflects popular opinion. Such a system could, at least in principle, exist through an international organization such as the European Union or the North American Free Trade Agreement, or even the World Trade Organization. The fact that the member states of the WTO, in practice, do not constitute a complete common market *may* be because such a loose organization is incapable of governing one, but it is more likely that member states are unwilling to give up trade barriers because of the domestic political benefits those barriers create.

My theory suggests that world government, driven by the potential benefits from market integration that Rodrik identifies, is likely only if two conditions hold. First, those countries that would be more vulnerable in a world common market, such as the smaller industrialized states and middle-income and poor countries, could credibly hold out for deeper political integration as a guarantee that their positions would not be further eroded under a system of complete market integration that ties them to regulatory decisions made in wealthier, larger states. That is, they would have to reject further trade liberalization as contrary to their interests, out of the fear that unequal dependence would leave them subject to exploitation. This first condition is not difficult to imagine; indeed, it was the basic rationale that many developing economies, particularly in Latin America, adopted for import-substitution policies.

The second condition is that the United States and other large, wealthy economies would value economic integration so highly and regard its potential benefits as so large that they would accede to demands for a world government even though its creation would be costly. This condition is less likely to hold in the foreseeable future. The United States, for one, is large enough and has enough potential trading partners—at least some of whom would probably not be able to hold out credibly for a world federation—that it is unlikely to be moved to agree to demands for a constitutional solution in the way that New South Wales was in Australia. Perhaps the potential benefits from economic integration over the very long run will grow to the point where the United States might contemplate such an arrangement, but it is difficult to imagine such a change any time soon.

What about motives other than market integration? Two current issues, global warming and transnational terrorism, do have the potential to become problems of central importance to the United States; however, projects to slow the rate of global warming (either by technological innovations in transportation and energy or by direct action to reduce carbon emissions) and projects to suppress terrorism (such as neutralizing terrorist organizations or eliminating or containing rogue states) are nonexcludable goods. That is, their benefits can be shared by all states, whether they contribute to the provision of the good or not. This means that the alternative to cooperation among states is free-riding, which would give smaller states an extremely favorable exit option and, hence, no need for a federal institution to protect their interests by contriving symmetry.

Although Daniel Deudney (2006) argues that the threat of uncontrolled nuclear weapons will lead states into a world republic out of fear for their safety, his thesis rests on the nonexcludability of the benefits from controlling nuclear terrorism. That is, since all states would benefit from the policing of nuclear activities, all have an incentive to join. But again, smaller states would be even better off free-riding on efforts by larger states to interdict nuclear arms and so would have little incentive to end their independence in exchange for free gains.[2]

Contrived Symmetry and the Study of Politics

Finally, my theory has implications for the study of international politics generally. Structural realism, dating from the work of Kenneth Waltz (1979), argues that insecurity drives states to form coalitions to balance against threats to their independence. As an alternative to forming a balancing coalition, however, states uncomfortable with the growing influence of a neighbor can use institutions to create credible assurances. Even though using institutional means to tame a potential partner is not necessarily inconsistent with traditional realism (Walt 2005), the logic does show that states have more options at their disposal than are commonly recognized. This understanding is actually more consistent with the traditional realist approach (Morgenthau 1954), which saw power as driving states to take measures for their own security but left open the possibility that states could use creative diplomacy to bind power in other ways, as Bismarck did, using institutions.

Although this book focuses on the origins of federal unions, its implications may also help us to understand some of the workings of federations. If federal constitutions are tools to contrive symmetry, then they must necessarily elicit more investments from some states—those that would otherwise be less vulnerable in cooperation—than from others. It is not a coincidence that many of the early prime ministers of Australia were politicians from New South Wales, nor is it a coincidence that they were integrated into federal parties that bound them into cross-state alliances, leading them to espouse positions on controversial issues (like tariffs) that alienated them from their home districts. Similarly, many of the early American presidents were Virginians, but they were drawn into a party system that organized competition between Federalists and Democratic-Republicans, parties competing for national constituencies that did not have strong regional bases (that is, they reflected neither a dominant North-South state divide nor a large-small state divide).

International relations theorists in the institutionalist tradition have often seen international organizations as devices to reduce transactions

---

[2] Wendt (2003) argues that world federalism is inevitable, and bases his argument on a combination of identity and security motives. I addressed these in Chapter 4.

costs. States that have already agreed to cooperate can make their cooperation more effective, or more rewarding, by enacting mechanisms that promote transparency, facilitate side-payments, or otherwise capture economies of scale in organizing negotiations or implementing decisions (Martin 1992). For example, some of the leading institutionalist theories of the European Union (e.g., Pollack 2003) describe the Union as a device to reduce transactions costs, thereby enhancing the gains to cooperation.

My argument suggests a broader possible motive for institutionalizing international politics. To the extent that IOs can be designed with higher or lower exit costs, it may be that some of the variations in institutional design are a result of different needs for groups of states seeking to contrive symmetry to make cooperation possible. When cooperation through an ad hoc arrangement is unappealing to potentially vulnerable states, a small institutional investment such as those states make in legalized regimes may be just enough to make cooperation possible. Institutions may raise exit costs for states, but, more important, they may raise those costs more for some states than for others. This means that international institutions may be more than just devices to facilitate cooperation for states that have already decided to cooperate; they may be tools to change the balance of bargaining power among states, making cooperation possible in the first place.

Even if international organizations are like smaller versions of federations (with some costs automatically imposed on states that exit, even if they are not as high as the exit costs in a federation), they still have limits. Counterintuitively, the limits may have more to do with trust and dependence than anything else: when the leaders of states are comfortable with their ability to bargain as equals in the future, they will be more willing to continue cooperating through these relatively anarchic organizations. For example, among the most significant challenges facing important organizations today, such as the World Trade Organization, the Asia-Pacific Economic Cooperation (APEC) forum, and the United Nations Security Council, is how best to elicit investments from those members who have the best outside options in order to make them less prone to demand changes in agreements later.

Some of the mechanisms at work in federal integration have also been hypothesized to have consequences for the operation of international organizations, such as the mobilization of political parties and social groups (Cortell and Davis 1996), the entrenchment of bureaucratic organizations (Barnett and Finnemore 1999), and changes in national political identity (Wendt 1999). Although current international organizations tend to hold only very small versions of these bonds (if any), the extent to which they differ could be an important source of variation among IOs, just as the difference in the size of the political investment is a critical difference between IOs and federations. Future work on international organizations, and in particular those that deal with excludable goods such as trade agreements, should examine the way these organizations are governed for evidence of variation in the use of political investments to contrive symmetry among members.

Political scientists are increasingly coming to the view that international politics is not a blank slate or complete anarchy. States follow rules, even constitutional rules (Ikenberry 1998), and relationships of authority are in fact quite common (Lake 2009). In situations where national leaders could potentially benefit from cooperation, they have a wide of range of options as to how to structure that cooperation, from ad hoc agreements to treaties to international organizations to federations.

Often, state leaders choose to cooperate through low-cost mechanisms such as treaties, or they simply refrain from cooperating at all. When they do choose to federate, though, it is not out of a harmony of interests. Creative leaders go through great difficulties to enact federal agreements when the stakes are high and they cannot achieve cooperation in any other way. States form federations because they mistrust one another, not because their interests are in harmony.

REFERENCES

Abdelal, R., and J. Kirshner. 1999. "Strategy, Economic Relations, and the Definition of National Interests." *Security Studies* 9 (1–2): 119–56.

Abizadeh, A. 2005. "Does Collective Identity Presuppose an Other? On the Alleged Incoherence of Global Solidarity." *American Political Science Review* 99 (1): 45–60.

Acemoglu, D., P. Antrāás, and E. Helpman. 2005. *Contracts and the Division of Labor*. Cambridge, Mass.: National Bureau of Economic Research.

Acemoglu, D., and J. A. Robinson. 2006. "Economic Backwardness in Political Perspective." *American Political Science Review* 100 (1): 115–31.

Adar, K. G., and M. Ngunyi. 1994. "The Politics of Integration in East Africa since Independence." In *Politics and Administration in East Africa,* ed. W. Oyugi, 395–428. Nairobi: East African Educational Publishers.

Adler, E. 1997. "Imagined (Security) Communities: Cognitive Regions in International Relations." *Millennium—Journal of International Studies* 26 (2): 249–+.

Albrecht-Carrie, R. 1958. *A Diplomatic History of Europe since the Congress of Vienna*. New York: Harper.

Aldrich, J. H. 1995. *Why Parties? The Origin and Transformation of Political Parties in America*. Chicago: University of Chicago Press.

Alesina, A., A. Angeloni, and F. Etro. 2001. "The Political Economy of International Unions." National Bureau of Economic Research. Cambridge, Mass.

Alesina, A., R. Baqir, and W. Easterly. 1999. "Public Goods and Ethnic Divisions." *Quarterly Journal of Economics* 114 (4): 1243–84.

Alesina, A., and E. Spolaore. 1997. "On the Number and Size of Nations." *Quarterly Journal of Economics* 112 (4): 1027–56.

———. 2003. *The Size of Nations*. Cambridge, Mass.: MIT Press.

Allin, C. D. 1907. "An Intercolonial Preferential Experiment." *Proceedings of the American Political Science Association* 4 (Fourth Annual Meeting): 57–68.

———. 1913. "The Genesis of the Confederation of Canada." In *Annual Report of the American Historical Association for the Year 1911*, 1:239–48. Washington, D.C.: American Historical Association.

———. 1918. *A History of the Tariff Relations of the Australian Colonies.* Minneapolis: University of Minnesota Press.

Allin, C. D., and W. Anderson. 1929. *Australasian Preferential Tariffs and Imperial Free Trade: A Chapter in the Fiscal Emancipation of the Colonies.* Minneapolis: University of Minnesota Press.

Alt, J. E., F. Carlsen, P. Heum, and K. Johansen. 1999. "Asset Specificity and the Political Behavior of Firms: Lobbying for Subsidies in Norway." *International Organization* 53 (1): 99–+.

Alter, K. J. 1998. "Who Are the 'Masters of the Treaty'? European Governments and the European Court of Justice." *International Organization* 52 (1): 121–+.

Anderson, B. 1983. *Imagined Communities: Reflections on the Origin and Spread of Nationalism.* London: Verso.

Angueira, M. d. C. 1989. *El proyecto confederal y la formación del Estado nacional, 1852–1862.* Buenos Aires: Centro Editor de América Latina.

Ansolabehere, S., J. M. Snyder, and C. Stewart. 2001. "Candidate Positioning in U.S. House Elections." *American Journal of Political Science* 45 (1): 136–59.

Arnold, R. 1970. "Some Australian Aspects of New Zealand Life, 1890–1913." *New Zealand Journal of History* 4 (1): 54–76.

———. 1981. *The Farthest Promised Land: English Villagers, New Zealand Immigrants of the 1870s.* Wellington: Victoria University Press.

———. 1987. "The Australasian Peoples and Their World, 1888–1915." In *Tasman Relations, New Zealand, and Australia, 1788–1988*, ed. K. Sinclair, 52–70. Auckland: Auckland University Press.

Aroney, N. 2000. "Mueller on European Federation: A Reply from the Perspective of Australian Federalism." *Public Choice* 105 (3–4): 255–72.

———. 2002. "'A Commonwealth of Commonwealths': Late Nineteenth-Century Conceptions of Federalism, and Their Impact on Australian Federation, 1890–1901." *Journal of Legal History* 23 (3): 253–90.

Artzrouni, M., and J. Komlos. 1996. "The Formation of the European State System: A Spatial 'Predatory' Model." *Historical Methods* 29 (3): 126–34.

Axelrod, R. M. 1984. *The Evolution of Cooperation.* New York: Basic Books.

Ayany, S. G. 1970. *A History of Zanzibar: A Study in Constitutional Development, 1934–1964.* Nairobi: East African Literature Bureau.

Bache, I., and M. V. Flinders. 2004. *Multi-level Governance.* New York: Oxford University Press.

Bache, I., and S. George. 2006. *Politics in the European Union.* New York: Oxford University Press.

Bache, I., S. George, and R. A. W. Rhodes. 1996. "Cohesion Policy, and Subnational Authorities in the UK." In *Cohesion Policy and European*

Integration: Building Multi-level Governance, ed. L. Hooghe, xiv, 458. New York: Oxford University Press.

Bailey, M. 1973. *The Union of Tanganyika and Zanzibar: A Study in Political Integration*. Syracuse: Program of Eastern African Studies, Maxwell School of Citizenship and Public Affairs.

Baker, R. 1891. *A Manual of Reference to Authorities for the Use of the Members of the National Australasian Convention, Which Will Assemble at Sydney on March 2, 1891, for the Purpose of Drafting a Constitution for the Dominion of Australia*. Adelaide, [S. Aust.]: W. K. Thomas.

———. 1897a. *The Executive in a Federation*. Adelaide: C. E. Bristow, Government Publisher.

———. 1897b. *Federation*. [Adelaide, s.n.].

Banfield, J. 1965. "The Structure and Administration of the East African Common Services Organization." In *Federation in East Africa: Opportunities and Problems*, ed. C. Leys and P. Robson, 30–40. London: Oxford University Press.

Barnett, M. N., and M. Finnemore. 1999. "The Politics, Power, and Pathologies of International Organizations." *International Organization* 53 (4): 699–+.

———. 2004. *Rules for the World: International Organizations in Global Politics*. Ithaca: Cornell University Press.

Barton, G. B. 1901. *The Troubles of the Australian Federation*. Canberra: National Library of Australia.

Basinger, S. J. 2003. "Regulating Slavery: Deck-Stacking and Credible Commitment in the Fugitive Slave Act of 1850." *Journal of Law Economics & Organization* 19 (2): 307–42.

Bastin, J. 1964. "Federation and Western Australia." In *Historical Studies: Australia and New Zealand*, ed. J. J. Eastwood and F. B. Smith, 199–214. Box Hill, Vic.: Melbourne University Press.

Battye, J. S. 1924. *Western Australia: A History from Its Discovery to the Inauguration of the Commonwealth*. Oxford: Clarendon Press.

Bazillon, R. 1990. "Economic Integration and Political Sovereignty: Saxony and the *Zollverein*, 1834–1877." *Canadian Journal of History* 25:189–213.

Beach, W. G. 1899. "The Australian Federal Constitution." *Political Science Quarterly* 14 (4): 663–80.

Bean, R. 1973. "War and the Birth of the Nation State." *Journal of Economic History* 33:203–21.

Bednar, J. 2007. "Valuing Exit Options." *Publius—The Journal of Federalism* 37 (2): 190–208.

———. 2008. *The Robust Federation*. New York: Cambridge University Press.

Bednar, J., W. N. Eskridge, and J. A. Ferejohn. 2001. "A Political Theory of Federalism." In *Constitutional Culture and Democratic Rule*, ed. J. A. Ferejohn, J. N. Rakove, and J. Riley, xi, 414. New York: Cambridge University Press.

Berg-Schlosser, D. 1994. "Ethnicity, Social Classes, and the Political Process in Kenya." In *Politics and Administration in East Africa*, ed. W. Oyugi, 244–96. Nairobi: East African Educational Publishers.

Bethell, L. 1993. *Argentina since Independence.* New York: Cambridge University Press.

Biden, J., and L. Gelb. 2006. "Unity through Autonomy in Iraq." *New York Times,* May 1.

Birch, A. H. 1965. "Opportunities and Problems of Federation." In *Federation in East Africa: Opportunities and Problems,* ed. C. Leys and P. Robson, 6–29. London: Oxford University Press.

Bismarck, O., and A. J. Butler. 1899. *Bismarck, the Man and the Statesman; being the Reflection and Reminiscences of Otto.* New York: Harper.

Blainey, G. 1964. "The Role of Economic Interests in Australian Federation." In *Historical Studies: Australia and New Zealand,* ed. J. J. Eastwood and F. B. Smith, 179–94. Box Hill, Vic.: Melbourne University Press.

Bloodgood, E. 2007. "Internet Politics: States, Citizens, and New Communication Technologies." *Millennium—Journal of International Studies* 35 (3): 763–65.

Blum, U., and L. Dudley. 1991. "A Spatial Model of the State." *Journal of Institutional and Theoretical Economics—Zeitschrift für die Gesamte Staatswissenschaft* 147 (2): 312–36.

Bollen, K., and J. D. Medrano. 1998. "Who Are the Spaniards? Nationalism and Identification in Spain." *Social Forces* 77 (2): 587–621.

Bolton, P., and G. Roland. 1997. "The Breakup of Nations: A Political Economy Analysis." *Quarterly Journal of Economics* 112 (4): 1057–90.

Bouillon, M. E., D. Malone, and B. Rowswell. 2007. *Iraq: Preventing a New Generation of Conflict.* Boulder, Colo.: Lynne Rienner.

Boxill, I. 1993. *Ideology and Caribbean integration.* Kingston, Jamaica: Consortium Graduate School of Social Sciences, University of the West Indies, Mona Campus.

Branch, A. P., and J. C. Ohrgaard. 1999. "Trapped in the Supranational-Intergovernmental Dichotomy: A Response to Stone Sweet and Sandholtz." *Journal of European Public Policy* 6 (1): 123–43.

British Parliament. Various years. *Accounts and Papers.* London: Darling & Son.

Brown, J. C. 1979. *A Socioeconomic History of Argentina, 1776–1860.* New York: Cambridge University Press.

Bryce, J. B. 1888. *The American Commonwealth.* New York: Macmillan.

Buchan, B. 2000. "The Government of Peace: Liberal Civilisation and the Problem of Violence." *Political Science.* Canberra: Australian National University.

Bunce, V. 1999. *Subversive Institutions: The Design and the Destruction of Socialism and the State.* New York: Cambridge University Press.

Bunkley, A. W. 1950. "Sarmiento and Urquiza." *Hispanic American Historical Review* 30 (2): 176–94.

Burgess, M. 2000. *Federalism and European Union: The Building of Europe, 1950–2000.* New York: Routledge.

——. 2006. *Comparative Federalism: Theory and Practice.* New York: Routledge.

Burgess, M., and J. Pinder. 2007. *Multinational Federations.* New York: Routledge.

Burgess, M., and H. Vollaard. 2006. *State Territoriality and European integration.* New York: Routledge.

Burr, R. N. 1955. "The Balance of Power in Nineteenth-Century South America: An Exploratory Essay." *Hispanic American Historical Review* 35 (1): 37–60.

Byman, D., and K. M. Pollack. 2007. *Things Fall Apart: Containing the Spillover from an Iraqi Civil War*. Washington, D.C.: Brookings Institution Press.

Calvert, R. L., M. D. McCubbins, and B. R. Weingast. 1989. "A Theory of Political Control and Agency Discretion." *American Journal of Political Science* 33 (3): 588–611.

Carr, W. 1991. "The Origins of the Wars of German Unification." In *Origins of Modern Wars*, ed. H. Hearder. London: Longman.

Cerny, P. G. 1995. "Globalization and the Changing Logic of Collective Action." *International Organization* 49 (4): 595–94.

Chapman, R. M. 1961. "No Land Is an Island: Twentieth-Century Politics." In *Distance Looks Our Way: The Effects of Remoteness on New Zealand*, ed. K. Sinclair. Auckland: University of Auckland Press.

Chhibber, P. K., and K. Kollman. 2004. *The Formation of National Party Systems: Federalism and Party Competition in Canada, Great Britain, India, and the United States*. Princeton: Princeton University Press.

Chu, Y. H. 2004. "Taiwan's National Identity Politics, and the Prospect of Cross-Strait Relations." *Asian Survey* 44 (4): 484–512.

Clark, M. 1963. *A Short History of Australia*. New York: New American Library.

———. 1980. *The Quest for an Australian Identity*. St. Lucia: University of Queensland Press.

Clark, V. S. 1908a. "Australian Economic Problems. I. The Railways." *Quarterly Journal of Economics* 22 (3): 399–451.

———. 1908b. "Australian Economic Problems. II. The Tariff." *Quarterly Journal of Economics* 22 (4): 576–601.

Clarke, H. D., A. Kornberg, and P. Wearing. 2000. *A Polity on the Edge: Canada and the Politics of Fragmentation*. Peterborough, Ont.: Broadview Press.

Clayton, A. 1981. *The Zanzibar Revolution and Its Aftermath*. London: C. Hurst.

Coase, R. H. 2000. "The Acquisition of Fisher Body by General Motors." *Journal of Law and Economics* 43 (1): 15–31.

Connolly, C. 1978. "Class, Birthplace, Loyalty: Australian Attitudes to the Boer War." *Historical Studies* 18 (71): 210–32.

Conradt, D. P. 2005. *The German Polity*. New York: Pearson/Longman.

Cooley, A. 2005. *Logics of Hierarchy: The Organization of Empires, States, and Military Occupations*. Ithaca: Cornell University Press.

Cortell, A. P., and J. W. Davis. 1996. "How Do International Institutions Matter? The Domestic Impact of International Rules and Norms." *International Studies Quarterly* 40 (4): 451–78.

Coulthald-Clark, C. 1988. "Formation of the Australian Armed Services, 1901–14." In *Australia: Two Centuries of War and Peace*, ed. M. McKernan and M. Browne. Sydney: Macarthur Press.

Cox, G. W., and M. D. McCubbins. 1994. "Bonding, Structure, and the Stability of Political-Parties—Party Government in the House." *Legislative Studies Quarterly* 19 (2): 215–31.

Craig, J. 1993. "A United-States of Australasia." *Australian Journal of Political Science* 28 (1): 38–53.

Craven, G. 2001. "A Liberal Federation and a Liberal Constitution." In *Liberalism and the Australian Federationed,* ed. J. R. Nethercote. Riverwood, N.S.W.: Federation Press.

Criscenti, J. T. 1961. "Argentine Constitutional History, 1810–1852: A Re-examination." *Hispanic American Historical Review* 41 (3): 367–412.

Crisp, L. F. 1979. *The Later Australian Federation Movement, 1883–1901: Outline and Bibliography.* Canberra: Research School of Social Sciences, Australian National University.

Crisp, L. F., and J. Hart. 1990. *Federation Fathers.* Carlton, Vic.: Melbourne University Press.

Crowly, F. 2000. *Big John Forrest, 1847–1918: A Founding Father of the Commonwealth of Australia.* Nedlands: University of Western Australia Press.

Dalziel, R. 1987. "'Misunderstandings Rather than Agreements': Intercolonial Negotiations, 1867–1883." In *Tasman Relations, New Zealand, and Australia, 1788–1988,* ed. K. Sinclair, 71–89. Auckland: Auckland University Press.

Davis, S. R. 1978. *The Federal Principle: A Journey through Time in Quest of a Meaning.* Berkeley: University of California Press.

Deakin, A. 1895. "The Federal Council of Australasia." *Review of Reviews,* 154–59.

Deakin, A., and J. A. La Nauze. 1963. *The Federal Story: The Inner History of the Federal Cause, 1880–1900.* Parkville, Vic.: Melbourne University Press.

de Figueiredo, R. J. P., and B. R. Weingast. 2005. "Self-Enforcing Federalism." *Journal of Law Economics and Organization* 21 (1): 103–35.

de Figueiredo, R., B. R. Weingast, and J. Rakove. 2000. "Rationality, Inaccurate Mental Models, and Self-Confirming Equilibrium: A New Understanding of the American Revolution." Typescript. University of California, Berkeley. http://faculty.haas.berkeley.edu/rui/ms1%5B1%5D.01.pdf.

Deudney, D. 1995. "The Philadelphia System—Sovereignty, Arms-Control, and Balance of Power in the American States-Union, circa 1787–1861." *International Organization* 49 (2): 191–228.

———. 2006. *Bounding Power: Republican Security Theory from the Polis to the Global Village.* Princeton: Princeton University Press.

Deutsch, K. W. 1968. *Political Community and the North Atlantic Area: International Organization in the Light of Historical Experience.* Princeton: Princeton University Press.

Dicey, A. V. 1885. *Lectures Introductory to the Study of the Law of the Constitution.* London: Macmillan.

Dickson, B. J. 2008. *Wealth and Power in Contemporary China: The Communist Party's Embrace of the Private Sector.* New York: Cambridge University Press.

Dion, S. 1996. "Why Is Secession Difficult in Well-Established Democracies? Lessons from Quebec." *British Journal of Political Science* 26:269–83.

Dixson, M. 1999. *The Imaginary Australian: Anglo-Celts and Identity, 1788 to the Present.* Sydney: University of New South Wales Press.

Donovan, P. 1990. "History of the Northern Territory." In *The Northern Territory in the Defence of Australia: Geography, History, Economy, Infrastructure, and Defence Presence,* ed. D. Ball and J. O. Langtry. Canberra: Australian National University Press.

Dougherty, K. L. 2001. *Collective Action under the Articles of Confederation.* New York: Cambridge University Press.

Douglas, A. P. 1909. *The Dominion of New Zealand.* London: Pitman.

Dowley, K. M., and B. D. Silver. 2000. "Subnational and National Loyalty: Cross-National Comparisons." *International Journal of Public Opinion Research* 12 (4): 357–71.

Doyle, M. W. 1986a. *Empires.* Ithaca: Cornell University Press.

——. 1986b. "Liberalism and World-Politics." *American Political Science Review* 80 (4): 1151–69.

Duchacek, I. D. 1970. *Comparative Federalism: The Territorial Dimension of Politics.* New York: Holt, Rinehart and Winston.

Duckworth, A. 1899. "The Economic Aspect of Australian Federation." *Economic Journal* 9 (34): 322–27.

Duffy, C. G. 1890. "Road to Australian Federation." *Contemporary Review* 57:153–69.

Eichengreen, B. 2007. "The Breakup of the Euro Area." National Bureau of Economic Research Working Paper 13393. Cambridge, Mass.

Elazar, D. J. 1988. *The American Constitutional Tradition.* Lincoln: University of Nebraska Press.

——. 1998a. *Constitutionalizing Globalization: The Postmodern Revival of Confederal Arrangements.* Lanham, Md.: Rowman & Littlefield.

——. 1998b. *Covenant and Constitutionalism: The Great Frontier and the Matrix of Federal Democracy.* New Brunswick, N.J.: Transaction.

Elkins, Z., and J. Sides. 2007. "Can Institutions Build Unity in Multiethnic States?" *American Political Science Review* 101 (4): 693–708.

Ellingsen, T. 1998. "Externalities vs. Internalities: A Model of Political Integration." *Journal of Public Economics* 68 (2): 251–68.

Emerson, R. 1960. *From Empire to Nation: The Rise to Self-Assertion of Asian and African Peoples.* Cambridge: Harvard University Press.

Enderlein, H. 2006. "Adjusting to EMU—The Impact of Supranational Monetary Policy on Domestic Fiscal and Wage-Setting Institutions." *European Union Politics* 7 (1): 113–40.

Etzioni, A. 1965. *Political Unification: A Comparative Study of Leaders and Forces.* New York: Holt, Rinehart and Winston.

Eyck, E. 1950. *Bismarck and the German Empire.* London: Allen & Unwin.

Fazal, T. M. 2004. "State Death in the International System." *International Organization* 58 (2): 311–44.

Fearon, J. D. 1994. "Domestic Political Audiences and the Escalation of International Disputes." *American Political Science Review* 88 (3): 577–92.

——. 2007. "Iraq's Civil War." *Foreign Affairs* 86 (2): 2–15.

Fearon, J. D., and D. D. Laitin. 2000. "Violence, and the Social Construction of Ethnic Identity." *International Organization* 54 (4): 845–77.

Feuchtwanger, E. J. 2002. *Bismarck*. New York: Routledge.

Filippov, M., P. C. Ordeshook, and O. Shvetsova. 2003. *Designing Federalism: A Theory of Self-Sustainable Federal Institutions*. New York: Cambridge University Press.

Finnemore, M. 2003. *The Purpose of Intervention: Changing Beliefs about the Use of Force*. Ithaca: Cornell University Press.

Flanz, G. 1968. "The West Indies Federation." In *Why Federations Fail: An Inquiry into the Requisites for Successful Federalism,* ed. T. M. Franck, xv, 213. New York: New York University Press.

Flockerzie, L. 1991. "State-Building and Nation-Building in the 'Third Germany': Saxony after the Congress of Vienna." *Central European History* 24 (3): 268–92.

Forsyth, M. G. 1981. *Unions of States: The Theory and Practice of Confederation*. New York: Leicester University Press Holmes & Meier.

Franck, T. M. 1964. *East African Unity through Law*. New Haven: Yale University Press.

———. 1968. *Why Federations Fail: An Inquiry into the Requisites for Successful Federalism*. New York: New York University Press.

Freeman, E. A. 1863. *History of Federal Government*. London: Macmillan.

French, M. 1978. "Ambiguity of Empire Day in New-South-Wales, 1901–21—Imperial Consensus or National Division." *Australian Journal of Politics and History* 24 (1): 61–74.

Frieden, J. A. 1994. "International Investment and Colonial Control—A New Interpretation." *International Organization* 48 (4): 559–93.

———. 1999. "Actors and Preferences in International Relations." In *Strategic Choice and International Relations*, ed. D. Lake and R. Powell, 39–76. Princeton: Princeton University Press.

Friedjung, H. 1935. *The Struggle for Supremacy in Germany, 1859–1866*. London: Macmillan.

Friedman, D. 1977. "A Theory of the Size and Shape of Nations." *Journal of Political Economy* 85 (1): 59–77.

Gall, L. 1986. *Bismarck: The White Revolutionary*. London: Allen & Unwin.

Galloway, W. J. 1899. *Advanced Australia: A Short Account of Australia on the Eve of Federation*. London: Methuen.

Garran, R. 1897. *The Coming Commonwealth: An Australian Handbook of Federal Government*. Sydney: Angus & Robertson.

———. 1933. *The Cambridge History of the British Empire*, Volume 7, Part 1, *The Federation Movement and the Founding of the Commonwealth*. Cambridge: Cambridge University Press.

Gartzke, E., and K. S. Gleditsch. 2004. "Why Democracies May Actually Be Less Reliable Allies." *American Journal of Political Science* 48 (4): 775–95.

Gehlbach, S. 2006. "A Formal Model of Exit and Voice." *Rationality and Society* 18 (4): 395–418.

Ghai, D. 1965. "Territorial Distribution of the Benefits and Costs of the East African Common Market." *Federation in East Africa: Opportunities and Problems,* ed. C. Leys and P. Robson, 72–82. London: Oxford University Press.

Gillingham, J. 2006. *Design for a New Europe.* New York: Cambridge University Press.

Goldstein, L. F. 2001. *Constituting Federal Sovereignty: The European Union in Comparative Context.* Baltimore: Johns Hopkins University Press.

Goldsworthy, A. K. 2003. *The Complete Roman Army.* New York: Thames & Hudson.

Goodwin, P. B., Jr. 1977. "The Central Argentine Railway and the Economic Development of Argentina, 1854–1881." *Hispanic American Historical Review* 57 (4): 613–32.

Gordon, D. 1984. "Foreign Relations Dilemmas of Independence and Development." In *Politics and Public Policy in Kenya and Tanzania,* ed. J. D. Barkan, 297–336. New York: Praeger.

Gordon, N., and B. Knight. 2006. "The Causes of Political Integration: An Application to School Districts." National Bureau of Economic Research Working Paper 12047. Cambridge, Mass.

Gould, D. M. 1994. "Immigrant Links to the Home Country—Empirical Implications for United-States Bilateral Trade-Flows." *Review of Economics and Statistics* 76 (2): 302–16.

Gourevitch, P. 1999. "The Governance Problem in International Relations." In *Strategic Choice and International Relations,* ed. D. A. Lake and R. Powell, 271. Princeton: Princeton University Press.

Gowa, J., and E. D. Mansfield. 2004. "Alliances, Imperfect Markets, and Major-Power Trade." *International Organization* 58 (4): 775–805.

Grey, J. 1990. *A Military History of Australia.* Cambridge: Cambridge University Press.

———. 2001. *The Australian Army.* South Melbourne: Oxford University Press.

Grey, J. G. 1901. *Australasia Old and New.* London: Hodder & Stoughton.

Grieco, J. M. 1982. "Between Dependency and Autonomy—India's Experience with the International Computer Industry." *International Organization* 36 (3): 609–32.

Griffith, S. W. 1896a. *Notes on Australian Federation: Its Nature and Probable Effects.* Brisbane, Queensland: Edmund Gregory, Government Printer.

———. 1896b. *Some Conditions of Australian Federation.* Brisbane, Queensland: Edmund Gregory, Government Printer.

Grodzins, M. 1966. *The American System: A New View of Government in the United States.* Chicago: Rand McNally.

Gross, A. 1948. *Attainment: Being a Critical Study of the Literature of Federation.* Melbourne: Bread and Cheese Club.

Grossman, S., and O. Hart. 1986. "The Costs and Benefits of Ownership: A Theory of Vertical and Lateral Integration." *Journal of Political Economy* 94 (4): 691–719.

Gruber, L. 2000. *Ruling the World: Power Politics and the Rise of Supranational Institutions.* Princeton: Princeton University Press.

Haftel, Y. Z., and A. Thompson. 2006. "The Independence of International Organizations—Concept and Applications." *Journal of Conflict Resolution* 50 (2): 253–75.

Hallerberg, M., and K. Weber. 2002. "German Unification 1815–1871 and Its Relevance for Integration Theory." *European Integration* 24 (1): 1–21.

Halperín Donghi, T. 1972. *Argentina: De la Revolución de independencia a la Confederación rosista.* Buenos Aires: Editorial Paidós.

Hamnett, B. R. 1997. "Process and Pattern: A Re-Examination of the Ibero-American Independence Movements, 1808–1826." *Journal of Latin American Studies* 29 (2): 279–328.

Hancock, K. 2001. "Surrendering Sovereignty: Hierarchy in the International System and the Former Soviet Union." Ph.D. thesis, University of California–San Diego.

Hanna, W. A. 1965. *Sequel to Colonialism: The 1957–1960 Foundations for Malaysia: An On-the-Spot Examination of the Geographic, Economic, and Political Seedbed Where the Idea of a Federation of Malaysia Was Germinated.* New York: American University Field Staff.

Harman, G. 1970. "Politics and Railway Development in New England." *Journal of the Royal Australian Historical Society* 56 (4): 281–95.

Harrison, S. S. 2002. *Korean Endgame: A Strategy for Reunification and U.S. Disengagement.* Princeton: Princeton University Press.

Hart, O. 2007. *Hold-up, Asset Ownership, and Reference Points.* Cambridge, Mass.: National Bureau of Economic Research.

Hart, O., and J. Moore. 1990. "Property-Rights and the Nature of the Firm." *Journal of Political Economy* (6): 1119–58.

———. 2005. "On the Design of Hierarchies: Coordination versus Specialization." *Journal of Political Economy* 113 (4): 675–702.

———. 2007. "Incomplete Contracts and Ownership: Some New Thoughts." *American Economic Review* 97 (2): 182–86.

Hart, R. 1998. *From Occupation to Independence: A Short History of the Peoples of the English-Speaking Caribbean Region.* London: Pluto Press.

Hazlewood, A. 1975. *Economic Integration: The East African Experience.* New York: St. Martin's Press.

Heckathorn, D. 1989. "Collective Action and the Second-Order Free-Rider Problem." *Rationality and Society* 1 (1): 78–100.

Helliwell, J. F. 1996. "Do National Borders Matter for Quebec's Trade?" *Canadian Journal of Economics—Revue Canadienne d'Economique* 29 (3): 507–22.

Herbst, J. I. 2000. *States and Power in Africa: Comparative Lessons in Authority and Control.* Princeton: Princeton University Press.

Hewett, P. 1969. "Aspects of Campaigns in South-eastern New South Wales at the Federation Referenda of 1898 and 1899." In *Essays in Australian Federation,* ed. A. W. Martin, 167–85. Carlton, Vic.: Melbourne University Press.

Hirschman, A. O. 1945. *National Power and the Structure of Foreign Trade.* Berkeley: University of California Press.

——. 1970. *Exit, Voice, and Loyalty: Responses to Decline in Firms, Organizations, and States.* Cambridge: Harvard University Press.

Hirst, J. 2000. *The Sentimental Nation: The Making of the Australian Commonwealth.* Melbourne: Oxford University Press.

Hiscox, M. J. 2002. *International Trade and Political Conflict: Commerce, Coalitions, and Mobility.* Princeton: Princeton University Press.

Hobbes, T. 1968[1651]. *Leviathan.* Baltimore: Penguin Books.

Hoffman, S. 1964. "The European Process at Atlantic Crosspurposes." *Journal of Common Market Studies* 3:85–101.

Hollander, E. 2006. "Swords or Shields? Collaboration and Resistance in Nazi-Occupied Europe." Ph.D. thesis. University of California–San Diego.

Holt, M. F. 1978. *The Political Crisis of the 1850s.* New York: Wiley.

Howard, P. 2004. "Why Not Invade North Korea? Threats, Language Games, and U.S. Foreign Policy." *International Studies Quarterly* 48 (4): 805–28.

Hudson, R. 1891. "The Formation of the North German Confederation." *Political Science Quarterly* 6 (3): 424–38.

Hudson, R. A., and D. Seyler. 1989. "Jamaica." In *Islands of the Commonwealth Caribbean: A Regional Study,* ed. S. W. Meditz and D. M. Hanratty, xxix, 771. Washington, D.C.: U.S. Government Printing Office.

Hughes, C. A., and B. D. Graham. 1968. *A Handbook of Australian Government and Politics, 1890–1964.* Canberra: Australian National University Press.

Huntington, S. P. 1957. *The Soldier and the State: The Theory and Politics of Civil-Military Relations.* Cambridge: Belknap Press of Harvard University Press.

Ikenberry, G. J. 1998. "Constitutional Politics in International Relations." *European Journal of International Relations* 4 (2): 147–77.

Irvine, R. F., and O. T. J. Alpers. 1902. *The Progress of New Zealand in the Century.* Philadelphia: Linscott.

Irving, H. 1999. *To Constitute a Nation: A Cultural History of Australia's Constitution.* Melbourne: Cambridge University Press.

Irwin, D. A. 2006. *The Impact of Federation on Australia's Trade Flows.* Cambridge, Mass.: National Bureau of Economic Research.

Jackson, P. T. 2006. *Civilizing the Enemy: German Reconstruction and the Invention of the West.* Ann Arbor: University of Michigan Press.

Jebb, R. 1905. *Studies in Colonial Nationaism.* London: E. Arnold.

Johnson, D. H. 1974. *Volunteers at Heart: The Queensland Defence Forces, 1860–1901.* St. Lucia: University of Queensland Press.

Jones, J. 2007. "The Report of the Independent Commission on the Security Forces of Iraq." *Center for Strategic and International Studies* (September 6). http://www.csis.org/media/csis/pubs/isf.pdf

Jones, R., and C. Fowler. 2007. "National Elites, National Masses: Oral History and the (Re)Production of the Welsh Nation." *Social & Cultural Geography* 8 (3): 417–32.

Josselin, J. M., and A. Marciano. 1999. "Unitary States and Peripheral Regions: A Model of Heterogeneous Spatial Clubs." *International Review of Law and Economics* 19 (4): 501–11.

Jung, J. K. 2008. "The Paradox of Institution Building after Civil War." *Political Science*. Ithaca: Cornell University.

Kabwegyere, T. B. 1974. *The Politics of State Formation: The Nature and Effects of Colonialism in Uganda*. Nairobi: East African Literature Bureau.

Kahl, C. H. 2000. "States, Scarcity, and Civil Strife in the Developing World." *Political Science*. New York: Columbia University.

Kahl, C., M. Flournoy, and S. Brimley. 2008. "Shaping the Iraq Inheritance." *Center for a New American Security* (June): 36–37.

Kahler, M., and S. L. Kastner. 2006. "Strategic Uses of Economic Interdependence: Engagement Policies on the Korean Peninsula and across the Taiwan Strait." *Journal of Peace Research* 43 (5): 523–41.

Kastner, S. L. 2003. "Commerce in the Shadow of Conflict." *Political Science*. La Jolla: University of California–San Diego.

Kastner, S. L., and C. Rector. 2008. "National Unification and Mistrust: Bargaining Power and the Prospects for a PRC/Taiwan Agreement." *Security Studies* 17 (1): 1–33.

Katulis, B., C. Kahl, and M. Lynch. 2008. "Thinking Strategically about Iraq: Report from a Symposium." *Middle East Policy* (Spring).

Katulis, B., M. Lynch, and P. Juul. 2008. "Iraq's Political Transition after the Surge: Five Enduring Tensions and Ten Key Challenges." *Center for American Progress* (September).

Kaufman, S. J. 1997. "The Fragmentation and Consolidation of International Systems." *International Organization* 51 (2): 173–+.

Keohane, R. O. 1971. "The Big Influence of Small Allies." *Foreign Policy* 2 (Spring): 161–82.

———. 1984. *After Hegemony: Cooperation and Discord in the World Political Economy*. Princeton: Princeton University Press.

Keohane, R. O., and L. L. Martin. 1995. "The Promise of Institutionalist Theory." *International Security* 20 (1): 39–51.

Kimei, C. S. 1987. "Tanzania's Financial Experience in the Post-War Period." Stockholm: Acta Universitatis Upsaliensis.

King, P. T. 1982. *Federalism and Federation*. Baltimore: Johns Hopkins University Press.

Klein, B., R. G. Crawford, and A. A. Alchian. 1978. "Vertical Integration, Appropriable Rents, and the Competitive Contracting Process." *Journal of Law & Economics* 21 (2): 297–326.

Klein, B., and K. M. Murphy. 1988. "Vertical Restraints as Contract Enforcement Mechanisms." *Journal of Law & Economics* 31 (2): 265–97.

Knightly, P. 2000. *Australia: A Biography of a Nation*. London: Jonathan Cape.

Koch, H. W. 1984. *A Constitutional History of Germany in the Nineteenth and Twentieth Centuries*. New York: Longman.

Koremenos, B., C. Lipson, and D. Snidal. 2001a. "Rational Design: Looking Back to Move Forward." *International Organization* 55 (4): 1051–82.

———. 2001b. "The Rational Design of International Institutions." *International Organization* 55 (4): 761–99.

Kornblith, G. J. 2003. "Rethinking the Coming of the Civil War: A Counterfactual Exercise." *Journal of American History* 90 (1): 76–105.

Krasner, S. D. 1983. *International Regimes.* Ithaca: Cornell University Press.

Kreps, D. M. 1990. "Corporate Culture and Economic Theory." In *Perspectives on Positive Political Economy,* ed. J. E. Alt and K. A. Shepsle, 90–143. New York: Cambridge University Press.

Kurtz, D. M. 1970. "Political Integration in Africa: The Mali Federation." *Journal of Modern African Studies* 8 (3): 405–24.

Laitin, D. D. 1986. *Hegemony and Culture: Politics and Religious Change among the Yoruba.* Chicago: University of Chicago Press.

——. 1994. "The Tower-of-Babel as a Coordination Game—Political Linguistics in Ghana." *American Political Science Review* 88 (3): 622–34.

——. 1998. *Identity in Formation: The Russian-Speaking Populations in the Near Abroad.* Ithaca: Cornell University Press.

——. 2007. *Nations, States, and Violence.* New York: Oxford University Press.

Lake, D. A. 1992. "Powerful Pacifists—Democratic States and War." *American Political Science Review* 86 (1): 24–37.

——. 1999. *Entangling Relations: American Foreign Policy in Its Century.* Princeton: Princeton University Press.

——. 2007. "Escape from the State of Nature—Authority and Hierarchy in World Politics." *International Security* 32 (1): 47–+.

——. 2009. *Hierarchy in International Relations: Authority, Sovereignty, and the New Structure of World Politics.* Ithaca: Cornell University Press.

Lake, D. A., and A. O'Mahony. 2004. "The Incredible Shrinking State: Explaining the Territorial Size of Countries." *Journal of Conflict Resolution* 48 (5): 699–722.

Lake, D. A., and D. S. Rothchild. 2005. "Territorial Decentralization and Civil War Settlements." In *Sustainable Peace: Power and Democracy after Civil Wars,* ed. P. G. Roeder and D. S. Rothchild. Ithaca: Cornell University Press.

La Nauze, J. A. 1972. *The Making of the Australian Constitution.* Melbourne: Melbourne University Press.

Lee, W. R. 1988. "Economic-Development and the State in Nineteenth-Century Germany." *Economic History Review* 41 (3): 346–67.

Lemco, J. 1991. *Political Stability in Federal Governments.* New York: Praeger.

Lerman, K. A. 2004. *Bismarck: Profiles in Power.* New York: Longman.

Lewis, G. 1976. "Australian Nationalism and the Queensland Tariff Debate." *Journal of the Royal Australian Historical Society* 62 (3): 168–78.

Lewis, P. 2002. *Surviving Small Size: Regional Integration in Caribbean Ministates.* Barbados: University of the West Indies Press.

Leys, C. 1965. "Recent Relations between the States of East Africa." *International Journal* 20 (4): 510–23.

Leys, C., and P. Robson. 1965. *Federation in East Africa: Opportunities and Problems.* London: Oxford University Press.

Liberman, P. 1996. *Does Conquest Pay? The Exploitation of Occupied Industrial Societies.* Princeton: Princeton University Press.

Lijphart, A. 1999. *Patterns of Democracy: Government Forms and Performance in Thirty-Six Countries.* New Haven: Yale University Press.

Lipson, C. 2003. *Reliable Partners: How Democracies Have Made a Separate Peace.* Princeton: Princeton University Press.

Lister, F. K. 1996. *The European Union, the United Nations, and the Revival of Confederal Governance.* Westport, Conn.: Greenwood Press.

———. 2001. *The Later Security Confederations: The American, "New" Swiss, and German Unions.* Westport, Conn.: Greenwood Press.

Livingston, W. R. 1932. "Australasia in Conference, 1883–1887." *Pacific History Review* 1:60–81.

Livingston, W. S. 1952. "A Note on the Nature of Federalism." *Political Science Quarterly* 67:81–95.

Lomas, P. 2005. "Anthropomorphism, Personification, and Ethics: A Reply to Alexander Wendt." *Review of International Studies* 31 (2): 349–55.

Loveday, P. 1972. "The Federal Convention: An Analysis of the Voting." *Australian Journal of Politics and History* 18 (2): 169–88.

Loveday, P., and A. W. Martin. 1966. *Parliament Factions and Parties: The First Thirty Years of Responsible Government in New South Wales, 1856–1889.* Melbourne: Melbourne University Press; New York: Cambridge University Press.

Loveday, P., A. W. Martin, and R. S. Parker. 1977. *The Emergence of the Australian Party System.* Sydney: Hale & Iremonger.

Lowenheim, O. 2003. "'Do ourselves credit and render a lasting service to mankind': British Moral Prestige, Humanitarian Intervention, and the Barbary Pirates." *International Studies Quarterly* 47 (1): 23–48.

Lowenthal, D. 1961. *The West Indies Federation: Perspectives on a New Nation.* New York: Columbia University Press.

Macfie, M. 1893. "Australia under Protection." *Economic Journal* 3 (10): 297–307.

MacLeod, I. 1985. "Iain MacLeod to Harold Macmillan, 22 September 1961." In *Select Documents on the Constitutional History of the British Empire and Commonwealth: The Foundations of a Colonial System Of Government,* ed. A. F. Madden, D. K. Fieldhouse, and J. Darwin, vols. 1–7; vol. 8, pt. 1. Westport, Conn.: Greenwood Press.

Maddox, W. P. 1941. "The Political Basis of Federation." *American Political Science Review* 35 (6): 1120–27.

Mandle, W. F. 1973. "Cricket and Australian Nationalism in the Nineteenth Century." *Journal of the Royal Australian Historical Society* 59 (4): 225–46.

Mansfield, E. D., and H. V. Milner. 1997. *The Political Economy of Regionalism.* New York: Columbia University Press.

Marks, G., L. Hooghe, and K. Blank. 1996. "European Integration from the 1980s: State-centric v. Multi-level Governance." *Journal of Common Market Studies* 34 (3): 341–78.

Martin, A. W. 1964. "Economic Influences in the 'New Federation Movement.'" In *Historical Studies: Australia and New Zealand,* ed. J. J. Eastwood and F. B. Smith, 215–25. Box Hill, Vic.: Melbourne University Press.

———. 1969. *Essays in Australian Federation.* Melbourne: Melbourne University Press.

———. 1980. *Henry Parkes: A Biography.* Carlton, Vic.: Melbourne University Press.

Martin, D. 1988. *Tanzanie: L'Invention d'une culture politique.* Paris: Presses de la Fondation nationale des sciences politiques.

Martin, L. 2003. *Iron Man: The Defiant Reign of Jean Chrâetien.* Toronto: Viking Canada.

Martin, L. L. 1992. "Interests, Power, and Multilateralism." *International Organization* 46 (4): 765–92.

———. 2000. *Democratic Commitments: Legislatures and International Cooperation.* Princeton: Princeton University Press.

Martin, L. L., and B. A. Simmons. 1998. "Theories and Empirical Studies of International Institutions." *International Organization* 52 (4): 729–57.

Mattli, W. 1999. *The Logic of Regional Integration: Europe and Beyond.* New York: Cambridge University Press.

Mattli, W., and A. M. Slaughter. 1998. "Revisiting the European Court of Justice." *International Organization* 52 (1): 177–+.

Mayer, F. 1998. *Interpreting NAFTA: The Science and Art of Political Analysis.* New York: Columbia University Press.

Mazrui, A. A. 1965. "Tanzania versus East Africa." *Journal of Commonwealth Studies* 3 (3).

Mazrui, A. A., and D. Rothchild. 1967. "The Soldier and the State in East Africa: Some Theoretical Conclusions on the Army Mutinies of 1964." *Western Political Quarterly* 20 (1): 82–96.

McKay, D. H. 2001. *Designing Europe: Comparative Lessons from the Federal Experience.* New York: Oxford University Press.

McKay, D. H. 1999. *Federalism and European Union: A Political Economy Perspective.* New York: Oxford University Press.

McLaren, J. 1997. "Size, Sunk Costs, and Judge Bowker's Objection to Free Trade." *American Economic Review* 87 (3): 400–420.

McLean, D. 1995. *War, Diplomacy, and Informal Empire: Britain and the Republics of La Plata, 1836–1853.* New York: St. Martin's Press.

McMinn, W. G. 1979. *A Constitutional History of Australia.* Melbourne: Oxford University Press.

Meighoo, K. P. 2003. *Politics in a "Half Made Society": Trinidad and Tobago, 1925–2002.* Kingston, Jamaica: Ian Randle.

Meyerson, B. B., D. Seyler, and J. Hornbeck. 1989. "Trinidad and Tobago." In *Islands of the Commonwealth Caribbean: A Regional Study,* ed. S. W. Meditz and D. M. Hanratty, xxix, 771. Washington, D.C.: U.S. Government Printing Office.

Millar, T. B. 1969. *Australia's Defence.* Melbourne: Melbourne University Press.

Milner, H. V. 1997. *Interests, Institutions, and Information: Domestic Politics and International Relations.* Princeton: Princeton University Press.

Mines, F. J. 1969. *Premiers' Conferences and Other Intercolonial Conferences in Australasia before Federation.* Canberra: Arrow Press.

Mitchell, A. 1979. "'A Real Foreign Country': Bavarian Particularism in Imperial Germany, 1870–1918." *Francia* 7:587–96.

Moore, W. H. 1910. *The Constitution of the Commonwealth of Australia.* Melbourne: C. F. Maxwell, G. Partridge.

Moravcsik, A. 1993. "Preferences and Power in the European-Community— A Liberal Intergovernmentalist Approach." *Journal of Common Market Studies* 31 (4): 473–524.

———. 1998. *The Choice for Europe: Social Purpose and State Power from Messina to Maastricht.* Ithaca: Cornell University Press.

———. 1999. "A New Statecraft? Supranational Entrepreneurs and International Cooperation." *International Organization* 53 (2): 267–+.

———. 2006. "Restructuring Europe: Centre Formation, System Building, and Political Structuring between the Nation State and the European Union." *West European Politics* 29 (3): 589–90.

Moravcsik, A., and M. A. Vachudova. 2003. "National Interests, State Power, and EU Enlargement." *East European Politics and Societies* 17 (1): 42–57.

Moreno, I. J. R. 1965. "El Litoral Despues de Pavon, septiembre–diciembre 1861." In *Pavon y la Crisis de la Confederation.* E. d. I. Historica, 311–462. Buenos Aires: Equipos de Investigation Historica.

Morgenthau, H. J. 1954. *Politics among Nations: The Struggle for Power and Peace.* New York: Knopf.

Mpangala, G. P. 1992. *Major Issues in Tanzanian Economic History.* Dar es Salaam: Dar es Salaam University Press.

Nethercote, J. R. 2001. *Liberalism and the Australian Federation.* Annandale, N.S.W.: Federation Press.

Newman, P. 1965. "The Economics of Integration in East Africa." In *Federation in East Africa: Opportunities and Problems,* ed. C. Leys and P. Robson, 56–71. London: Oxford University Press.

Nexon, D., and T. Wright. 2007. "What's at Stake in the American Empire Debate." *American Political Science Review* 101 (2): 253–71.

Nielson, D. L., and M. I. Tierney. 2003. "Delegation to International Organizations: Agency Theory and World Bank Environmental Reform." *International Organization* 57 (2): 241–+.

Niou, E. M. S. 2004. "Understanding Taiwan Independence and Its Policy Implications." *Asian Survey* 44 (4): 555–67.

Nixson, F. I. 1973. *Economic Integration and Industrial Location—An East African Case Study.* Harlow: Longman.

Norris, R. 1969. "Economic Influences on the 1898 South Australian Federation Referendum." In *Essays in Australian Federation,* ed. A. W. Martin. Carlton, Vic.: Melbourne University Press.

———. 1975. *The Emergent Commonwealth: Australian Federation, Expectations, and Fulfilment, 1889–1910.* Carlton, Vic.: Melbourne University Press.

Nye, J. S. 1965. *Pan-Africanism and East African Integration.* Cambridge: Harvard University Press.

——. 1968. "Comparative Regional Integration: Concept and Measurement." *International Organization* 22 (4): 855–80.

Oates, W. E. 1972. *Fiscal Federalism.* New York: Harcourt Brace Jovanovich.

Okoth, P. G. 1994. "The Foreign Policy of Uganda toward Kenya and Tanzania." In *Politics and Administration in East Africa,* ed. W. Oyugi, 359–94. Nairobi: East African Educational Publishers.

Oliver, P. E., and G. Marwell. 1988. "The Paradox of Group-Size in Collective Action—A Theory of the Critical Mass." *American Sociological Review* 53 (1): 1–8.

——. 2001. "Whatever Happened to Critical Mass Theory? A Retrospective and Assessment." *Sociological Theory* 19 (3): 292–311.

Olson, M. 1965. *The Logic of Collective Action: Public Goods and the Theory Of Groups.* Cambridge: Harvard University Press.

Olson, M., and R. Zeckhauser. 1966. "An Economic Theory of Alliances." *Review of Economics and Statistics* 48:266–79.

Ordeshook, P. C., and E. Niou. 1998. "Alliances versus Federations: An Extension of Riker's Analysis of Federal Formation." *Constitutional Political Economy* 9:271–88.

Orwa, D. K. 1994. "Change and Continuity in Kenya's Foreign Policy from Kenyatta to Moi." In *Politics and Administration in East Africa,* ed. W. Oyugi, 297–330. Nairobi: East African Educational Publishers.

Osborne, M. J., and A. Rubinstein. 1990. *Bargaining and Markets.* San Diego: Academic Press.

Parent, J. 2006. "E Pluribus Unum: Political Unification and Political Realism." *Political Science.* New York: Columbia University.

Parker, R. S. 1964. "Australian Federation: The Influence of Economic Interests and Political Pressures." In *Historical Studies: Australia and New Zealand,* ed. J. J. Eastwood and F. B. Smith, 152–78. Box Hill, Vic.: Melbourne University Press.

Parsons, C. 2003. *A Certain Idea of Europe.* Ithaca: Cornell University Press.

Parsons, H. G. 1899. "Australian Federation—From the Inside." *Fortnightly Review* 66:612–21.

Pflanze, O. 1963. *Bismarck and the Development of Germany: The Period of Unification, 1815–1871.* Princeton: Princeton University Press.

Piddington, A. B. 1929. *Worshipful Masters.* Sydney: Angus & Robertson.

Pierson, P. 1996. "The Path to the European Integration—A Historical Institutionalist Analysis." *Comparative Political Studies* 29 (2): 123–63.

Pollack, J. D., and C. M. Lee. 1999. *Preparing for Korean Unification: Scenarios and Implications.* Santa Monica, Calif.: RAND.

Pollack, M. A. 2003. *The Engines of European Integration: Delegation, Agency, and Agenda Setting in the EU.* New York: Oxford University Press.

Poole, K. T., and H. Rosenthal. 1997. *Congress: A Political-Economic History of Roll Call Voting.* New York: Oxford University Press.

Porritt, E. 1922. *The Fiscal and Diplomatic Freedom of the British Overseas Dominions.* Oxford: Clarendon Press.

Pringle, R. 1975. "The Federation Issue in New South Wales Politics, 1891–99." *Australian Journal of Politics and History* 21 (2): 1–12.

Proctor, J. H. J. 1956. "The Functional Approach to Political Union: Lessons from the Effort to Federate the British Caribbean Territories." *International Organization* 10 (1): 35–48.

Pye, L. 1971. "Identity and Political Culture." In *Crises and Sequences in Political Development: Studies In Political Development*, ed. L. Binder, 7:xi, 326. Princeton: Princeton University Press:

Raiffa, H. 1982. *The Art and Science of Negotiation*. Cambridge: Belknap Press of Harvard University Press.

Rauch, J. E. 1999. "Networks versus Markets in International Trade." *Journal of International Economics* 48 (1): 7–35.

Rauch, J. E., and J. Watson. 2004. "Network Intermediaries in International Trade." *Journal of Economics and Management Strategy* 13 (1): 69–93.

Rector, C. 2001. "Buying Treaties with Cigarettes: Internal Side-Payments in Two-Level Games." *International Interactions* 27 (3): 207–38.

Reeves, W. P. 1899. "Protective Tariffs in Australia and New Zealand." *Economic Journal* 9 (33): 36–44.

———. 1901. "The Attitude of New Zealand." *Empire Review* 1 (1): 111–15.

———. 1902. *State Experiments in Australia and New Zealand*. London: A. Horing.

Reid, G. H. 1917. *My Reminiscences*. London: Cassell.

Riker, W. H. 1957. *Soldiers of the States: The Role of the National Guard in American Democracy*. Washington, D.C.: Public Affairs Press.

———. 1964. *Federalism: Origin, Operation, Significance*. Boston: Little, Brown.

———. 1975. "Federalism." In *Handbook of Political Science*, Vol 5, ed. F. Greenstein and N. Polsby. Reading, Mass.: Addison-Wesley.

———. 1980. "Implications from the Disequilibrium of Majority Rule for the Study of Institutions." *American Political Science Review* 74 (2): 432–46.

———. 1987. *The Development of American Federalism*. Boston: Kluwer Academic.

Riordan, M. H., and O. E. Williamson. 1985. "Asset Specificity, and Economic Organization." *International Journal of Industrial Organization* 3 (4): 365–78.

Risse, T. 1995. *Cooperation among Democracies: The European Influence on U.S. Foreign Policy*. Princeton: Princeton University Press.

———. 2004. "Social Constructivism, and European Integration." In *European Integration Theory*, ed. A. Wiener and T. Diez, xvi, 290. New York: Oxford University Press.

Robertson, A. N. 1897. *Federation and Afterwards: A Fragment of History, A.D. 1898–1912*. Sydney: Angus & Robertson.

Robertson, C. G. 1918. *Bismarck*. London: Constable.

Rock, D. 1985. *Argentina, 1516–1982: From Spanish Colonization to the Falklands War*. Berkeley: University of California Press.

Rodrik, D. 2000. "How Far Will International Economic Integration Go?" *Journal of Economic Perspectives* 14 (1): 177–86.

Roeder, P. G. 2007. *Where Nation-States Come From: Institutional Change in the Age of Nationalism*. Princeton: Princeton University Press.

Roeder, P. G., and D. S. Rothchild. 2005. "Dilemmas of State-Building in Divided Societies." In *Sustainable Peace: Power and Democracy after Civil Wars,* ed. P. G. Roeder and D. S. Rothchild. Ithaca: Cornell University Press.

Rose, A. K. 2006. "Size Really Doesn't Matter: In Search of a National Scale Effect." National Bureau of Economic Research Working Paper 12191. Cambridge, Mass.

Rothchild, D. S. 1960. *Toward Unity in Africa: A Study of Federalism in British Africa.* Washington, D.C.: Public Affairs Press.

———. 1964. "East African Federation." *Transition* 12:39–42.

———. 1966. "The Limits of Federalism: An Examination of Political Institutional Transfer in Africa." *Journal of Modern African Studies* 4 (3): 275–93.

———. 1968. *Politics of Integration: An East African Documentary.* Nairobi: East African Publishing House.

Ruane, K. 2000. *The Rise and Fall of the European Defence Community: Anglo-American Relations and the Crisis Of European Defence, 1950–55.* New York: Macmillan.

Russett, B., and J. Sullivan. 1971. "Collective Goods and International Organization." *International Organization* 25 (4): 845–65.

Rustow, D. A. 1967. *A World of Nations: Problems of Political Modernization.* Washington, D.C.: Brookings Institution.

Sadleir, R. 1999. *Tanzania, Journey to Republic.* New York: Radcliffe Press.

Sandler, T. 2004. *Global Collective Action.* New York: Cambridge University Press.

Saunders, M. 1985. "Parliament and the NSW Contingent to the Sudan in 1885: The Dissection of a Debate." *Journal of the Royal Australian Historical Society* 70 (4): 227–50.

Sawer, G. 1969. *Modern Federalism.* London: Watts.

Sawer, M. 2001. *Elections: Full, Free, and Fair.* Annandale, N.S.W.: Federation Press.

Schelling, T. C. 1966. *Arms and Influence.* New Haven: Yale University Press.

———. 1978. *Micromotives and Macrobehavior.* New York: Norton.

Schwartz, A., and J. Watson. 2004. "The Law and Economics of Costly Contracting." *Journal of Law Economics and Organization* 20 (1): 2–31.

Schwartzberg, M. 2004. "Athenian Democracy and Legal Change." *American Political Science Review* 98 (2): 311–25.

Seckinger, R. L. 1976. "South American Power Politics during the 1820s." *Hispanic American Historical Review* 56 (2): 241–67.

Serle, G. 1969. "The Victorian Government's Campaign for Federation, 1883–1889." In *Essays in Australian Federation,* ed. A. W. Martin, 1–56. Carlton, Vic.: Melbourne University Press.

Shannon, V. P. 2005. "Wendt's Violation of the Constructivist Project: Agency and Why a World State Is Not Inevitable." *European Journal of International Relations* 11 (4): 581–87.

Shivakoti, G., and E. Ostrom. 2002. *Improving Irrigation Governance and Management in Nepal.* Oakland, Calif.: ICS Press.

Shivji, I. G. 1990. *The Legal Foundations of the Union in Tanzania's Union and Zanzibar Constitutions.* Dar es Salaam: Dar es Salaam University Press.

Shortus, S. P. 1973. "'Colonial Nationalism': New South Welsh Identity in the Mid-1880s." *Journal of the Royal Australian Historical Society* 59 (1).

Sidgwick, H., and E. M. Sidgwick. 1903. *The Development of European Polity.* New York: Macmillan.

Silver, M. S. 1984. *The Growth of Manufacturing Industry in Tanzania: An Economic History.* Boulder, Colo.: Westview Press.

Simon, S. 2008. "The Price of the Surge." *Foreign Affairs* (May/June).

Sinclair, K. 1970. "Australian Inter-Governmental Negotiations 1865–80: Ocean Mails and Tariffs." *Australian Journal of Politics and History* 16 (2): 151–76.

———. 1986a. *A Destiny Apart: New Zealand's Search for National Identity.* Wellington, N.Z.; North Sydney: Allen & Unwin, with Port Nicholson Press.

———. 1986b. *The Native Born: The Origins of New Zealand Nationalism.* Occasional Publication Number 8. Auckland, N.Z.: Massey University.

———. 1987. "Why New Zealanders Are Not Australians: New Zealand and the Australian Federation Movement, 1881–1901." In *Tasman Relations: New Zealand and Australia, 1788–1988,* ed. K. Sinclair, 90–103. Auckland: Auckland University Press.

Slapin, J. B. 2008. "Bargaining Power at Europe's Intergovernmental Conferences: Testing Institutional and Intergovernmental Theories." *International Organization* 62 (1): 131–62.

Smith, A. 1776. *An Inquiry into the Nature and Causes of the Wealth of Nations.* London: Printed for W. Strahan and T. Cadell.

Smith, A. 1998. "International Crises and Domestic Politics." *American Political Science Review* 92 (3): 623–38.

Smith, J. M. 2000. "The Politics of Dispute Settlement Design: Explaining Legalism in Regional Trade Pacts." *International Organization* 54 (1): 137–+.

Smith, M. 1923. *Bismarck and German Unity.* New York: Columbia University Press.

Snidal, D. 1985. "The Limits of Hegemonic Stability Theory." *International Organization* 39 (4): 579–614.

Snyder, G. H. 1997. *Alliance Politics.* Ithaca: Cornell University Press.

Snyder, J. L. 1991. *Myths of Empire: Domestic Politics and International Ambition.* Ithaca: Cornell University Press.

Snyder, J. M., and M. M. Ting. 2002. "An Informational Rationale for Political Parties." *American Journal of Political Science* 46 (1): 90–110.

Spillman, L. 1996. "'Neither the Same Nation nor Different Nations': Constitutional Conventions in the United States and Australia." *Comparative Studies in Society and History* 38 (1): 149–81.

Springer, H. 1962. "Federation in the Caribbean: An Attempt That Failed." *International Organization* 16 (4): 758–75.

Spruyt, H. 1994. *The Sovereign State and Its Competitors: An Analysis of Systems Change.* Princeton: Princeton University Press.

Steinberg, S. H. 1961. *The Statesman's Year-Book: Statistical and Historical Annual of the States of the World for the Year 1961–1962.* New York: St. Martin's Press.

Stepan, A. 1999. "Federalism and Democracy: Beyond the U.S. Model." *Journal of Democracy* 10 (4): 19–34.

Stern, F. R. 1977. *Gold and Iron: Bismarck, Bleichröder, and the Building of the German Empire.* New York: Knopf.

Stole, L. A., and J. Zwiebel. 1996. "Intra-Firm Bargaining under Non-Binding Contracts." *Review of Economic Studies* 63 (3): 375–410.

Stone Sweet, A., and W. Sandholtz. 1997. "European Integration and Supranational Governance." *Journal of European Public Policy* 4 (3): 297–317.

Stuart-Cansdell, C. 1891. *Federation, Colonial and British; being an exposition of the federal systems of Switzerland, the United States of America, Canada, and Germany, in aid of the formation of Australasian and British federation, with suggestions as to many direct and indirect advantages.* Sydney: Edwards, Dunlop.

Thompson, R. C. 1974. "James Service: Father of Australian Foreign Policy?" *Historical Studies* 16 (63): 258–76.

Tilly, C. 1990. *Coercion, Capital, and European States, AD 990–1990.* Cambridge, Mass.: Blackwell.

Tordoff, W. 1967. *Government and Politics in Tanzania: A Collection of Essays Covering the Period from September 1960 to July 1966.* Nairobi: East African Publishing House.

Trainor, L. 1970. "British Imperial Defence Policy and the Australian Colonies, 1892–96." *Historical Studies* 15 (54): 204–18.

Travers, R. 2000. *The Grand Old Man of Australian Politics: The Life and Times of Sir Henry Parkes.* East Roseville, N.S.W.: Kangaroo Press.

Trollope, A. 1968 [1873]. *Australia and New Zealand.* London: Dawsons of Pall Mall.

Truman, D. B. 1962. "Federalism and the Party System." In *Federalism, Mature and Emergent,* ed. A. W. Macmahon, 557. New York: Russell & Russell.

Turner, H. G. 1904. *A History of the Colony of Victoria from Its Discovery to Its Absorption into the Commonwealth of Australia.* London: Longmans Green.

Vale, B. 2000. *A War betwixt Englishmen: Brazil against Argentina on the River Plate, 1825–1830.* New York: I. B. Tauris.

van Houten, P. 2003. "Globalization and Demands for Regional Autonomy in Europe." In *Governance in a Global Economy: Political Authority in Transition,* ed. D. A. Lake and M. Kahler. Princeton: Princeton University Press.

Veit-Brause, I. 1986. "German-Australian Relations at the Time of the Centennial International Exhibition, Melbourne, 1888." *Australian Journal of Politics and History* 32 (2): 142–59.

———. 1988. "Australia as an 'Object' in Nineteenth-Century World Affairs—The Example of German Consular Representation in the Australian Colonies." *Australian Journal of Politics and History* 34 (2): 142–59.

Verhofstadt, G. 2005. *De Verenigde Staten van Europa: Manifest voor een nieuw Europa.* Antwerp: Houtekiet.

Voeten, E. 2004. "Resisting the Lonely Superpower: Responses of States in the United Nations to U.S. Dominance." *Journal of Politics* 66 (3): 729–54.

Vogel, J. 1898. "The Prospects of Australian Federation." *Contemporary Review* (74): 275–79.

Walford, A. J. 1939. "General Urquiza and the Battle of Pavon, 1861." *Hispanic American Historical Review* 19 (4): 464–93.

Wallander, C. A. 2000. "Institutional Assets and Adaptability: NATO after the Cold War." *International Organization* 54 (4): 705–35.

Walt, S. M. 1987. *The Origins of Alliances.* Ithaca: Cornell University Press.

——. 2005. *Taming American Power: The Global Response to U.S. Primacy.* New York: Norton.

Walter, B. F. 2002. *Committing to Peace: The Successful Settlement of Civil Wars.* Princeton: Princeton University Press.

Waltz, K. N. 1979. *Theory of International Politics.* Reading, Mass.: Addison-Wesley.

Ward, J. M. 2001. *The State and the People: Australian Federation and Nation-Making, 1870–1901.* Marrickville, N.S.W.: Federation Press.

Warden, J. 1992. "Federalism and the Design of the Australian Constitution." *Australian Journal of Political Science* 27:143–58.

Watson, J. 2002. *Strategy: An Introduction to Game Theory.* New York: Norton.

Watts, R. L. 1966. *New Federations: Experiments in the Commonwealth.* Oxford: Clarendon Press.

Weber, K. 1997. "Hierarchy amidst Anarchy: A Transaction Costs Approach to International Security Cooperation." *International Studies Quarterly* 41 (2): 321–40.

Weichlein, S. 2000. "Saxons into Germans: The Progress of the National Idea in Saxony after 1866." In *Saxony in German History: Culture, Society, and Politics, 1830–1933,* ed. J. Retallack. Ann Arbor: University of Michigan Press.

Weingast, B. R. 1997. "The Political Foundations of Democracy and the Rule of Law." *American Political Science Review* 91 (2): 245–63.

Wendt, A. 1992. "Anarchy Is What States Make of It: The Social Construction of Power Politics." *International Organization* 46 (2): 391–425.

——. 1999. *Social Theory of International Politics.* New York: Cambridge University Press.

——. 2003. "Why a World State Is Inevitable." *European Journal of International Relations* 9 (4): 491–542.

Westgarth, W. 1887. *The Battle between Free Trade, and Protection in Australia; Free-trading New South Wales and Protectionist Victoria the Chief Combatants.* Melbourne.

——. 1889. *Half a Century of Australasian Progress: A Personal Retrospect.* London: Sampson Low Marston Searle & Rivington.

Whigham, T. 1988. "Cattle Raising in the Argentine Northeast: Corrientes, C. 1750–1870." *Journal of Latin American Studies* 20 (2): 313–35.

Wildavsky, A. B. 1967. *American Federalism in Perspective.* Boston: Little, Brown.

Will, W. M. 1991. "A Nation Divided—The Quest for Caribbean Integration." *Latin American Research Review* 26 (2): 3–37.

Williams, E. 1959. *The Economics of Nationhood.* Trinidad: Office of the Premier.

Williamson, O. E. 1983. "Credible Commitments: Using Hostages to Support Exchange." *American Economic Review* 73 (4): 519–40.

———. 1985. *The Economic Institutions of Capitalism: Firms, Markets, Relational Contracting.* New York: Free Press.

———. 1994. "Visible and Invisible Governance." *American Economic Review* 84 (2): 323–26.

Willoughby, H. 1891. *Australian Federation, Its Aims and Its Possibilities: With a Digest of the Proposed Constitution, Official Statistics, and a Review of the National Convention.* Melbourne: Sands & McDougall.

Windell, G. 1970. "The Bismarckian Empire as a Federal State, 1866–1880: A Chronicle of Failure." *Central European History* 2 (4): 291–311.

Wise, B. R. 1909. *The Commonwealth of Australia.* London: Pitman.

Wittman, D. 1991. "Nations and States—Mergers and Acquisitions—Dissolutions and Divorce." *American Economic Review* 81 (2): 126–29.

Yarbrough, B. V., and R. M. Yarbrough. 1992. *Cooperation and Governance in International Trade: The Strategic Organizational Approach.* Princeton: Princeton University Press.

Ziblatt, D. 2006. *Structuring the State: The Formation of Italy and Germany, and the Puzzle of Federalism.* Princeton: Princeton University Press.

INDEX